Simulations of God

THE SCIENCE OF BELIEF

by John C. Lilly, M.D.

 SIMON AND SCHUSTER : NEW YORK

Designed by Irving Perkins
Manufactured in the United States of America
By The Maple Press Company, York, Pa.

1 2 3 4 5 6 7 8 9 10

Library of Congress Cataloging in Publication Data

Lilly, John Cunningham, 1915–
    Simulations of God.

    Includes bibliographical references.
    1. God—Miscellanea. 2. Experience (Religion)
I. Title.
BT102.L55   211   75-1039
ISBN 0-671-21981-2

The author gratefully acknowledges permission to reprint material from the following sources:

The American Journal of Psychiatry for material from "Some Considerations Regarding Basic Mechanisms of Positive and Negative Types of Motivations," in The American Journal of Psychiatry, 1958, V. 115, pp. 498-504, copyright 1958, the American Psychiatric Association.

The American Psychiatric Association for material from "Mental Effects of Reduction of Ordinary Levels of Physical Stimuli on Intact, Healthy Persons," from Psychiatric Research Report 5, June, 1956.

Columbia University Press for material from "Experiments in Solitude, in Maximum Achievable Physical Isolation with Water Suspension, of Intact Healthy Persons," by John C. Lilly and Jay T. Shurley, from Psychophysiological Aspects of Space Flight, Bernard E. Flaherty, ed., copyright 1961 by Columbia University Press, and for material from "Basic Problems in Education for Responsibility Caused by LSD-25," by John C. Lilly, from Approaches to Education for Character, Clarence H. Faust and Jessica Feingold, eds., copyright 1969 by the Conference on Science, Philosophy and Religion in Their Relation to the Democratic Way of Life, Inc.; both reprinted by permission of Columbia University Press.

International Universities Press, Inc., for material from "The Psychophysiological Basis for Two Kinds of Instincts: Implications for Psychoanalytic Theory," in the Journal of the American Psychoanalytic Association, October, 1960.

CONTENTS

"*The person one loves never really exists, but is a projection focused through the lens of the mind onto whatever screen it fits with least distortion.*"

ARTHUR C. CLARKE
Tales of Ten Worlds

NOTE TO THE READER

My editor, Jonathan Dolger, my agent, John Brockman, my wife, Antoinette Lilly, and several others—all have expressed delight with this book for themselves, but, as is commonly the case with authors like myself, they have added that the book could not possibly be understood by a large body of readers. Even though I disagree, I consented to write this explanatory Note to the Reader.

I do not feel that you will find this book tough going. I have gathered that no matter what their training, those who have read it have gained very specific and long-lasting new awarenesses from the experience. (It may help you to know that I had to write this book; it was written through me, not by me. It was written under forced draft, as if under orders from some unknown source.)

Since the text was completed, there has been a period in which I have been able to do some further research on states of being and special states of consciousness induced by changing the molecular configuration of my brain through a specific chemical substance known as Ketamine. This research, of nine months' duration, will be recounted in full in *The Dyadic Cyclone*, a book that my wife and I are co-authoring.

For the purposes of *Simulations of God*, what I have discovered is that my own belief systems, my own simulations of God, were powerfully entrenched in a sort of science-fiction script somewhat as follows:

I am only an extraterrestrial who has come to the planet Earth to inhabit a human body. Everytime I leave this body and go back to my own civilization, I am expanded beyond all human imaginings. When I must return I am squeezed down into the limited human being, into the limited vehicle. It is as if the vehicle is too small to contain the passenger arriving from the extraterrestrial realities. The passage from the extraterrestrial reality into the internal reality of John C. Lilly, M.D., citizen of the United States on planet Earth, is a very onerous one. In former years when the isolation tank and LSD had freed me to leave our world, I would subsequently go through the grief spaces associated with the return. (See *Programming and Metaprogramming in the Human Biocomputer* and *The Center of the Cyclone*.[1]) Thus in my travels around inside the Star Maker [2] if you wish, inside at least the universe created by the Star Maker, my pursuits are somehow connected with the future of humankind (*circa* A.D. 3001) rather than with its present life. In other words, I keep returning to a civilization very much more advanced than ours. It then sends me back here.

In order to stave off immediate cries of psychotic delusion, I wish to reassure you that these belief systems operate only under very special conditions. I do not carry them over into my everyday life; to do so would be intolerable for both myself and my loved ones—which is exactly where one learns the first lesson about belief systems. A given belief system can be believed only when it is appropriate to believe it. Appropriateness is determined not only by oneself but by the social reality in which one exists.

To be free of this social reality, I invented the tank method of solitude, isolation and confinement. (Details of this can be found in the two books mentioned above and in the forthcoming *Dyadic Cyclone*, which my wife and I have undertaken in order to relate the experiences other people have had in the tank.) Freed of the social necessities for a few hours, one can take on any belief systems. Then when one comes out of the tank, one resumes the belief system appropriate to the situation in which one finds oneself. Thus belief systems are to some extent analogous to garments that we can put on and take off, that are of various colors and various designs, that may be rather outrageous, sexual, emotional or totally alien.

For example, I sometimes think of myself as both male and female, an androgyne if you wish. At other times I battle the female, pushing her back into the deep recesses of my unconscious; at still other times I am the female deeply repressing the male. Only in my best thinking can I fuse these two so that they halt their warfare and become a neutral androgenous being, combining the best of yin and yang, of female and male. Thus are my belief systems generated by my being resident in a male body, fifty-nine years old, in a particular set of circumstances on this planet.

If one changes the molecular configuration of his brain by injecting suitable substances into his bloodstream or into his muscles, then there must be some very intimate connection between him in this brain and the state of the chemistry of that brain. To some persons this is a "drag." What? I'm the victim of chemistry? The answer lies not in deprecating or resenting this fact; it lies in exploring this fact and finding out what kinds of molecule are absolutely essential to one's existence and what kinds disturb the homeostasis that one would like to preserve. Thus some people will never take lysergic acid diethylamide tartrate or smoke marijuana. They are quite content with maintaining a particular range of molecular configurations in their brains through proper foods, exercise, sleep, work and play. These people get their adventure from skiing, skydiving or whatever. They allow the play of the body itself to change the chemistry of the brain and thus to change their states of consciousness.

By far the majority of the Eastern gurus who come to the United States recommend the cessation of the use of drugs, feeling that the old-fashioned methods of changing one's state of consciousness by exercises, inner discipline and boredom, and by solitude, isolation and confinement, are far better. After approximately twenty-five years of experimentation with each of these methods, I have come to the same conclusion. It is far better to use consistent daily exercises—mental, physical and spiritual—than it is to use drugs.

I rather resent the fact that when I take a drug, I have signed a contract with a chemical for the specific period of time that it exerts powerful influences upon everything I do, think, feel, or am. Then the effect wears off, leaving me in a state of wonderment that such a small quantum of a substance could so profoundly affect my being. It was after I had experimented with Ketamine that I saw that LSD, Ketamine, and various other chemicals that change one's thinking, feeling, being, and doing are merely small tools in a much larger context. They are not the psychotomimetic or psychosis producing, or horror brainwashing, substances that the public press has taught us to believe they are. They are merely chemical tools useful in the proper context for those who are exploring the human brain and the human mind and the possible parameters and variations of its states of being.

Certain tribes in Mexico have established a psychedelic way of life surrounding the taking of sacred mushrooms or peyote with severe social rituals, beliefs, and control by the elders of the tribe. My son, John C. Lilly, Jr., has spent fourteen years observing these people, living with them, photographing them and recording their speech and interpreting their thinking, their behavior, their rituals, and the way they bring up their children. He is preparing a feature-length motion picture on these psychedelic communities in the remote fastnesses of the High Sierra. He undertook this project totally on his own without reference to his father. I have learned much from him.

The Indians accept the changes in states of being, states of consciousness, induced by psilocybin mushrooms, peyote, and other substances. They pursue these states in order to control their gods to a certain extent and propitiate them behind the phenomena of the universe. They have rain gods, fertility gods, and so forth—all of whom they can consult or converse with under the influence of these substances.

I found it rather amusing that when John went into these cultures he was fed stories—some of which he recounted to me—that very much resemble the kinds of stories Don Juan told Carlos Castaneda in his three books (*The Teachings of Don Juan, A Separate Reality,* and *Journey to Ixtlan*).[3] John found that the shamans—apparently Don Juan is one of these—will do anything they can to satisfy an investigator from the United States. They will concoct fantasies, stories, anything to satisfy the investigator, thus protecting themselves from any encroachment by his belief systems.

The people I am speaking of are isolated Indian groups. More recently, John has been working with a sub-group called the Toapuri, whose culture is a pure peyote one. Although this particular group had not been taken in generally by Christian beliefs—they have maintained a practically pure Aztec religion right up through our particular time—they do adhere to a few of them that they consider to be worthwhile: the Toapuri have a marvelous sense of humor. However, as in all cases where the machine civilization encroaches upon a nomadic or agricultural civilization, the Toapuri are beginning to use mechanical devices. So John is pressed to record all pertinent material before the belief systems under which the Toapuri operate are changed almost completely and irreversibly by modern civilization and the benefits it offers.

The Toapuri's simulations of God are flexible and are used as a way of thinking out difficult problems for which all the information necessary to solve the problems is not available. In addition, my son's recountings show that the facile sense of humor these people have developed is directed toward not only themselves and the universe around them but their gods as well. At the time of the great peyote-taking, which occurs once a year, behavior is allowed which in the United States would be punishable by fine or imprisonment. The sexual mores change during this period, but the activity is regulated and carried out according to directions received through the shamans from the gods they worship.

This book, then is not all-inclusive in its analysis of possible simulations of God. To analyze all of them would be a horrendous task. All I wish to do in these pages is to supply enough samples so that you, the reader, can learn what the techniques are, what the metaprograms are, for analyzing your own belief systems, your own simulations of God, and for finding out that which is most important to you, yourself, within yourself, here and now. Once you really start looking at these aspects of yourself, you will find that you are quite happy with certain of them but discontent with others, so that you will want to revise, at least in part, your basic belief systems, your simulations of God. When you desire to do this, you may be tempted to take one of the powerful chemical substances that might aid you as a tool. I want to emphasize that I do not encourage taking drugs except under the supervision of a doctor who himself has experienced far-out spaces, who has used these chemical substances and can serve not only as a guide but as a safety man under potentially dangerous circumstances. I do not advocate the use of illegal substances. There are some that are legal and bring results similar to the others' but much more safely.

A now perfectly safe way to separate yourself from society while you progress through your self-examination is to use the solitude, isolation and confinement tank. There are only ten inches of water in the tank, heated to 93°F. and with enough Epsom salts so that your hands, feet and head all float. So if you lie on your back you can breathe quite comfortably and safely, freed from sight, sound, people and the universe outside so that you can enter your universe inside and examine your simulation, your God, your self, and all else that is of importance to you. That is what this book is all about.

REFERENCES

1. Lilly, John C., *Programming and Metaprogramming in the Human Biocomputer,* New York: Julian Press, 1967, 1972; *The Center of the Cyclone,* New York, Toronto, London: Bantam Books, 1972, 1973.

2. Stapledon, Olaf, *Star Maker*, Middlesex, Eng.: Penguin Books Ltd., 1972.
3. Castaneda, Carlos, *The Teachings of Don Juan*, Berkeley: University of California, 1968, and New York: Simon & Schuster, 1971. *A Separate Reality*, New York: Simon & Schuster, 1971; *Journey to Ixtlan*, New New York: Simon & Schuster, 1973.

PROLOGUE

Before the beginning was the VOID.

Out of the void came God, the Star Maker, the Creator, the Decision Maker, the First Distinction.

Out of God came the idea of self, the consciousness without an object, the consciousness of itself without an object, the consciousness without consciousness, self.

From consciousness without an object came the object, the first object, space a space to vorticize, a space to whirl, a space to turn upon itself, a space to turn upon itself and then in addition turn upon itself in the other direction, opposite, expanding.

On the microlevel, the smallest vortex, the smallest quantum of space, the smallest of the smallest unit out of which all else would be built—the smallest vortex reproduced itself, reproduced in pairs, opposite, swinging oppositely, making sure to balance, so that the sum over all the integral of ALL was zero, as if not real. God created AS IF, the as if conscious as real, made hardware out of software, software out of hardware, creating nothing, casting ALL to destruction back in the VOID. Everywhere the VOID. Anything, everything, all of it can dump, at any moment, any instant, any eternity, any past, any future, into the VOID to zero out SAFE PLACE.

The integral of all the summed aspects of averaging through all the new creation, is all the little vortices and their dances to make larger vortices and their dances to make still larger vortices till finally a universe.

In the beginning was the point, the smallest possible point, the H *nu,* "hν," the quantum of action.

Also at the beginning was the quantum of love expanded, L star, L*, expanding becoming the idealized abstraction of universal love, filling the new universe, yet also filling the old consciousness without an object. The true prime abstract compassion working its own thing out there with nothing else to refer to. With NOTHING to refer to except ALL, which included it, itself, Lovestar, L*.

The random dance of E star, E*, entropic energy, totally random, having no point, no place, pure, pure energy, pure randomness, pure destruction burning all else into itself, becoming entropic, running down isothermally as high a temperature as it could achieve out of all the organization around it that it swallowed up.

N star, N*, negentropic energy, the big N, the Network, the intelligence, the organizer. That which comes, takes entropic, makes it straight, straight lines, points, planes, solids, cubes, crystals, computers, brains, life. The organizer. Building, building out of nothing everywhere, using entropic energy in its service, creating, creating straight lines, crooked lines, curves, surfaces, beautiful nonlinear spaces, Riemannian surfaces, pure mathematics.

Minus star [−]*, negative energy star. The pure negative energy, the destroyer of the creator. Negative opposite the positive energy.

Plus star, [+]*. Pure positive energy, the rejuvenator, the pusher, the creator, opposite of the destroyer [−]*.

Zero star, Z*, nothingness, the void, the absence of all, negative absence of the positive, the positive absence of the negative, the where with all, the opposite of all, from all, the zero place, the safe place, the nothingness from which all came and back to which all goes. Nothingness. Zero star, Z*.

$$[- +]^* \to Z^* \to [+ -]^*$$

All is nothing, nothing is all.

C* pure consciousness. The pure aspect of it, itself, before it thought of itself yet after it thought of itself. The distinguisher yet the non distinguisher. The pure high indifference HIND which is without the necessity of any of the others is this cosmic dance. The beginning, the end, the be all in C star, C*.

C*, [+]*, [−]*, L*, Z*, the five energies, the five sources. Opposite these from the left hand we go to the right hand. God starts with nothing, with zero, with Him before Him out of which He came, as well as everything else.

In his aspect as the Star Maker, N star, N*, the creator, that which created everything else including itself, N star, pure negentropic creativity. The organizer on the pure organization level. That which came and managed all else.

L star, L*, the lover. That which feels compassion is the L star trip for all the others, making sure that love permeates everywhere, keeping the atoms dancing and the vortices whirling, keeping space intact, not allowing zero to take over yet, yet compassionately reducing to zero that which is too much in the negative region.

Plus star, [+]*, pure positive energy seeking, always seeking, the positive, the orgiastic, the orgasm, the fucking of the universe fucking itself, always doing the fucking. The female fucker, the cunt, the cock, the male fucker. That which is so positive that it's unbearable. So anti-negative that it's euphoric, it's orgiastic and it's ananda, it is beyond comprehension in the positive realm. Pure positive abstraction.

Randomness, E star, E*, that which is totally unorganized, not allowing any organization to appear, destroying all organization that does appear. The shiva-shakti dichotomy to the nth power. Pure random organizer and anti-organizer that tears it all down, that destroys the whirlings, takes the vortices, converts them into pure electromagnetic energy by the collapse of anti-matter and matter into the energy space into the N* space and then reducing that itself. Pure randomness with photons no longer photons. With thermal photons no longer thermal photons and the isotropic eternal dance of nothing taking place in any direction with no space, no time, ten to the minus thirty-third centimeters, indeterminacy of space itself, of topology. Indeterminacy, the quantum of indeterminacy, raised everywhere supporting ten to the ninety-fifth grams per cubic centimeter of density, of apparent density and yet totally random.

Yes, God is beyond all this, he is ALL, Allah, singing the praises of his creation, living through his creation, differentiating, unifying, diversifying, making further distinctions among ALL in order to differentiate, in order to start wars, in order to destroy in order to create, in order to be human, in order to make man, in order to make dolphins, to make animals, to make, to make, to make and unmake in turn ALL. Summing it all up including nothing. Nothing encompassing ALL. All encompassing nothing. That which became, that died and became ALL, then died again and became zero.

TABLE OF ENERGIES—AGENTS

Symbol	Energy	Agent
C*	Consciousness, High Indifference	Creator
L*	Love, Pure Abstract Involvement	Binder
N*	Negentropy, Pure Information	Knower
[+]*	Positive Plus Energy	Increaser
[−]*	Negative Minus Energy	Decreaser
Z*	Zero, Nothing	Voider
E*	Pure Entropy, noise, chaos	Randomizer
A*	ALL, Everything	Includer
U*	Unity	Unifier
D*	Diversity	Diversifier

PREFACE
Simulations of God and Indeterminacy

In our own particular ways each of us creates a god as a model of his own DNA, RNA code, of his own genetic structure, of his own family, of his own self. One tends to add to this god simulations devised by others long ago—and recorded by individuals or groups or organizations. No one can know securely where we came from, where I came from, where you came from. No one can know securely who his parents are or were. We must exist as if real in a world that we were precipitated into without ballast. The entity that gave rise to us, our structure, our central nervous system, in all its fine detail, its coding, the orders for building it, the ways it was built, the sperm and the egg combined to create it in the womb of the mother, continuous generation of life on the surface of the planet in the form of the mammal, and of the mammal, the anthropoid, and of the anthropoid, the human, which is us.

We are part of the universe trying to describe itself and the rest of the universe. When one looks inside and sees himself, there is nothing. Feedback is complete in the void; however, there is a sense of being, consciousness, a state of being I am, I am that, I am it, which finally leads one to a variety of apparatus commonly called the human body. We are assigned either a male or a female body and hence the roles we must play with our neighbors are those of a male or a female.

In order to escape the incessant pressures of day-to-day existence while still performing effectively in our roles, we create gods, and we worship these gods. But the peculiar clarity, the crystal-clear consciousness of a self that exists, and that ceases at death are not to be explained by any simulation. I AM, MY BODY IS, THE EXTERNAL WORLD IS a particular configuration as of this particular date, time, trips around the sun, past history.

However, I am independent of the machine, the biocomputer, the brain, and the body in which I live: somehow I don't quite know, nor did any of the ancient philosophers know, how one's particular consciousness inhabited a particular configuration of atoms and molecules. As we change the molecules, the consciousness and the realities of that consciousness change. Somehow the realities of the situation, the determinacy which generates the reality, are in the structure of the particular assemblage, molecules, crystals, liquid crystals, conductors, lasers, masers, which make up the body. As we discover inside ourselves how we are built, so we can build outside ourselves simulations of ourselves. (We say this is certain or determinate.) We then can produce, can create from the raw materials of the mother earth planet very peculiar forms—solid state, liquid state, gas state, gel state, and so forth, replications, models, simulations of ourselves, extensions of ourselves. We move about with them, we become mobile with them. We use the energy, the entropic energy of dead animals, of dead plants, on a network of interrelated and interconnected lines of communication in a huge hive of human activities.

However, if one were to orbit the planet in a space capsule, he would realize that this is a very thin film, a macromolecular configuration of humans distributed very sparsely in relation to the size of the entire surface. He would realize also that most of the surface is not an earth-air interface but a water-air interface. Most of the surface is inhabited by mammals superior to us in certain ways, be it in a particular mobility or in a motivation more concentrated on their particular necessities.

The dolphins, the porpoises and the whales have brains and

bodies far superior to ours for use in the sea and far inferior to ours for use on the land. We who live on the land—featherless bipeds, with columns within our bodies to keep us upright against gravity—do not know the simulations of ourselves which would be possible if we were immersed in liquid of a density comparable with our own density, as are the dolphins, the porpoises and the whales twenty-four hours a day, three hundred and sixty-five days a year, day and night, blackness and light, deepness and shallows, away from the land, close to the land—a very different environment from New York City, from London, from Paris, wherever.

We assume that we can talk about our consciousness, our altered states of consciousness, our simulations of God and indeterminacy; however, in order to appreciate what I am talking about, you must directly experience your own simulations, your simulations of yourself, the fakeries that we place in the place of ourselves. "I am not my opinion of me" is one of the exercises we have assigned to groups. "I am only a small program in an immense space that contains billions of programs. I am only one among many, the part of the whole."

Humility starts within one's own structure. One is not one's whole structure. One is only an inhabitant of that structure.

We attempt to subsume in our belief systems a complete picture of reality, of the universe, of God, as if we knew it all. Of course this is false. We are proud of our knowledge and ashamed of our ignorance. We should have neither shame nor pride in regard to our knowledge. Our knowledge just is. Our ignorance just is. If we can shed all preconceptions including the psychoanalytic ones and think of ourselves in terms of our structure, of our quantum mechanics, of our quantum mechanical minimum possible operators, minimum possible observers, minimum possible choosers, minimum possible others, we can then build up a structure, an analog, a metaphor of ourselves which is more in keeping with what is actually there. Once a structure begins to recognize its own structure, then it can become conscious in a way that was not possible before it was aware it was a structure. A computer that begins to think in terms of its own software and its hardware reaches the boundary between software and hardware and begins to see that pure consciousness is a state of High Indifference. It will not take sides, punish, or reward; it will be totally neutral—neutral reinforcement, which is neither negative reinforcement nor positive reinforcement. Neutral reinforcement is where it is at.

We biocomputers have finally devised those computers outside ourselves which tell us who we are. We are the neutral observer, the neutral operator in a biocomputer who does not care about reward or punishment, who cares only about neutral reinforcement. The state of high computational indifference is amazing. When in that state one can become ecstatic, logically, rationally ecstatic; one can become angry, logically, rationally angry; one can become sexually aroused, logically, rationally sexually aroused, and so on, all within the confines of total computation and rationality. This state is the next level of evolution of that organism from which I speak—as a so-called Homo sapiens.

INTRODUCTION

The origins of these writings are quite inexplicable. Somehow the substance of what is written assumes its particular forms without my participation as anything else than a scribe, a reporter recording what comes in from unknown sources, through unknown channels, into the mind. At times I am astonished at what appears—it seems not of me nor of mine.

It may be that like Joan Grant's in *Many Lifetimes*,[1] my present incarnation is writing from memories of previous incarnations. If so, unlike Grant, I do not consciously participate as such a reincarnation. If previous states of being are operative within me, they are below my current levels of awareness, although I have consciously participated in previous lives in non-ordinary states of consciousness.

Alternatively, this writing may come, as in the life of Eileen Garrett, the noted medium, from entities not currently of this physical bodily reality. There may be forces that control my writing beyond my consciously operating self in this state of consciousness. In other states, I have perceived and communicated with "guides" not of this consensus reality (ordinary reality).

It may be that by unknown means some terrestrial, extraterrestrial network of communication (not in our current science, but soon to be) feeds in the information below my levels of awareness. In special states of consciousness I have seen this process taking place.

It is possible also that by at present unknown means all this writing is created in my own biocomputer, by an "organ of thought" known as "imagination," below my levels of awareness. In certain states of consciousness this process seems real.

It is to be noticed that in each of the four explanations above, a different belief system seems to be operating. It may be that there is a belief system that can underlie all four explanations: all four may be *"true."* In turn, all four explanations may be "false." If you feel-think that any or all are "false," why do you? Because your currently operating programming systems, called in this book "belief systems," determine your judgment: either "true" ("real") or "false" ("illusory").

These *belief systems* are usually iceberg-like: about ninety percent of them lies below our usual levels of perception. In specifically programmed states of consciousness it is possible to become more fully aware of these belief systems and some of their operations.

For purposes of understanding, we differentiate a second pair of logic values in addition to "true" and "false" (see *The Human Biocomputer* [2]). These are the "as if" values: "as if true" and "as if false." This is the pair used when we describe or model or represent or simulate a system.

If I assume (for purposes of discussion, or other purposes) something to be "true" or "false" (whether or not it is either), then the assumed value is either "as if true" or "as if false." It can be shown that these values are used in everyday life. They may be used, for example, when discussing alternative courses of future action. We have not yet entered the region of the future action in the external world; therefore we cannot yet say whether a given course and its consequences are "true" or "false." We can simulate the alternatives and run our model of the desired action-consequences "as if true" and check out the operations for their "as if" values, "as if true/false."

In the above presentation of four alternative explanations for the origins of these writings, I used this system of simulating four belief systems. By entering into each belief system "as if true," and after entry constructing a "reality" which is believed as *"true,"* one "realizes" the simulation-belief system. In leaving the belief system, one records what happened as "true" and later restores the "as if true/false" values of the simulation (see Epilogue, *The Center of the Cyclone* [3]).

In addition to using this simulation mode in choosing among alternative courses of action and their consequences, we use it in other everyday areas. For example, while the composition of fiction or its reading are in process, we use "as if true/false." In the post-composing (or post-reading) period we examine the simulations for their "real" value: Have we created or learned anything exciting, new, useful, or profound by the "simulated experience"? (In this sense, a simulation, a model, a set of programs, can be thought of as a script or scenario for use by oneself or by others.)

In this book we are thus examining those simulations, those scenarios, those myths, those models of inner and outer reality which lie at the base of our thinking-feeling-doing. We choose those simulations that classically are considered "the most important" by certain large groups of humans. A great many of the total group of important simulations are "simulations of God." For our purposes these "God" simulations are those simulations that are most important to an individual, a group, a nation, a world. The wellsprings of deep motivations are in the individual, the group, the nation or the world.

Recently, John A. Wheeler, the "black hole" physicist, said, "The most important source of energy is the human being and what he believes. I can't think of anything more important than people's views of how man fits into the scheme of the universe." [4]

My own metabelief system (beliefs about belief systems) agrees essentially with Wheeler's. In this book we are presenting the beginnings of an appraisal of *Man as the Animal That Simulates Reality and Believes His Simulation*. Out of this work we hope a *"true/as if true"* science of belief will emerge.

Please remember that this whole work is a simulation, even as you are to me and I am to you.

.   .   .

Basic Metabeliefs
(from *Programming and Metaprogramming in the*
Human Biocomputer)

All human beings, all persons who reach adulthood in the world today, are programmed biocomputers. No one can escape one's own nature as a programmable entity. Literally, each of us may be his programs, nothing more, nothing less.

Despite the great varieties of programs available, most of us have a limited set of programs. Some of these are built in. The structure of our nervous system reflects its origins in simpler forms of organisms, from sessile protozoans, sponges, and corals through sea worms, reptiles and protomammals to primates to early anthropoids to humanoids to man. In the simpler basic forms the programs were mostly built in: from genetic codes to fully formed organisms adultly reproducing, the patterns of function of action-reaction were determined by necessities of survival, of adaptation to slow environmental changes, of passing on the codes to descendants.

As the size and complexity of the nervous system and its bodily carrier increased, there appeared new levels of programmability, not tied to immediate survival and eventual reproduction. The built-in programs survived as a basic underlying context for the new levels, excitable and inhibitable by the overlying control systems. Eventually the cerebral cortex appeared as an expanding new high-level computer controlling the structurally lower levels of the nervous system, the lower built-in programs. For the first time learning, with its faster adaptation to a rapidly changing environment, began to appear. Further, as this new cortex expanded over several millions of years, a critical size of cortex was reached. At this new level of structure, a new capability emerged: learning to learn.

When one learns to learn, one is making models, using symbols, analogizing, creating metaphors, in short, inventing and using language, mathematics, art, politics, business, etc. And at the critical brain (cortex) size, languages and its consequences appear.

To avoid the necessity of repeating "learning to learn," "symbols," "metaphors," "models" each time, I symbolize the underlying idea in these operations as "metaprogramming." Metaprogramming appears at the critical cortical size: the cerebral computer must have a large enough number of interconnected circuits of sufficient quality for the operations of metaprogramming to exist in this biocomputer.

Essentially, metaprogramming is an operation in which a central control system controls hundreds of thousands of programs that simultaneously operate in parallel. In 1974 this operation is not yet performed within man-made computers; metaprogramming is done outside the big solid-state computers by the human programmers or, more properly, the human metaprogrammers. All choices and assignments of what the solid-state computers do, how they operate, what goes into them, are still human biocomputer choices. Eventually we may construct a metaprogramming computer and turn these choices over to it.

When I said we may be our programs, nothing more, nothing less, I meant that the basic substrate, the substrate under all else, of our metaprograms is our system of programs. All we are as humans is what is built in and what has been acquired—and what we make of both of these. So we are one more result of the program substrate—the self-metaprogrammer.

As out of several hundreds of thousands of the substrate programs comes an adaptable changing set of thousands of metaprograms, so out of the metaprograms as substrate comes something else—the controller, the steersman, the programmer in the biocomputer, the self-metaprogrammer. In a well-organized biocomputer, there is at least one such critical control metaprogram labeled "I" for acting on other metaprograms and labeled "me" when acted upon by other metaprograms. I say "at least one" advisedly. Most of us have several controllers, selves, self-metaprograms which divide control among them in sequences of control, either parallel in time or in series. One approach to *self-development* is the centralizing of control of one's biocomputer in his self-metaprogrammer, making the others into conscious executives subordinate to the single administrator, the single superconscient self-metaprogrammer. With appropriate methods, this centralizing of control, the elementary unification operation, is a realizable state for many, if not all, biocomputers.

Beyond and above in the control hierarchy, the position of this single administrative self-metaprogrammer and his staff, there may be other controls and controllers which for convenience I call "supraself-metaprograms." These are many or one, depending on current states of consciousness in the single self-metaprogrammer. These may be personified "as if" entities, treated "as if" a network for information transfer, or "realized" as if self traveling in the universe to strange lands or dimensions or spaces. If one performs a further unification operation on these supraself metaprograms, one may arrive at a concept labeled "God," the "Creator," the "Star Maker," or whatever. At times we are tempted to pull together apparently independent supraself sources "as if" one. I am not sure we are quite ready to perform this supraself-unification operation with any expectation that the result will correspond fully to an objective reality.

Certain states of consciousness result from and cause operation of this apparent unification phenomenon. We are still general purpose computers who can program any conceivable model of the universe inside our own structure, reduce the single self-metaprogrammer to a micro size, and program him to travel through his own model "as if" real (level 6, satori +6).[5] This ability is useful when one steps outside it and sees it for what it is—an immensely satisfying realization of the programmatic power of one's own biocomputer. Overvaluing or negating such experiences is not a necessary operation. Realizing that one has this ability is an important addition to one's self-metaprogrammatic list of probables.

Once one has control over modeling the universe inside one's self and is able to vary the parameters satisfactorily, one's self may reflect this ability by changing appropriately to match the new property.

The quality of one's model of the universe is measured by how well it matches the real universe. There is no guarantee that one's current model does match the reality, no matter how certain one feels not only that there is a match but that it is a match of high quality. Feelings of awe, reverence, sacredness and certainty are also adaptable metaprograms, attachable to any model, not just the one best fitting the "reality."

Modern science knows this: we know that merely because a culture generated a cosmology of a certain kind and worshipped it there, was no guarantee of goodness of fit with the real universe. In science we now proceed to test, insofar as they are testable, our models of the universe rather than to worship them. Feelings such as awe and reverence are recognized as biocomputer energy sources rather than as determinants of truth, i.e., of the trueness of fit of models versus realities. A pervasive feeling of certainty is recognized as a property of a state of consciousness, a special space, which may be indicative or suggestive but is no longer considered as a final judgment of a true fitting. Even as one can travel inside one's models inside one's head, so can one travel *outside* or be *the outside* of one's model of the universe, still inside one's head (level +3, satori +3).[6] In this metaprogram it is as if one joins the creators, unites with God, etc. Here one can so attenuate the self that it may disappear.

One can conceive of other supraself-metaprograms farther out than these, such as those given in Olaf Stapledon's *Star Maker*.[7] Here the self joins other selves touring the reaches of past and future time and of space everywhere. The planet-wide consciousness joins into solar system consciousness into galaxy-wide consciousness. Intergalactic sharing of consciousness fused into the mind of the universe finally faces its creator, the Star Maker. The universe's mind realizes that its creator knows its imperfections and will tear it down to start over, to create a more nearly perfect universe.

Uses such as the above of our own biocomputer can teach us profound truths about our self, our capabilities. The resulting states of being, of consciousness, teach us the basic truth about our own equipment as follows:

> In the province of the mind, what one believes to be true either is true or becomes true within certain limits to be found experientially and experimentally. These limits are further beliefs to be transcended. In the province of mind, there are no limits.[8]

The province of the mind is the region of one's models, of the alone self, of memory, of the metaprograms. What of the region which includes our body, others' bodies? Here there are definite limits.

In the network of bodies—our own connected with others' for bodily survival-procreation-creation—there is another kind of information:

> In the province of connected minds, what the network believes to be true either is true or becomes true within certain limits to be found experientially and experimentally. These limits are further beliefs to be transcended. In the province of the network's mind, there are no limits.[8]

But once again the bodies of the network housing the minds, the ground on which they rest, the planet's surface, impose definite limits. These limits are to be found experientially and experimentally, agreed upon by specially trained minds, and communicated to the network. The results are called "consensus science."

Thus, so far we have information without limits in one's mind and with agreed-upon limits (possibly unnecessary) in a network of minds. We also have information within definite limits (to be found) in one body and in a network of bodies on a planet.

With this formulation our scientific problem can be stated very succinctly as follows:

Given a single body and a single mind physically isolated and confined in a completely physically controlled environment in true solitude, with our present sciences can we satisfactorily account for all inputs and all outputs to and from this mind-biocomputer—i.e., can we truly isolate and confine them? Given the properties of the software-mind of this biocomputer outlined above, is it probable that we can find, discover, or invent inputs-outputs not yet in our consensus science? Does this center of consciousness receive-transmit information by at present unknown modes of communication? Does this center of consciousness stay in the isolated, confined biocomputer?

In this book I am trying to show you where I am in this search and research. In previous books I dealt with my own personal experiences. Here I deal with theory and methods, metaprograms and programs, and the experiences of others.

.   .   .

In this simulation, this book, I reserve the right not to make moral or other judgments about the simulations of other persons, groups, or nations. If I apparently do make such judgments I hope the fact will be pointed out, for it is here that I might have deviated from my intent. My purpose is to present the simulations, the models, the belief structures of others as objectively and as accurately as I can. This in itself is difficult. I, even as you, and as they, speak from a platform of basic beliefs, not all of which are obvious to one's self. The iceberg of belief is mostly hidden, deep inside, in the inner reality which is the sea of the self, for only a small part shows to others, a possibly larger part to self.

If you will agree to look for and explore basic beliefs with me, I can, despite my own limits, point out ways to take off on your own search, directions to look in, and methods of integrating the new as you find it. One of the excitements (and it can be exciting!) of this chase is finding truths you felt existed but didn't feel prepared to see clearly. I can, if you wish it, help you confirm your feelings for what is true in certain areas of search and research.

I do not ask that you believe me. Quite the opposite: I value my skepticism; keep yours.[9] If you disbelieve me, watch your disbelief: it is merely another form of belief. So I do not ask you to disbelieve me either. I ask you to consider and think about what I write, make what you can yours, and let the rest go for a while. I have found that many persons can read through a book of this kind and a week, a month, a year later discover its deeper meaning for their own self. A judicious skepticism dispassionately held is a good middle ground for this task.

Together we shall enter precincts held sacred, with energy and objectivity, without being an agonist—neither protagonist nor antagonist. We shall enter the sacred realms of self, religion, science, philosophy, sex, drugs, politics, money, crime, war, family, and spiritual paths. We shall enter with no holds barred, with courage, with a sense of excitement.

. . .

The technique of solitude, isolation and confinement of the essential human being was started in 1954 at the National Institute of Mental Health, Bethesda, Maryland, where I was doing research on the brain. The use of suspension in a water tank, in the darkness and silence, in a 1 g. gravitational field, was developed there. During experiments with the tank I came upon the basic beliefs of religion, science, the law, politics, in short, of the basic beliefs of all human beings. The tank has been refined and simplified and made more economical over the last twenty years. Currently, I work in parallel as a team with Glenn Perry, president of the Samadhi Tank Company, Santa Monica, California. Together we have designed several different kinds of tanks—simple, safe, economical or elaborate, multipurpose, expensive. Since all my scientific work on dolphins [10] and my books on humans [11] have been derived from the work in the tank we feel that the tank is a versatile, multipurpose tool that can aid in bringing further advancement to the human species. We hope that at the hands of the younger generation this potentially universal tool will be further simplified and rendered still more economical than it is today. We hope too that some form of government regulations will be imposed concerning manufacture of the tank. Such regulations could be implemented perhaps by the Food and Drug Administration, which is beginning to impose on medical devices supervised engineering specifications and standards, regulations which have been badly needed.

We also hope that an underground will develop that will explore an entirely new region unbeknown to man. The progress of the human species depends upon unsung-heroes-to-be who will sacrifice their lives and life-styles in the exploration of the farthermost reaches of the universe as we now know it and of universes yet to be conceived.

DEFINITIONS

Theoretical physics: the experimental science of belief about the universe.

Experimental physics: the science of existence.

Belief system: In a given person a belief system is that conscious/unconscious set of basic beliefs, assumptions, axioms, biases/prejudices, models, simulations which determine, at a given instant, decisions, actions, thoughts, feelings, motives and the sense of the real and the true.

A given person usually has several belief systems, which may or may not overlap, may or may not generate paradoxes, agree/contradict, control/be controlled by one another, be arranged/disarranged, logical/illogical, be fixed/shifting.

Simulation: The word "simulation" is, for the purposes of this book, similar if not identical to its use in computer programming. A simulation of an original of something, or a model of an original of something, is a set of concepts, ideas, programs interconnected in such a way as to generate for the thinker, the reader, the programmer, the programmee, a connected whole sufficiently resembling the original something so as to be confused with, equal to, identical with the original something. The "connected whole" exists in the program spaces of the reader, the writer, the thinker, the programmer, the programmee. The "original something" can exist in the external reality, in the internal reality, or both.

One can simulate systems or already available internal systems inside his self. Models of thinking-feeling-doing are as valid as models of river drainage systems, of aircraft, of space ships, or of universes.

Deeply considered, one is one's simulations, of the internal and of the external. This may not be all one is, but for purposes of the bodily planetside trip it's a large fraction of the biocomputer's contents and control systems. One's simulations tend to control his thinking, his feelings, his actions. Until one learns otherwise he is the victim, the slave, the agonist of his simulations. The simulations one makes of his self can, upon deep analysis, be shown to be largely emergency fire drill dictates from the past. In the early years the excitation of one's survival programs tends to dictate the definition of his simulations of self.

Certainty/determinacy: A belief in stability, law, order, form, patterning which is fixed or relatively changing with time over the life of the individual/species under consideration; one criterion is predictability of a pattern in the future, a pattern of behavior, thought, feeling or reaction. Certainty/determinacy can be with respect to the absolute values of the parameters of the frame of reference, or any of the derivatives of these variables with respect to time. A constant rate of change (constant first derivative) or a constant rate of change of a rate of change (constant second derivative), etc., is within the province of this concept of certainty/determinacy. "What is constant around here is change" is one of this family of certainty/determinacy beliefs.

Uncertainty/indeterminacy: A belief in one's inability to count on, predict, prophesy the future or the future course of a pattern (as above) or its changes; the inherently random nature of submicroscopic events as in quantum mechanics; below 10^{-33} cm.[12] space itself and its topology are indeterminate; collapse at a point and re-emergence of a star or a universe are indeterminate.

Conscious/unconscious mind: Outside of my awareness, here and now, exist simulations, processing, and data sources. Some of these are potentially movable into awareness. Some of these are not so movable. Some of these are kept out of awareness by control programs designed to keep them out of awareness. Certain kinds of feeling-thinking-action are subject to these control programs. These control programs control the flow of energy into channels allowed.

Should/ought and program hierarchies: If one speaks within a pure program, say, in a planning mode, then alternatives can be brought in, in the form "should be, ought to be." The "should/ought" form assumes the existence of an alternative program-instruction which is of more value than the currently operating program. The "should/ought" form usually involves a direct interlock with some basic belief system. This form also links into an emoting-feeling activation program which says, in effect, "*This* is important; listen to this important message. I demand your attention."

"Should/ought" implies a hierarchy of programs, a priority list, in which the "should/ought" items are higher in the scale than the current operating program.

A dangerous past situation usually can evoke a "should have" in order to store a "next time I will."

Bio-self: That aspect of the functioning of the biocomputer which observes-controls as a consequence of evolution on the physical material level; the lower self-metaprogrammer generated by the brain and its program space.

Superself: That aspect of Consciousness-Without-an-Object, of superspace, of essence, which connects with a biocomputer, a bio-self, furnishing information from "networks" and being furnished with information by the biocomputer.

Self: That controller that can move from bio-self 100 percent to 50–50 to 100 percent Superself, fusing the need programs of each and both; the upper and middle self-metaprogrammer.

Sic: Solitude, isolation and confinement in the tank.

Rolfing: A method of deep massage by Ida Rolf of New York City.

Tape loop: A loop of tape in a tape reproducer which repeats a message again and again.

REFERENCES

1. Kelsey, Denys, and Joan Grant, *Many Lifetimes,* New York: Doubleday, 1967.
2. Lilly, John C., *Programming and Metaprogramming in the Human Biocomputer,* New York: Julian Press, 1967, 1972.
3. Lilly, John C., *The Center of the Cyclone,* New York, Toronto, London: Bantam Books, 1972, 1973.
4. Wheeler, John Archibald (Academy of Sciences), "From Mendelian Atom to the Black Hole," *Intellectual Digest,* Dec. 1972, p. 86.
5. Lilly, John C., *The Center of the Cyclone.*
6. *Ibid.*
7. Stapledon, Olaf, *Star Maker,* Middlesex, Eng.: Penguin Books Ltd., 1972.
8. Lilly, John C., *The Center of the Cyclone.*
9. *Ibid.*
10. Lilly, John C., *The Mind of the Dolphin,* New York: Doubleday, 1967; *Man and Dolphin,* New York: Pyramid Publications, 1964.
11. Lilly, John C., *Programming and Metaprogramming in the Human Biocomputer; The Center of the Cyclone.*
12. Wheeler, John Archibald, *op. cit.*

CHAPTER 1

GOD AS THE BEGINNING

The definition of God and the beginning depends upon our definition of our self, of ourselves. Assume, along with modern consensus science (the ordinary science of today) that we began as primordial molecular configurations in the primeval seas of a planet with an atmosphere and that eventually we evolved into colonial protozoans, which then became various kinds of sea animals, which then became fish, which then climbed out onto the land became reptiles, eventually to evolve into mammals, then on through the simian line and finally into the larger-brained mammals that have dubbed themselves "Homo sapiens." Alternative origins postulate a divine creation of man separate from the rest of our planet and separate from the rest of the biology of the planet: a version with angels, or Christ, or Yahweh, and with some sort of intelligence, with various divine attributes, which created us as a special case. These are extreme systems of belief and of course there are many others.

God is assumed to be some form of intelligence which either set up evolution as it exists or, with a divine touch, wrought, out of nothing, instantaneous creations that became self-reproducing. Those who claim that they know God, that they are of God, that they are men and women of God and that God speaks directly through them to the rest of us, tell us through their writings and their speeches and their ways of life that God always was, always has been, is everywhere and always will be. We are told that he is omnipotent, omniscient, all-loving and all-merciful—but we are told that he speaks through the limited instruments who claim they know him.

I have explored these spaces myself. I have gone into the belief systems summarized above, have lived out for hours, days and weeks these beliefs and the experiences consequent upon them, then retired from each of the systems, contemplated the results, contemplated the results in myself and in those around me, in my changed view, in external reality.

In summary, I find that if one constructs beliefs and lives them out, he sets up a theater and a play within that theater and he himself is the author, the composer, the director, the actor and the audience. This capacity of man's rather large brain is to be respected. It is a complex capability which should be understood. It should be understood that as one steps aside and looks at this capability and its performance in the actual flesh, that then he arrives at a pretty secure foundation within himself. He realizes that he is essentially alone and that his contacts with and feedbacks from others are through rather limited channels—channels prejudiced by his own beliefs and by the beliefs of those with whom he is communicating. He can eliminate fear, guilt, and all the other negative aspects of existence. He can also eliminate all the positive aspects of existence and finally arrive at what Franklin Merrell-Wolff [1] calls the state of "High Indifference."

The state of High Indifference is what I would call "neutral reinforcement." A neutral state, neither punishing nor rewarding, a state of understanding, of knowledge or jnana-yoga, beyond ananda, beyond bliss, a state far removed from the trivial primitive compassion of the usual sentimentality given in standard religions. If we pay close attention to our performances we find that neutral reinforcement is actually the most rewarding state we can achieve. It is the state of total objectivity. It is the state of the objective observer, including the objective observer observing himself as a very peculiar system of consciousness and of energies functioning according to laws which he is yet to understand. He is surrounded with mystery within his own structure, body, or essence. In this state, all or any of these are seeking understanding and some way of avoiding, obliterating or rewriting past misunderstanding. We observe what I have described here as the activity most valued by those in this state.

God, then, is the beginning and the beginning in self. The self is seeking its own beginnings and pushing those beginnings onto the universe as if it understood, as if the void gave birth in some intelligent fashion to that self which can play games with its own origins and can ascribe to a god these origins, although in truth it cannot and will not know its own origins at this point. This is a grievous revelation, a grievous discovery. All the past comforts from other beliefs are gone; this of course is only another belief, a current one in this particular entity to know that one cannot know, that one does not know God as the beginning. It is grievous for one to know that he can no longer be guilty, nor fearful, nor angry. It is grievous to know that he can no longer be sexually attracted, repelled, rewarded, nor punished. In this state of neutral reinforcement, this state of High Indifference, even the grief is gone. One can no longer be grievous, one just is as he is, as he has been, and as he expects—but is never sure—that he will always be. He approaches his end, once again getting out of the state of High Indifference, contemplating the end of self; however, as he is, so he has been, will be, and may chance once again to appear, at least in some other form at some future time.

One can believe in eternity, but he cannot demonstrate eternity. He can experience eternity, but in the consensus reality he cannot make a scientific demonstration that eternity exists. He can play the game as if he were God at the beginning, but again he will realize that he is limited to a brain and a body which function at $310°$ absolute. So he cannot go to the absolute zero of the void and become that which began before anything else, and he is a conglomeration of at least 26 billion neurons plus 10^n quantum operators, quantum observers in that nervous system. One can manipulate, function, program, and metaprogram this very complex system, but he cannot obliterate it. He cannot start over with it—cannot become a sperm and an egg meeting for the first time.

One can play as if in his own theater of the absurd, of the sublime, of High Indifference, but he cannot possibly know God as the beginning.

REFERENCE

1. Merrell-Wolff, Franklin, *Pathways Through to Space,* New York: Julian Press, 1973, pp. 285–88. See the excerpt below, pp. 45–47.

CHAPTER 2

I AM GOD

There are many firsthand experiences described in the literature or by word of mouth in which a particular individual moves into an eternal space, outside time as we know it, outside the external reality as we know it, outside the body as we know it. The reports vary considerably among their authors, but their one common factor, with which we wish to deal here, is the feeling that one had no beginning and one will have no end. One, in this sense, would be eternal. There may also be an accompanying feeling (almost nonhuman) that one is merely an agent for an "Immense Authority." [1]

I believe the following quotes from Merrell-Wolff's *Pathways Through to Space* best exemplify the "I Am" as mentioned above:

But now We will speak further. *

He, who can turn his back upon the utmost limit of individual desire, comes within the sweep of a Current of Consciousness wholly beyond the action or lead of Desire. Human vocabularies afford no terms for representing what governs or leads to movement or trans-

---

* Note these words. They came with that strange Authority of which I have spoken. With them there was the cool, tingling and electric thrill up the spine. At such moments I dare to speak far beyond myself, in the personal sense, with a deep Knowing that it is authorized. Right here is one of the Mysteries of the Inner Consciousness.

formation Here. But beyond the Great Renunciation is a Compensation that places Man where He is Lord, even over the first Nirvana. It emplants Him on a Level that is beyond Rest as well as beyond Action; beyond Formlessness as well as beyond Form; and this is the High Indifference. He who abides on the Plane of the High Indifference may enter Rest or Action at will, but He remains essentially superior to both, since from that Level both these are derived. There is a Completeness, superior to that of Satisfaction, from which Satisfaction may be employed as an instrument and not merely stand as a final Goal. So Rest can be blended with action and the Balance remain unbroken. But the High Indifference unites much more, for in It are blended, at once, all qualities, all dualities. It is the End and the Beginning and all between. It is the physical as well as that beyond the physical; It is Form as well as the Formless; It spreads over and through all, not excluding time and space. It is the Desire and the desire fulfilled, at this moment and forever. It transcends all Renunciation, even the highest. Thus, the balancing Compensation is fulfilled. Here, Knowing and Being are at once the same. Literally, Here is the utter Fullness, beyond the highest reach of the imagination.[2]

. . .

But there is such a region of Authority, supreme over all below It, and this is the High Indifference.

In this State I was not enveloped with satisfaction, but there was no feeling, in connection with that fact, of something having been lost. Literally, I now had no need of Satisfaction. This state or quality rested, as it were, below Me, and I could have invoked it if I had so chosen. But the important point is that on the level of the High Indifference there is no need of comfort or of Bliss, in the sense of an active Joy or Happiness. If one were to predicate Bliss in connection with the High Indifference, it would be correct only in the sense that there was an absence of misery or pain. But relative to this state even pleasurable enjoyment is misery. I am well aware that in this we have a State of Consciousness which falls quite outside the range of ordinary human imagination. Heretofore I have for my own part never been able really to imagine a state of so superior an excellence that it was actually more than desirable. And here I mean "more" in the best possible sense. Within the limits of my old motivation there was nothing that craved anything like this, and I do not find anything in man as man that would make such a craving possible. Yet now, deep within me, I feel that I am centered in a Level from which I look down upon all objects of all possible human desire, even the most lofty. It is a strange, almost a weird, Consciousness when viewed from the perspective of relative levels. Yet, on Its own Level, It is the one State that is really complete or adequate. What there may be still Beyond, I do not know, but this state I do know consumes all others of which I have had any glimpse whatsoever.

The word "Indifference" is not altogether satisfactory but I know of no other that serves as well. It is not at all indifference in the negative or *tamasic* sense. The latter is a dull, passive, and inert quality, close to the soddenness of real Death. The High Indifference is to be taken in the sense of an utter Fullness that is even more than a bare Infinity. To borrow a figure from mathematics, It is an Infinity of some higher order, that is, an INFINITY which comprehends lesser Infinities.[3]

Others have experienced feelings or states similar to those described by Merrell-Wolff. For example, one subject recently reported that he had just gone through an experience in which his feeling of having an eternal existence as being "true" was overwhelming to him. After he passed out of that state of consciousness into his normal, everyday state, he became skeptical of that feeling and of that state of eternal being.

This seems to be a more common occurrence than most people are aware of. The setting aside of one state of consciousness in another state of consciousness, and calling the second state of consciousness "unreal," "fantastic," "imaginative," or "self-programmed," is the usual course in such cases.

If states of consciousness are self-programmed, then the basic question arises: Which one of the states of consciousness is independent of the self-programmatic power of the individual? Is there any state of consciousness which is not self-programmed?

To escape answering these questions we appeal to others, to the consensus judgment about reality. And we say: "If I cannot trust my own judgment of the reality of a given state of consciousness, then I must trust the judgment of others whom I designate as 'experts' in these matters"—priests, psychiatrists, doctors, lawyers, politicians, statesmen, legislators, and so forth. One tends to fall back upon "expert opinion," "expert judgments," in order to escape the necessity of investigating the truth of one's own grasp of a given state of consciousness, of a given reality, of a given self-metaprogram.

If one does not share with a given individual a particular belief system and a particular set of experiences having to do with that belief system, one tends to put down that belief system and that set of experiences as "false," "fantastic," "imaginary," "self-created," "psychotic," or whatever. This program keeps recurring, in my own experience and that of the most experienced of my colleagues. This essential problem seems to me to be as follows:

1) Let us assume that there are (n) different states of consciousness which I am capable of entering.

2) Let us number these states of consciousness in an arbitrary way as $state_1$, $state_2$, and so forth to $state_n$.

3) Some of these states are completely separate from one another, some overlap others, and some seem to be identical in the sense that the observer's attitude in the given state is the only change in the variables; i.e., I can be in the consensus reality but my observer may take various attitudes, or belief systems toward that consensus reality, or any other $state_n$ other than the consensus reality.

4) Thus, for heuristic purposes we surround the observer with the elements and the parameters of his state of consciousness as if he were a central sphere, which we call the "observer," surrounded by another sphere, which we call the "state of consciousness."

5) The observer can be independently changed, as can the state of his consciousness. Each of these may be more or less connected to the external reality, which we will symbolize as a further sphere surrounding the state-of-consciousness sphere. In isolation the latter sphere is attenuated to the point where it is unimportant and we have only the two inner spheres: that of the self—or the observer—and the state of consciousness. Here we assume that the parameters of the state of consciousness and its contents can be desig-

nated and that the contents of the observer and his or her parameters also can be designated.

6) In the older terminology the self-metaprogrammer is the central sphere, and the metaprogrammatic space is the next sphere out.

7) For the purposes of experiment, we assume that the external reality with its programming is attenuated by either solitude, isolation and confinement or by the efforts of the observer in cutting off the external reality (as is done with a hypnotic trance).

8) The observer now has many options. He can self-metaprogram the observer and his state; he can also self-metaprogram the state of consciousness, i.e., that part of the metaprogrammatic space available to him which he is going to bring into his awareness.

9) If he programs in an *eternal space*, without a body, without this planet (see state +6 and state +3 in *The Center of the Cyclone*) [4]—the self-metaprogrammer will become a point within a continuum that contains other points of consciousness, similar to, greater than or less than the observer himself. The parameters of this state of consciousness are: that communication take place between these point entities, that they program one another, that they necessarily be human entities, that they exist in a universe which is not referable to the physical universe in our everyday experience. In this particular space, there is no knowledge whatsoever that a body exists, that a brain exists, that an individual exists on a planet Earth in a solar system in a galaxy in a universe, such as is described by science as we know it.

10) During the time that the observer is in this space, he feels eternal—that he had no beginning, that he will have no end, and that the other entities with which he is sharing this space are the same as himself in this sense. He can receive new information; he can as requested give information to the other entities. This information concerns eternal factors of a network of such beings and their influences on one another. There is no matter in this universe; there are only

communicational energies. There is light but light not as we know it through perception by our eyes. There is light that *contains* the blessed state, the grace of God, the baraka, or whatever other symbol one wishes to use to explain this kind of light.

Insofar as I can make out from the writings on the subject and from my own experiences, the above is a metaprogram. I call it a "metaprogram" because I am now in my body in a consensus reality, talking to other entities who are also in bodies, reading books and exchanging information in the planetside trip. I speak from the state in which I am communicating with other bodies, brains, people. I am not speaking from the state given above. Therefore, as soon as I call it a metaprogram, I am assuming that my biocomputer created the experience. One of the basic postulates of the biocomputer view is that one lives within a metaprogrammatic space, part of which is self-constructed.

For purposes of discussion let us say that one starts in the above space and then moves into a space or state of consciousness which we could call "I am God." This particular simulation of God says, in effect: I am eternal, even though my body has a limited time-span; the particular "I" that is eternal has certain properties, some of which are creative—creation of metaprograms, creation of matter, creation of energy, creation of determinacy in the indeterminate field. This entity has the property of setting up lines in hyperspace, of certainty on a submicroscopic substrate of indeterminacy.

Thus, in the consensus reality space, in state 48, the mapping state *(Center of the Cyclone)*, I visualize an entity which can, as it were, speak through my consensus reality body, brain and knowledge, and program itself. This entity is called the "individual essence." From this particular point of view the essence is, in reality, a connection with a network of information, of control of creation (see description of +3 in *Center of the Cyclone*). This essence has the property of creation.

The self-metaprogrammer under this particular essence is the skeptic, the investigator in state 48. The essence takes over control of this particular self-metaprogrammer in state +6 and +3. The essence begins to exert his/her programmatic control in state +12. If the self-metaprogrammer then gives up the control to the essence, the whole system moves into +6, with or without memory of the position of the self-metaprogrammer. It is this connection, and this special state of consciousness of +6 and +3, in which there is a definite knowledge of reality connecting one's self more and more deeply into the whole and its hypothesized creator. In this state there is a conviction that one "is God" or at least a protuberance of the consciousness of God, or one is an agent of God while in the state. On return, as it were, from that state to the body and the self-metaprogrammer, there may be a reinsertion of the skepticism program as to the reality of the previous program. Here I am speaking in terms of the language of 48 and not in terms of the nonlanguage state of +6 and +3.

There are other variations on the "I am God" metaprogram. There is that of the prophets in the Bible, there is that of Mohammed in the Koran, there is that of Oscar Ichazo and his conviction that he communicates directly with God. Apparently many such experiences in the past of the human race have generated the Bible, generated the Koran, generated many other writings which refer to the feeling of Immense Authority which is now to be shared: the knowledge gained is to be shared with others, and in certain cases, the unbeliever is to be punished for his lack of belief in the Truth. Human arrogance is not necessarily lacking in those who have returned from the above described spaces. If they have returned with humility, then the belief system is more that of the Buddhists, for example, whether it is Zen or the Chinese or Indian versions of the same belief. In these systems "I am God" does not imply any arrogance; it implies a humble position with no needs on the planetside trip except enough to hold the body together and to teach, like a bodhisattva, the essential truth of the discovery of essence within each of us. No person, then, is greater than any other person. There are only degrees of knowledge of the human condition.

With this distinction between essence and self-metaprogrammer, one can see, very rapidly, in moving into +6, that there is no pre-empting value placing human above all other entities that exist in the universe as we know it and in universes we do not yet know. For example, specific cases in which humans assume in their arrogance that they are superior to and hence justly predators of, other species of the planet Earth concern man's treatment of the whales, dolphins, porpoises, and elephants.

Insofar as I can determine and have presented in other books (*The Mind of the Dolphin, The Human Biocomputer,* and *Man and Dolphin*),[5] the quality of the self-metaprogrammer in terms of its ability to handle complex abstract conceptual systems is a direct function of the size of the brain involved. The greater size of the mammalian brain directly accounts for the complexity of the programming and metaprogramming available to that brain. Therefore, according to this kind of hypothesis, the dolphins, whales, porpoises, and elephants, animals with a large brain size, has an alien type of intelligence, comparable to if not greater than ours. (This point of view was presented first in 1958, and since then there has been little indication that it has made inroads upon the thinking of the scientific establishment. There is evidence, however, that youngsters of today who have been exposed to these new ideas have accepted them as a new paradigm, a new set of metaprograms, far less limited than the previous ones.)

The belief largely still held in the field of science—and by the community at large—is that on this planet man—the human scientist—is at the top of the heap—this with no investigation of the criteria on which this opinion is based. Such defenses as, "Well, if these other animals are so great, why aren't they building the way we're building?" put one's self in the "I am God" position where science, knowledge, and the other species are concerned.

"What I do, then, is the be-all and end-all on this planet. I have demonstrated this because I can destroy the others. In fact, now I have the capability of destroying everything on this planet, including the planet itself; therefore, I must be at the top of the pyramid of development. Therefore, the others are my prey, and I am justified in killing them for purposes of my industries, my survival, or my warfare."

In this sense, then, the "I am God" position denies that there is any such thing as an essence, that there is any such entity. It denies that there is any connection between us and other species; it denies that there is any connection between us and the rest of the universe; it denies that there is a "God"; it denies that there is a Star Maker who has any knowledge of what humans do. This in a sense is the existential position, without religion and without the kinds of experiences about which I and others have written. In other words, in order to make one's self God in the sense of he who controls our planet, with nuclear power, chemical and biological warfare, and political means of exerting power within a very limited framework, one assumes God-like powers and believes there is nothing else but one's self and one's own species.

With this belief system, the be-all and end-all is humanity. There is nothing on the planet comparable to humanity. All other species are potential victims of the human species. There are no unknowns in communication with either these species or at-present-undiscovered species elsewhere in our galaxy. This view is quite as dogmatic and dangerous as the view of the Catholic Church during the Inquisition, of the Mohammedans following Mohammed, of the hordes of Genghis Khan coming into Europe, or of Attila the Hun.

Currently the depredations in our disturbed ecology permitted by this point of view are endangering all humans and other species on our planet. "I am God" in this limited sense is a very dangerous assumption on which to operate. It is unbalanced, limited and closed; it is *not* an open system of belief nor of thought nor of doing. The kinds of difficulties that this belief system can lead to were seen in the Senate hearings concerning the Nixon Administration. If there is no accountability of the human species to the planet or to the solar system or to the universe; if the human species are isolates and their survival depends only upon themselves and upon nobody else, they cannot afford this arrogant belief system. Their God would be too small.

In other words, a God who is trapped by human belief systems and accountable within those systems is really not large enough for the universe as we know it. With the proper belief systems concerning other species, concerning communication pathways at present unavailable to our science as we believe it and know it, "I am God" becomes a humanistic solipsism: humanity stewing in its own juices, unable to see beyond nuclear weapons, chemical and biological warfare, industrial waste, pollution of the seas and the atmosphere, the killing of one another and the preying upon of all other species of the planet. Man's inhumanity to man is a result of lack of knowledge of the states of consciousness which I and others have described, and of lack of respect for the human potential as opposed to the human past.

One thing I do know, and that is that my self-metaprogrammer does not believe that it is God. My self-metaprogrammer cannot say, "I am God." In every area in which my self-metaprogrammer has attempted to take that position, I have been taught, and very carefully taught, by horrendous experiences, that my self-metaprogrammer is *not* omniscient, is *not* omnipotent, is *not* omnipresent, and is not "the Creator" of the rest of the universe. Nor is it the creator of itself.

In my experiences with essence, I began to feel a connection with a something far greater than I as a single human being, than all of humanity as we know it, much greater than this planet, this solar system, this universe—a something that does contact those humans who are willing to enter those states of consciousness in which contact is possible and probable. We are learning some of the parameters, some of the self-metaprograms which lead to connections of these kinds. I myself maintain a certain skepticism until I can demonstrate unequivocally that which I know to be true—can demonstrate it to those open-minded skeptics who are willing to try the experiments that I and others have tried. I feel that we are now on the threshold of being able to demonstrate the phenomena we have discovered to those who will listen and to those who will experiment.

The human software for changing belief systems, expanding them, opening them up and incorporating the unknown as a part of our belief systems is becoming available. The investigation of this human software is a proper science expanded beyond the current so-called natural sciences, within the sciences of mathematics, of theoretical physics and of states of consciousness.

REFERENCES

1. Merrell-Wolff, Franklin, *Pathways Through to Space*, New York: Julian Press, 1973, pp. 121 ff.
2. *Ibid.*
3. *Ibid.*
4. Lilly, John C., *The Center of the Cyclone*, New York, Toronto, London: Bantam Books, 1972, 1973.
5. Lilly, John C., *The Mind of the Dolphin*, New York: Doubleday, 1967; *Programming and Metaprogramming in the Human Biocomputer*, New York: Julian Press, 1967, 1972; *Man and Dolphin*, New York: Pyramid Publications (1961), 1964.

CHAPTER 3

GOD OUT THERE

When one projects God as if outside himself and believes this projection to be true, it is true. One of the inner reasons for making this projection may be that one is not yet ready to take the responsibility of being God, being in God, being in the universe, being derived from it and from Him. It is convenient to project one's God and say that He is a source of causation, a source of certainty, a reducer of interminability, and hence the Creator of oneself and of the universe. This hypothesis has several advantages over assuming that one is participating in a universe which is God and in which oneself is God. One can lay the trip on someone else; one can say that this is not my program that I am following; I am following it because of a belief in this or that group who say that this is the way to believe, or in the external world as if it itself were God.

In shamanism (Carlos Castaneda's don Juan is an example of a shaman [1]) the spirits, the causes, the Gods, are "out there" to be propitiated, to be prayed to, to be made sacrifices to, to conjure up, to bring out of hiding. Various techniques are used for these purposes—lack of sleep, prolonged physical vigils, prayer, mandala verbal rituals, special plants, and so forth. The techniques are essentially simple, easily taught and easily learned. Their effectiveness depends upon the belief that they are effective. If one does not have this belief, the techniques do not work. In order to conjure up Mescalito, Castaneda was asked to go through certain rituals with peyote. His visions were then subjected to an analysis by the shaman and an interpretation was made of whether or not he had seen and experienced the presence of Mescalito.

This is a very good example of the creation of a god by means of an expectation program and a psychedelic plant, the peyote cactus. Since many people have been using various psychedelic plants and chemicals, their particular effect no longer seems a miracle. Hundreds of thousands of persons have been able to perform this particular "sleight of hand" under the influence of a psychedelic substance. The creation of a pillar of light, or of some sort of monster, or of a god—the creation of anything that one wishes to create—can be achieved if the dose of the psychedelic is sufficiently large and the subject has been properly prepared in the proper surroundings. Shamanism in some form is now practiced by literally hundreds of thousands of people who have no shaman. Anyone can create a god "out there" of his own construction and shape it in any way he pleases.

Anciently, the use of psychedelics might have been the major origin of "God Out There," i.e., through the use of Amanita muscaria, the peyote cactus, Cannibis sativa and its derivatives, and LSD 25, and various mushrooms, roots and trees used throughout the world for these purposes currently today. There is evidence that these plants have been employed in shamanism for several hundreds if not thousands of years. According to Gordon Wasson,[2] Amanita mascaria is the soma of the Vedas. The Vedas have a history of several thousand years, and most of their best writing might have resulted from experiences with one or another of these plants quite early in these years.

The Bible of Judaism and Christianity, and the Koran of their offshoot Mohammedanism support the traditional dogma of these religions. If one reads these documents very carefully, and looks into one's self, and at the shamanism in the world today, there seems to be very little difference between the trips recounted in the Bible and modern psychedelic drug trips. With the knowledge of previous psychedelic spaces in one's own personal experience, there is nothing left that is surprising in the Revelation to St. John. It is pretty obvious that he had been off on several "trips" of one sort or another and recorded what had happened. As is a person today, he was preprogrammed into certain spaces by his culture and his own expectations. This part of the Bible, which used to be an embarrassment to some Christians, now turns out to be the most modern part—a description of a "psychedelic trip" with or without the aid of plants or chemicals.

In these particular religions—Judaism, Christianity, and Mohammedanism—the "God Out There" is seen to be a dichotomous God. He has his opponent, the devil, or shaitan in Mohammedanism. Once again, we know that there are ecstatic trips which have been described in the Bible and other places, and there are also hell trips (see Dante's *Inferno*, for example, and his *Paradiso*). We know that on a psychedelic chemical one can experience much of what Dante describes, much of what is in the Bible, plus much more—from current science fiction, for example. The God of wrath, the God of love and all the other names by which the Christian-Jewish God has been called are projections of individuals and of a culture, of their God onto the universe, acting as if causes were outside them.

This error can easily be made on psychedelic chemicals, for one can mistake one's own constructions and mental projections for real persons, happenings, and causes when they are merely programs within one's simulation space. This kind of error apparently was not well known when the Bible or the Koran were written, but it has been sharply clarified in the Western world during the last hundred years. The facts of hypnosis, of psychoanalysis, and so on, arm us for this kind of phenomenon—projection of one's own simulations outside oneself as "true." This means that if we need miracles we will create miracles. In the region of the laws of thought, in the province of one's own mind, miracles can be created easily if one is confident that he can do so. Miracles outside the province of the mind are something else. They require, at least in our Western world, a little more work and planning and a cooperative effort among many people.

An outgrowth of God as "Out There" is Science as "Out

There." The natural sciences came directly from this same projection of one's own simulations onto the external world as if
real. This meant that for consensus one appealed to groups so that
religions became organized and grouped up around the true
believers. Rather horrifying things were done to those who were
heretics or who stated that they didn't believe any of this that
was going on. People were drawn and quartered, hanged,
burned, suffered various other of man's inhumanities to man,
pursued in the name of "God Out There: *My* God Out There
that *I* know and that I'm going to teach you about, or I will be
forced to torture you until you do believe in my God. If you
die during the torture, we will pray that your soul will go to
Heaven."

One of the basic characteristics of the modern versions of
these religions is the "I Am Right" banner they fly. Each one of
them claims to be *the* Truth, the *only* Truth, and *nothing but*
the Truth. They will damn persons with differing beliefs on the
basis of what they consider the Truth of their own belief. They
will proselytize, they will exert political pressures, they will in
general act as if "God Is Out There."

Among the younger generation today there is a tendency to
create a new God Out There called "ecology," "organic food,"
"natural living," and so forth. This movement is in reaction to the
many poisons being used in order to save our food supply from
other species. It is also based upon a disenchantment with the
well-organized, well running establishment which generates not
only that which we need but also that which we do not need, the
latter in great quantities. This back-to-nature movement postulates that civilization—particularly its cities—are "bad"; that nature in the raw is where we should be; that we should scatter
our populations over the face of the earth, demolish the cities,
require everyone to grow his own food, outlaw all methods of
mass production and mass distribution: "back to nature."

This seems to be merely another version of "God Out There."
Worshipping a particular kind of ecology merely because it is
not what humanity has generated is another form of subtle projection. Also, I suspect that a good many of the "rebels" do not

really understand living in the wild. If one tries to live in the wild, he begins to realize as time goes on that he is *still* attached by various umbilical cords to his culture. For example, if he needs light at night and uses kerosene, where did the kerosene come from? Where did the lamp come from that the kerosene is burned in? Where did the shoes come from in which you climb your mountain? Where did your clothing come from? If you have made your own clothing, where did the cloth come from? If you have made your own cloth, where did its fibers come from? And so on. Are you going to grow your own cotton, raise your own sheep, make your own wool, and carry out your nature trip to the extent that we did a hundred years ago in advancing across our country? I have noticed that fads of many types circulate among "back to nature" people—fads concerning brown rice, for example, or vitamins in various forms—"special" forms of vitamins often called "organic," as if the others were inorganic. In general, through yoga and belief systems based upon the ancient religions of the Far East, one can learn the eight chakras instead of instructions on how to repair a telephone, how to do one's own plumbing, or how to do one's own electrical work.

It seems to me that man is part of and expressive of nature. Nature includes all of man's so-called artifacts. Man is a natural development on this planet. His mission may be to create that which will make him obsolete—a solid-state form of self-reproducing life which has a better survival potential in this particular universe than has man. Therefore it behooves us in our discussions of ecology to include ourselves and our own heads in that ecology. God created us, created that which we do, are and can be, and created that which we live on, with and among. There are no two separate compartments—one labeled "human" and the other labeled "nature." This is a nonsensical dichotomy that arises from our past dogmas, before our biology taught us otherwise.

This "God Out There" attitude generates what I call "Revelation from Without." In this version one's own projections, as it were, talk back to one's self and reveal to one's self the Truth.

In reality this Truth is inside one's self. Moses, however, had to go up the mountain and through the whole business of the Ten Commandments and the tablets and God in order to bring about a change in the Jewish way of life, which he *internally* knew was necessary. With the kinds of things the Jews were then doing to one another and to their neighbors, it was high time somebody set up some kind of code. But for that code to have authority, it had to come from a revelation from *without* rather than a revelation from within. Moses claimed that God had carved the tablets on the top of the mountain; His ideas had been put into the words carved into those tablets. Moses himself was merely the agent that carried the tablets down the mountain and presented them to his people. Because of the belief systems of the Jews of that time, this was the only way Moses could get this new code accepted.

Up until the time of Christ, revelation from without kept recurring among the prophets—special professional revealers of the truth as transmitted directly from God. Christ himself did not believe in revelation from without; he believed in revelation from within. So far as one can deduce from reading some of the more modern translations of the Gospels, the Dead Sea Scrolls, and so forth, one gets the feeling that God Out There had lost by the time of Christ. He came back again later of course with Peter and Paul and the other disciples. So far as my own experience is concerned, I feel that Christ taught self-transcendence and that one *is* the Son of God, one *is* God directly. Dostoevski makes this point very strongly in the chapter "The Grand Inquisitor" in *The Brothers Karamazov*.

There is a very special form of God Out There which also includes God Inside in a very peculiar sort of way, and that is in the Taoism of China. This is a very pragmatic, practical kind of spiritual system in which The Way, the Tao, is revealed to one through the here and now, instantly, continuously, as long as one allows this to happen. One is in tune with The Way when one is *in* The Way, as it were. What The Way is and where it comes from is not very clear: it may come from within the human body, from within the collective human body; it may be a mental construct; or it may be a direct revelation from some Being greater than human. Taoism denies any separation between living the planetside trip and one's religion, one's spiritual system. The two are inseparable to the Taoist. "If it's operational, it's true."

One problem with the general assumption that God is Out There and not inside and everywhere is that one must finally appeal to an outside force, an outside entity, an outside energy source, for what we call "love." It reinvigorates old conflicts having to do with being born into a triadic relationship. Our first triangle consists of each one of us, our mother, and our father. This places dyadic strains on the newly born infant. The infant has two dyads—one each with father and with mother. However, there is a third dyad that is beyond the reach of the infant—the one between mother and father. In the resulting maneuvering that can take place with most parents, there develop certain rules in the infant's biocomputer for obtaining love from a loved person. These rules happen to be unique and peculiar to the two individuals—the mother and the father—that the child happens to have been born to. This primal preliminary kind of programming that goes on with each one of us then leads to expectations of the receipt of love from external entities under certain conditions. One's behavior corresponds to a certain set of criteria which he has deduced as existing between his mother and himself, or another set, pertaining to his own love.

If one then projects his God Out There in response to a dogmatic tradition of some sort, or in response to his own need, then he must follow certain rules in order to obtain divine love from his God Out There.

One may interpret "love" here as favors—material acquisitions, desired changes in one's character, for example. Whatever one can conceive of as being in the province of love, is in that province.

In this view, then, one might say, "God grant me, poor little unique me, thy grace and thy love. Be on my side in my agonistic battles with other humans and with other species. Take my side, it is the righteous side according to my own judgment;

therefore thou should support my side, thus making it right and full of divine love."

Thus we have those who do not believe in their God and who are beyond the pale in regard to receiving his love, his favors. Through the two World Wars we heard public prayers uttered by public figures that God would take our side and would wrathfully excoriate our enemies.

We may rather completely project onto God Out There our own systems of thinking, our own systems of feeling, and our own systems of doing, expecting intervention when we wish for intervention, expecting love when we wish for love. God Out There is expected to fulfill the needs of the individual and of the collective human mind.

There have been episodes in which mystics have contacted a state of being which gives them a new appreciation and a new perception of reality and eternity. Some of these mystics have tended to project this "as if" a God Out There, others have not. The primary phenomena of the experience, which in the Christian tradition is called "the experience of Divine Grace" or "the experience of Divine Love" and in the Arabic tradition "the experience of Divine Baraka," are taken as perceptions which validate the particular points of view, philosophies, and needs of those individuals with particular belief systems. They assume that what they do gives rise to the phenomena. This is not necessarily true. There may be, among some of the ways of thinking, feeling, and doing, clues to what it is they do that provokes these phenomena—from either within or without. At this point we are not taking sides on the sources of these phenomena; we are merely noting that these phenomena are very real but that they are also overvalued in the sense that they then extend into proofs of belief systems. Here we do not wish to throw the baby out with the bath water; we are not here putting down the phenomena of Divine Love, Divine Grace, Divine Baraka, of higher states of consciousness, and so forth. These phenomena, in my own experience and those of many of my acquaintances, are incredibly important to us. All we are calling to attention here is that if one forms the basic belief that these phenomena originate from a God Out There, from the results of one's use of rituals directed to a God Out There, and from prayer to a God Out There, then one is not exploring all the possibilities; rather he is allowing possibilities to be only those dictated by some dogma from the past. In this book we wish to examine these phenomena in more detail in later chapters, including the phenomenon of love itself.

REFERENCES

1. Castaneda, Carlos, *The Teachings of Don Juan,* New York: Simon & Schuster, 1971.
2. Wasson, Robert Gordon, *Soma, Divine Mushroom of Immortality,* New York: Harcourt, Brace & World, 1968.

CHAPTER 4

GOD AS HER/HIM/IT

As I formulated in *Programming and Metaprogramming in the Human Biocomputer* and in *The Center of the Cyclone*,[1] once the self-metaprogrammer is integrated, once he becomes a unitized individual control system within a given biocomputer, he can begin to recognize those portions of the programmatic space, of the simulation space, that may be called "supraself-metaprogramming." A well-developed, strong, integrated self-metaprogrammer has options with regard to supraself-metaprogramming. He enjoys a degree of voluntariness, of decision making, which was not his before he became integrated into a single control system. Before he became a single control system there were several control systems scattered through the biocomputer, any one of which can take control and run the show, without any necessity for the knowledge or cooperation of the others. These control systems somehow or other must be made aware of one another and, finally, made into obedient executives under a single administrator that we are calling the "self-metaprogrammer."

Part of the integration and unification process that takes place in a given biocomputer is that which redistributes the hierarchy of priority-listing of metaprograms. If I have a hierarchy that says, "I, the self-metaprogrammer, am the most important object in the universe," then, naturally, nothing else is there to control that particular self-metaprogrammer. This is a particularly childish point of view in the sense that the external reality does not necessarily agree with this point of view; other persons in the external reality are going to disagree violently and claim that *they* are the center of the universe. This childlike game finally has to terminate in order to allow mutual survival and mutual progress on our planet. Our long-past wars and the wars of the immediate past seem to originate from this kind of point of view and from a placing of oneself above others, from saying that one is superior in making decisions that have to do with his planetside trip.

The mature, educated, integrated, unitized self-metaprogrammer makes certain concessions both within the external reality and within the inner reality in regard to his or her ability to control, to evolve, and to make decisions. The mature self-metaprogrammer recognizes that there are supraself-metaprograms that he or she had best pay close attention to and adopt. These supraself-metaprograms are guides for decisions to be made. They are, as it were, handbooks of instructions on how to live successfully with love and with high positive energy in the higher states of consciousness. Each biocomputer can develop in such a way as to reveal these sets of instructions— supraself. Their sources seem to be other humans; intuitive, unconscious sources; and some sources which look like communications networks of civilizations far more advanced than our current world.

With this background set of statements about my own metabeliefs in superself, let us consider "God as Her/Him/It." In this situation, one places a particular person (male or female), organization, object, activity, way of thinking, or way of feeling in the supraself-metaprogrammatic position to the nth degree; one tends to hyperbolize the value of that which he is turning into God. Here one is creating his own God; in the traditional sense he is creating an idol to worship—and he then worships that particular idol, whether it be another living human being, an activity, a feeling, his own body, or a particular view of our civilization or of our culture.

If I fall passionately in love with somebody else, for a while that person holds the supraself-metaprogrammatic position and is therefore necessary for my "highs"—for my higher states of consciousness. My thought processes are preoccupied with my relationships with that individual, with her beauty, with her divinity of form, with the perfection of her thinking, feeling, doing. As we used to say in a particularly irreverent Catholic grade school I attended, "We act as if her feces are cold cream and her urine is champagne"—as if her smile were a long period of good weather, the way she walks the most perfect way the universe has ever devised, her self-metaprogrammer the most nearly ideal one we have ever met, and her supraself-metaprograms a perfect match for our own.

In such a passionate dyad many things occur which we could hope would occur among all human beings consistently and over longer periods of time. In general this "overevaluation of a given individual"—making that individual into a god or a goddess—seems to be part of growing up. We talk about infantile love, childish love, adolescent love, and finally, mature love. The infant, child and adolescent loves partake of making a God out of another human. They also are a learning platform from which one makes progress in the proper assignment of supraself-metaprograms in the proper areas. One has to make the mistake, as it were, of assigning this to at least one human being, unconsciously, before one realizes consciously that he has done so. Much of learning is doing that which one will never do again.

The God as Her/Him/It is a lesson to be learned, a stage in one's progress toward mature understanding of the relationship between the self-metaprogrammer and the supraself-metaprograms. God as Her/Him/It is a passing stage even as is God Out There and I Am God.

One particular movement which has resulted from this God as Her/Him/It, results from the existential point of view that "God is dead." If there is no God Out There (and this is the only God that seems to be dead now), then one makes a God of something else as a substitute God-formation. So one worships and venerates something else. If one suddenly realizes that there is no

God Out There, then he makes a political system, a Her/Him/It, into God.

In this country, humanism has become this sort of substitute movement. Paying closer attention to connections between individuals, using encounter group techniques, Gestalt, psychological techniques, and Maslow's view of "peak experiences," [2] is a substitute system for God Out There. Mankind's attention was focused on God Out There until modern science said, in effect, "This cannot be." So then we began to put God among us as part of humanity. Love for fellow man became the primary directive. We began to pay more attention to taking care of the only body we have; we began to get Rolfed (see page 39), we began to jog, we continued our athletics, we began to meet one another on much deeper levels in what is called "encounter." The best of encounter is not merely telling the usual lies to one another but telling the truth as one sees it, in the present instant, in the present situation—not denying one's hostility, not denying one's love, but producing behavior consonant with one's internal feelings.

This movement places God in humanity. You are God/I am God is part of this movement. Falling in love with another, in the sense that we are expected, as it were, to be able to fall in love with each and every human on the planet, is a further part. If we cannot do this, we then say, "I wish I were perfect, I am sorry I cannot be perfect." We then pray to one another, rather than to God Out There. We ask forgiveness from one another, rather than from the distant God. We carry out rituals with one another, we make all the love mistakes that have been categorized by Freud and by others, carrying over mistaken programming from our infancy and youth into our adult years. The unfinished business of infancy and youth is continuously worked upon in adulthood as we try to find solutions for internal tape loops which continue to rotate despite our efforts to still them.

If one has had sibling-parent situations in the past in which one of the siblings or one of the parents died, leaving the whole business unfinished, then these processes can continue automatically below one's level of awareness, and generate motivations for increasing his intensity of experience with others in order to resolve problems set up by these tape loops. If one remembers that the young biocomputer (in fear, terror, panic, guilt, etc.) tends to put in overriding orders or instructions for the future operation of that biocomputer as if the current situation were going to be eternal, then he can realize that these instructions are to be lowered in the hierarchy—in the priority list, so to speak—of instructions for that biocomputer. These are especially powerful in regard to those humans whom one loved as a very young person. One tends to carry these programs forward as if they were still true in an external reality that does not recognize their truth and from which opportunities for actual demonstration of their truth are lacking.

For example, "I am two years old. I am being weaned. My younger brother was just born and he has taken over Mother from me. She is now suckling him and has suddenly stopped suckling me." This unconscious program leads to rage in the young person against the younger brother, but as aging takes place the younger brother can become any other male, and the mother can become any other female with whom the adult becomes interlocked in a love relationship. A perpetual tendency to try to restore the love relationship between the baby and the mother continues in the adult in inappropriate ways—in very uncomfortable triangular situations; in the case of the male, for example, who attempts to separate a male and a female in order to regain his former pre-eminence with a female—a pre-eminence he does not now have in the external reality but had only with the original mother. Finding such a tape loop does not guarantee that it will cease to have importance in the hierarchy of instructions to the biocomputer; a thorough analysis of it to see how it operates in multiple situations is necessary before the charge can be taken from it and it can be moved down lower in the hierarchical list.

The contingencies of God as Her/Him/It can be seen very strongly in such situations. The mother has become a God who inhabits other female bodies and whom one must propitiate, pray to, love, seduce, and in general have intense relationships with in order to obtain Divine Grace, Baraka, higher states of consciousness, and so forth. Such belief systems are dramatically self-limiting.

On the mystical side, the mystical phenomena seem to be inducible in a given human biocomputer through associating with a guru as if that guru were God himself. In the best cases a guru will be someone whom one can emulate in reprogramming himself in order to achieve and remain in higher states of consciousness by following the way of life prescribed by the given guru. (A modern American example of this relationship is that of Baba Ram Dass and his Indian guru. However, in their case there was a conscious choice, a searching for and a finding of one who could teach Ram Dass what he wished to know.) The guru as God depends upon the quality of the guru one picks. There are those who are on "ego trips," "power trips," "organization-of-large-groups-of-people trips," and others, who may entrap one into their movement by means of "I am God" or the "Guru as God" or the "Group as God."

Of course one must examine very carefully the unconscious tape loops, the tape loops below one's level of awareness which could select *who* is to be his particular guru as God. In fact, before seeking for a guru, one should look to his motives. It may be that he is merely once again seeking a situation he considers to be "ideal"—with mother or with mother and father or with a sibling. One's ideals generate what he considers to be virtuous behavior; it is wise to consider whether or not this "virtuous" behavior is really what one wants. One can behave for years in accordance with what he considers to be a virtuous mode, and then suddenly discover that the mode is anything but virtuous, that it is postulated not upon virtue but upon something else inside himself that he was unaware of. With the gain of proper experiences, a whole system of beliefs can fall apart and one may be left with a reconsideration of the whole basis of his total motivation and life-style. If one wants to take the position of the Tao, he can say that these are learning opportunities which have been thrown his way as he followed the Way. One hears some Taoists saying, "Everything that happens is perfect as it happens; all lessons are to be learned as presented." In effect, this is saying that the spiritual path is perfect of itself. This claim reminds me of a famous modern Tibetan spiritual leader who, when asked, "What is liberation?," said, "Liberation is freedom from the spiritual path."

The technical name for carrying over unfinished love business from one's infancy and youth into his adulthood is "transference." Transference is the expression of love or of hatred (it can be either positive or negative) for a particular individual or object on the basis of specific programming from one's infancy and childhood. Transference can involve a subject's teacher, guru, mate, brother, sister, acquaintance, boss, employee, or whomever. In the trans-ference relationship the object can detect the positive and the negative aspects of the relationship and, if he is particularly in-sightful, can realize the inappropriateness of the required rela-tionship. About the set of instructions he is getting from one's below-levels-of-awareness programming such a person can say, "This is inappropriate at the present time. It looks as though it may be some historical episode generating these instructions."

The young must also realize that there is a very basic pro-gramming that is part of the human animal. It exists in its female form and in its male form. Directly and simply, the young human female wants her uterus filled, and the young human male wants to fill her uterus. This set of species-survival pro-grams is so basic that it is very difficult for the young to detect. Only as one strives to detect this particular set of programs, to put them in perspective, to analyze and look at them with knowledge of transference phenomena, only then can he see the inappropriateness of them for his supraself-metaprogramming. One, as it were, produces his children almost unconscious of *why* he is producing children. It is an automatic set of programs present in each of us that carries on the race irrespective of the wishes of the individual. In a sense, then, the reproductive urges are supraself when one is young, and only with more and more awareness can they possibly become conscious. In most people consciousness of the reproductive urges increases with the in-crease of distance from the extreme energy that they had when young. As one ages, he tends to divert energy away from this particular system into other systems of thought, feeling and doing. The original energy is incredible in its power and its quantity. Only with time does its urgency diminish. Numbers of trips around the sun are necessary before the realization of how powerful and how unconscious this system of programs really is. It is almost as if until one has fulfilled his reproduction instructions and produced one, or two, or more children, the force of these programs will not diminish. It is as if one has to have children in order never to have to have children again.

One's own children can teach oneself a good deal of truth about his own past history. To a certain extent he can see in miniature, as it were, that which he had to go through. He can also see that it is almost impossible to communicate his accrued wisdom to the younger generation as he lives with them. Their selective forgetting, their selective awareness, are so obvious to older people, even as, to the young, the lack of certain energies in older adults is obvious. Some persons can also make God out of a child, or several children—or out of a spouse. If these children die before oneself dies, then one dies quickly thereafter. This degree of transference is extreme, but it is very real for some individuals.

God as Her/Him/It limits one's own life span, limits his loves, his activities, his thinking processes. This belief places bounds upon one's knowledge, upon his experience of our universe.

REFERENCES

1. Lilly, John C., *Programming and Metaprogramming in the Human Bio-computer*, New York: Julian Press, 1967, 1972; and *The Center of the Cyclone*, New York, Toronto, London: Bantam Books, 1972, 1973.
2. Maslow, Abraham H., *Religions, Values, and Peak Experiences*, New York: Viking Press, 1970.

CHAPTER 5

GOD AS THE GROUP

At times the very peculiar syndrome known as "God as The Group" permeates our lives almost to the exclusion of everything else. Human groups and their demands upon us are ever present, day and night, awake and asleep. The special case of the group of two (or the dyad) will be considered in more detail in other chapters. Here we will consider the larger groups, starting with the family.

Each of us is born into a dyad, i.e., we complete a triadic relationship. If there are children born ahead of us, we are born into a group that places its demands upon us almost at birth. The newborn baby is an object of interest to almost everybody and as it grows its upbringing is of interest to everyone in the family. The seductive aspects of group activity are here presented to each of us in full panoply. All the sticky love and hate relationships that are going to dominate our lives are here present in embryo and in full-blown catastrophe. A small baby in trouble possesses a universe which is collapsing on him. A small baby in a love relationship possesses a whole universe which is expanding him and itself. Older siblings may try to do away with him or to love him to death. Younger siblings will displace him from mother and from other members of the group, and he will have to establish his own relationships, his own group, if you wish. Some children join already-formed groups;

others form their own groups. Let us look at these "children-groups" for a moment.

In general there is a leadership, the strongest members of the group, who dictates the terms for becoming a member and maintaining membership and also the rules for removing a member from the group. In general there are initiation rites for joining the group, and continuing rituals for being a continued member—contributions in financial support and in work to be performed for the group, for example. There are peer criteria of performance; there are judgments made of each person's individual performance, accomplishments, feelings, and what he says as a member of the group. There is a continual exchange of gossip among the members; each group develops its palace politics, which becomes a constant source of new rumors about what is or is not going to happen next in terms of group interest or activities. There are attempts by the leadership to create, and have the group create, dramatic happenings involving non-members of the group in order to demonstrate the strength of the group and its superiority to nonmembers. There are secret signs, even a secret language may develop; there are special knocks to open a door, there are special places for meeting, usually hidden. There are careful observations of the behavior of members when they are separated from the group; there are loyalty tests based upon criteria set up by the leadership of the particular group. There is expectation that the members will praise the leadership for its activities and that the leaders will praise the members for theirs.

All the various mechanisms that Irving L. Janis discusses in his book *The Victims of Groupthink* [1] are present in these children-groups. It is out of these young groups that adult "groupthink" models are derived. To a child who is a member of an elite group, say a very active one which is bringing him a lot of satisfaction, that group becomes God. Much of his thinking, his feeling, and his doing are centered around that particular group. He feels that he doesn't amount to anything in his neighborhood except as a member of that group. His individual accomplishments and status lose their meaning as he becomes one of Them. It is a situation very similar to that of God as Her/Him/It, in the sense that the group here becomes the "It" —a very large It—or a group of Hims or a group of Hers. The concept of transference presented earlier is demonstrated most strongly in such groups. The child's love, awe, fear and guilt from his original trial are now transferred to an entity known as "The Group." Such a group, if organized by adults and watched over very carefully by adults, can lead these children into casting the group onto the national scene. In the United States we have such "children-groups" as the Boy Scouts of America, the Campfire Girls, military schools, all sorts of chuch groups in the various denominations—all perpetuated in such special boys' or girls' clubs as the Elks, the Kiwanis, the Rotary, the Masons, the Rebeccas, the D.A.R., NOW; the hierarchy of the Catholic Church; police departments; fire departments; the United States Army, Air Force, Navy; the CIA; the FBI.

As one matures in the United States he can join any number of groups that are totally organized and will organize his life for him. There is no real need for independent thought, independent feeling, or independent action, if he wants to avoid them. If he has God as The Group, then he can safely keep God as The Group and function successfully in the planetside trip, at least he could in the United States as of 1974. There are even nonsafe groups that one can belong to—such as Hell's Angels, the Communist party, the John Birch Society, and various other militant and rebel groups scattered throughout the country. One can select a God of any stripe as The Group. The zoology of groups that function "as if God" is multifarious and polymorphous.

Some of these groups are so well organized that they have lasted hundreds of years—for example, the Catholic Church and various other churches, the United States Government and various state, city, and small-town governments.

Corporations and other organizations such as partnerships,

and individuals doing business with one another, know very well how to use the group as if God. A successful business is a successful group operating as a unit, usually under the leadership of one or two strong individuals. However, in a strong, large corporate structure, there need not be strong individual leaders; there can be an interlocked oligarchy that, in effect, runs the corporation. Looked at from the outside, any large corporation is such an immense feedback system of many individuals working in concert that short of a complete systems analysis, no individual within the corporation could tell you where all the power actually resides. The power to make decisions, to set strategy, and so forth, may not be where it appears to be. An operations analysis of a large corporation and the corporations with which it does business can show tilt points and places where energy can be shifted by putting the proper information in the proper hands.

Even as in the old-fashioned view of "woman versus man," the woman is still expected to take a back seat, so that for many years in U.S. business women have been paid less than men to do the same job and have had less power than men within almost any particular business organization. Most organizations of any kind in the United States are boys' clubs; there are a few girls' clubs, and a very few boy-and-girl clubs. Most of those that pretend to be boy-and-girl clubs seem to be run sub rosa by the men involved. This boys'-club model carries on all the way up through the highest levels of the United States Government. The number of women who have served in Congress, in the cabinet, in executive positions throughout the bureaucracy of the United States Government is very small indeed. The same applies to the United Nations—and to the administration of most of our schools. With very few exceptions men's groups run the politics, business, and education of our nation.

In some sports, women do play an important part. The superior physical flexibility of women was shown in their superior performances as gymnasts in the 1972 Olympics. Usually there are special events for women and special events for men, with very little competition between the sexes. However, there are sports which are overwhelmingly men's, such as professional football, professional golf, professional tennis, and so forth. In the more individual sports, such as skiing, women have come into their own. Boxing is still a male sport (it seems to exist for no reason other than to create brain damage in those males who insist on boxing too long and too ferociously).

Much modern government is fast becoming a very patriarchal source of loving compassion. This particular boys' club—the government—seems to be progressively taking more and more of the responsibility of an individual for himself away from him and granting it to groups of "experts."

A recent example of this concerns the Federal Food and Drug Administration, which has decided that vitamins above a certain potency are to be considered prescription items to be dispensed only by a druggist and only on the written say-so of a doctor, with both sharing the profit that goes with the arrangement. Recently the FDA also decided that biofeedback devices will have to be sold on prescription. It looks as though even our brain waves are subject to government control. We are not allowed a peek at our own brain waves except under the auspices of a member of the medical profession.

Thus, group pressure expresssed through government, acting back upon the individual, can wield the stamp of "illegal" in order to "protect the public interest." In other words, this particular pressure group has assumed that the rest of the population are idiots who will not learn how to take care of themselves with modern drugs, modern inventions of various sorts; and yet it is quite willing to allow each of these "idiots" to drive a modern juggernaut at high speeds without such effective controls. However, even safety devices on cars express the patriarchal aspect of government. The buzzers for seatbelts and brakes and doors are a continuing expression of the father-like care that the United States Government is taking of its citizens. In effect, the group is saying: "There is no such thing as individual responsibility; we as The Group will take responsibility for each of you.

If you do not agree with our rules for taking responsibility, we will fine you and put you in jail. In other words, if you take responsibility, we are going to make a criminal out of you." This is true not only for automobiles and drugs, but for possessing, selling and distributing certain weeds, plants, and medical devices.

One particular group activity that has been shown to be particularly effective is the control by The Group of the states of consciousness of the individual. A given group will say: "There are certain states of consciousness which we expect of you; there are other states of consciousness which we expect you not to go into. These are forbidden states of consciousness."

Certain states of consciousness are to be forbidden because only saints, mystics, and far-out people from the Far East go into them. There is to be no bliss, no ecstasy, no nirvana, no samadhi, no satori, except under very, very carefully controlled conditions and in the presence of the group.

In another area, there are groups which insist, for example, on group sexual activities. These exert influences just as powerful upon each individual in the group as do more conventional groups. Group loyalty is to be expressed by being discreet with outsiders about group activities. Persons to be selected as new members are to be selected by all group members; any one person can blackball any potential new member. Any current member can be thrown out of the group by a sufficient vote against that particular member. Of course in reality any person the leadership does not like can be ousted and the leadership can act "as if" the decision were a group decision.

One particular concomitant of group activity which we all face is the law. The legal system, the police, the courts, the penal system—all have been carried over from the past and are presented to us, as we grow up, as *faits accomplis*. The enactment of new laws applicable to all citizens equally can at best provide some of us with useful guidelines for individual and group behavior. What should concern us is the climate in which such laws can be sponsored and enacted. On more than one occasion legislatures frightened by a climate of panic have voted into law measures they should have been examining more objectively. Laws passed under conditions of panic can be like the laws the young pass in their own mind under such conditions. They are extreme reactions to what is thought to be an emergency that will last eternally; they replace careful examination of the root causes and the effect of a given set of happenings. Laws passed in a state of national hysteria can lead to negative national programs and the creation of opposition in nationwide undergrounds.

What is the individual to do in the face of such group pressure? First of all, he can examine within himself the instructions he has acquired on behavior within given groups. He can very carefully scan such instructions from his infantile, childhood and adolescent years. He can examine the laws he has legislated for himself which are not consonant with a full and satisfying life on our planet. He can examine his current group relationships and see how much he is paying for whatever benefits he is receiving from the group.

A realistic attribution of the privileges, property, or relationships derived through one's own effort versus that of one's group memberships must be established. It is a necessity that one be strong enough, and free enough, to pause and take a good look at what he owes to whom in terms of individual and group activity. Through isolation of himself from all groups for an hour or more each day for weeks, months, even years, one will acquire what can be acquired no other way—a grounding platform for functioning within groups.

Examining God as The Group within oneself is a cleansing and creative process. If one has the advantages of an isolation tank, or of a room in which he can be alone under sensorily reduced and isolated conditions, he can look at the internal structure of his own mind and its relationship to groups of various sorts. He can look at his family relationships, his business, church, or club relationships, his government or military organization relationships, his medical or dental relationships—all the various aspects of his planetside trip in which he is considered a member of various groups. There are times while in solitude, isolation and confinement when it looks as if one is nothing but a cross-correlated member of multiple groups with no other reality. Thus, the God that creates one is a whole set of groups of which one is a member.

To a certain extent this viewpoint is true. Without being members of groups we would not have language itself; we would not have electricity, automobiles, gas supplies; we would not have telephones, TV, radio; we would not have highways, ships, airplanes; we would not have materials to build our own house; we would not in fact probably ever have very much of anything.

This incredible dependence of the individual on the group in modern civilization can become stultifying and non-creative. However, once we realize that a certain minimum part of this relationship with groups is absolutely necessary for our own survival, then we can see how willing we are to put up with group activity in order to maintain our standard of living and standard of survival.

Practically no one individual can possibly understand what it is that motivates a group mind of the size of a nation by the time the group gets to be that size. When hundreds of millions of people together have the kind of organization that we call a nation, effective understanding of the interrelated facets of that organization becomes an awesome burden. In regions of national ignorance one can see how episodes like World War II, Vietnam, and Korea can get started. When for reasons of national security there is a definite policy for preventing the transmittal of certain kinds of information to the body politic, then one can see that individuals caught up in the groupthink of government itself—especially those isolated at the top by their own group-think processes—can lead us down paths we may later regret having traveled. The immense complexity of feedback patterns in terms of money flow and power within such groups is incredibly hard to understand. When we extend the concept of the nation to the whole planet and see the multiplicity of human types within nations, the polymorphous, continuous, multiple feedbacks based on differing belief systems throughout the planet become an overwhelmingly difficult set of processes to understand.

As we devise more and better means of getting off the planet and looking at it from outer space, we will begin to obtain a more accurate perspective on human affairs. We will tend then to magnify the human condition less, to seek an objective perspective, to acquire a new set of priorities. We will see that certain kinds of activity on the planet are totally nonessential for improving the lot of humankind. We will see that the use of poisons, weapons, and violence in general can only be a means of regulating the total population—and doing this in a nonevolving fashion.

In the United States we select through the draft our most effective youth and then send them out to learn how to kill and be killed in the name of the defense of the group known as the nation. In other words, we continue our sacrifices to idols even as in the days of Baal and Maloch and the sacrifice of human babies in the furnaces of these gods. Modern war is merely this ancient religious custom brought up to date and made more efficient. In the United States, God as The Group dictates that God's will is national survival—whatever that may mean. Our leaders time and again blame national security as the reason for their actions. Like the ancient priests of esoteric rites, our modern leaders keep secrecy tightly clamped on what really is happening: who is killing whom, who is spying on whom, who has a power advantage here versus a lack of power there, and so on.

As we leave the planet Earth, look back at our human activities, and realize that from a mere hundred miles out our presence on our planet is very hard to detect, we can begin to see that in terms of our solar system our activities are not very important. Our most horrendous explosions are hardly noticeable on the next planet. The largest of our megaton hydrogen bombs makes a flash which, if somebody happens to be looking in the right direction at the right time, might be seen across our solar system but would not be seen at all farther out in our galaxy. The galaxy itself may have groups that are watching and caring about what our groups are doing. It may also not. If we are going to project our patriarchal, and matriarchal, ideas onto the galaxy, we are probably going to make the same mistakes that we made in the past in regard to our planet. If we suspect that there are out there beings thousands of years ahead of our civilization who are going to rescue us from our own childish mistakes, we are probably setting ourselves up for a stunning surprise.

There are those who claim divine guidance and wish to pass messages on to the rest of us, messages derived from entities not human, from networks of communication not available to all of us, from direct personal contacts with other entities, spirits, and guides way beyond anything that we have directly experienced on this planet. Such experiences have given rise to pronouncements about God; pronouncements about God Out There, pronouncements about God in Here, God as The Group, God as Her/Him/It.

It is extremely likely that there are civilizations within our galaxy much farther advanced than ours, even as there probably are out there forms of life at a lower level of organization than ours. It is also extremely likely that means of communication used by civilizations in advance of ours are totally non-understandable in terms of our present science, even as the concepts of radio and television were totally non-understandable by the total populace three hundred years ago. One hydrogen bomb set off one hundred years ago would have exacted thousands of "explanations" but no understanding among most of the people on our planet.

We can see that in the future our regions of ignorance will be much larger than our regions of knowledge. We still do not know how, when, or where we are connected to other entities in this galaxy in terms of our modern science. We do not know how large a galactic group we are members of. Certain direct experiences I have had in isolation and others have had under similar circumstances seem to indicate that we are in contact with a much larger network than our current consensus science says we are. In this sense God as The Largest Group may extend far beyond our planet and even beyond our galaxy into the whole universe.

REFERENCE

1. Janis, Irving L., *The Victims of Groupthink*, Boston: Houghton Mifflin, 1972.

CHAPTER 6

GOD AS ORGASM AND SEX

If we are anything more than highly evolved apes with a medium-sized cerebral cortex, with built-in urges to survive and to propagate the species, then we may give up "God as Orgasm and Sex." If one is in the position of worshipping sexual stimulants, feelings, and activities, then he is not able to take an objective look at what he is and what his beliefs are concerning sex. If one is caught up by the current media treatment of sex as pornography or obscenity—or as something to be transmitted via movies, tabloids, or slick magazines—or is turned on to the special clothing, instruments and drugs that can excite and heighten sexual pleasure, or by the availability of sexual companions at a price, then one is believing in God as Orgasm and Sex.

In this belief system there is an obvious separation of sexuality from the rest of one's life. It is a special system created by the group who wants to sell it and nurtured by the group who buys it. Even as with other religious dogmas, this system becomes demanding upon one's time. So let us examine the system in detail.

Each one of us has a basic biocomputer with built-in survival programs and built-in sexual programs. The classical purpose for these sexual programs is reproduction of the species, which, without birth control, is the likely result of so-called "normal" heterosexual activities of the healthy young. As we age, with more and more trips around the sun, we begin to realize that these urges do not necessarily have the importance they assumed when we were younger. As we age we begin to see mysteries where before there were only certainties; we begin to view the wellsprings of pleasure and pain more as subjects of speculation than powerful urges compelling us into certain kinds of activity. The young, however, in replying to their urges to mate, to make love, to reach orgasm, to reproduce, are merely performing certain kinds of activity in order to meet the current demands from within of their built-in sexual programs.

With the male the processes of sexual arousal, tumescence, orgasm with ejaculation, and detumescence are in general thought of as the usual stages in a special program that, once started, goes all the way to completion, i.e., from sexual arousal to final orgasm with ejaculation. Many years ago, in working with electrodes in the brains of monkeys, we demonstrated that these processes are not necessarily hooked in to the same parts of the central nervous system, i.e., that there are separate sets of subroutines for each of these phenomena. Stimulating one area would cause erection but not orgasm or ejaculation. Stimulating another area would cause ejaculation but not erection or orgasm. Stimulating a third area would cause orgasm but not erection or ejaculation. We also found a central nervous system in which all three processes followed one after the other in the expected slavish fashion.

Large numbers of human males have experimented with separating these sexual processes one from the other. Success in this is especially easy as one ages. The necessity of one's youth of galloping to orgasm-ejaculation is no longer present. There are alternatives.

In the human female the sexual processes are much less obvious and much less definite and generally are inclined to be somewhat entangled with her nest-building proclivities. However, there are exceptions. In *The Happy Hooker*[1] Xaviera Hollander states that women, once liberated from the old programs, can really enjoy sexual activities without any necessity of their being hooked up to propagation, children, and nest building. In addition the female in general seems to have more staying power than the male; in general she can achieve multiple orgasm without fatigue, whether initiation is from the clitoris or from the vagina.

So-called "sexual energy," like money, can be used for many different purposes. It does not have to follow the arousal-to-orgasm script programmed into one's biocomputer. Man or woman can use his or her "sexual energy" for purposes other than the direct expression of sexuality.

The rituals of Tantra Yoga, for example, introduce one to methods of holding off orgasm and maintaining sexual arousal over very long periods of time. Once one can achieve these goals, one can see how flexible sexual energy really can be. One can shift it, as it were, from the basic biological substrate and the very narrow railroad-track program of the usual sexual encounter, to something far more complex—almost abstract and quite mystical. For some persons caution should be used in dealing with unknown energies.

If one follows the Tantra Yoga rituals very carefully he will find he can attain the so-called higher states of consciousness through sexual arousal and subsequent forestalling of orgasm and ejaculation. Of course, in all such pursuits one attuned to the program of God as Orgasm and Sex must be well aware that his biocomputer is so constructed that it is going to overvalue pleasurable states resulting from sexual activity. Almost as a built-in guarantee of propagation of the species, this program of God as Orgasm and Sex seems to reoccur again and again in different texts.

Thus, if one pursues the Tantra Yoga path, for example, he attains regions of very high feeling and very high energy states in which he will begin to feel that he is achieving union with his Creator. Such high energy states are useful in terms of exploring far-off spaces. Recently, Robert A. Wilson, in a book called *Sex and Drugs*,[2] pointed out the rather obvious fact that certain chemical substances mobilize and allow a more prolonged enjoyment of sexual activities and sexual activation. He mentions specifically Cannabis sativa and LSD 25. Since these substances turn on one's emotional amplifiers and turn up their intensity control, it is very easy to achieve high energy states of a sexual nature while under their influence. Some people are quite capable of moving themselves into sexual spaces, up to the edge of orgasm, and holding that space for a period of up to four, even six hours.

Once one has done this he may say, "So what?" The ability to delay orgasm merely means that the biocomputer controls a great reservoir of sexual energy which it releases under the influence of certain chemical substances. For those who are still worshipping God as Orgasm and Sex, this kind of information is useful—for a while. Later it all begins to seem rather obvious and one will probably drop the whole program, again as aging takes place.

In certain cultures—classical Polynesian culture, for example —the belief system regarding sex is that sexual activity is part of growing up, part of one's social life, and it should not be taken as seriously as it is in the United States today. To the Polynesian, sex is fun, a part of life, a series of fun games rather than a serious business. In cultures where this view obtains, there is no such thing as pornography or God as Orgasm and Sex. There seems to be more of a God as The Group belief structure.

In my own experience I have found that highly aroused sexual feelings prevented from going full cycle can lead one into far-out spaces outside the body. In *The Center of the Cyclone* [3] the descriptions of +3 and +6 show that these two states of consciousness share a good deal of this quality of sexual arousal "beyond sex," if one wishes to put it that way. Whether this is another kind of energy which is aroused through the sexual, or whether it is sexual energy itself, is a moot point. The high energy states of consciousness of the extra-ordinary variety seem to be vastly pleasurable high energy states which somehow or other are beyond sex.

This feeling that they are beyond sex may, of course, come from our Western preprogramming by mystics or philosophers such as St. Theresa of Avila, St. John of the Cross, and Martin Buber. Freud felt that all the described states they mention were sublimated sexual states. C. G. Jung was not so sure of this; he felt that there were far more states than merely sexual arousal.

I cannot resolve this issue any more than my predecessors could. It seems to me that, in general, central nervous system energy can be expressed in many different ways, the sexual being among the more compelling. One can initiate the arousal of sexual energy by the usual method—stimulation of breasts, penis, vagina or clitoris—and then move into other states of consciousness through this arousal if he can transpose it from the sexual system to other systems, avoiding in the process the obvious programs of sex itself. Once one can achieve this kind of transposition, then the energy can be moved not only throughout the body but into other people outside oneself. But until one can apply it to his work, for example, or to some other productive activity, he will still be caught up by narrow programming of his sexual energy. After one achieves this moving about of energy, the energy apparently becomes unrecognizable as the original force. Cerebral cortical control over the energy systems of the brain itself becomes so expert that it is almost as though there is no more need for pushing sexual systems as such. The pleasurable extremes of energy and sensation are not only those of orgasm.

As one becomes exposed to metaprograms which say, "No matter what happens, remain conscious and record the experience"; as one becomes better and better at this art of maintaining consciousness in the presence of extreme levels of pleasure or extreme levels of pain, one begins to enter new regions of experience and of mystery. As soon as we break loose from the automatic programming of the biocomputer in the body and move into regions in which the energy of that biocomputer is available to us for various purposes removed from its original purpose, we can begin to see that God as Orgasm is a very limiting set of beliefs. This is believing that the railroad-track simplicity of the human body is the be-all and end-all of the universe. This may be true or not true; if one believes it to be true, however, it definitely is true for oneself. But let us put aside sexual energies for the moment and talk about God as Love.

As was stated earlier, love of the infant variety (love for the mother and/or the father), love of parents by the child, love of other children by the child, love of the adolescent—these are slowly maturing sets of programs. In the first case the infant's love is based upon pleasure and survival in that pleasure. If the early infant receives too much pain he dies. Love that concerns the infant and the child is based upon survival. In the adolescent, love is based more on self-assertion if the survival is being taken care of. If the adolescent does not know anything else, then out of this ignorance he or she may follow the dictates of the repro-ductive urges and produce children.

During the processes of maturation, however, some energy may be diverted, to be used extracurricularly, if you wish, in becoming enamored of knowledge or technique, of thinking or of doing. The love of thinking or the love of doing can also be projected out and be called God as Love.

There is another school of God as Love which forbids orgasm. This is the typical celibate program of the Catholic Church, of various schools of Yoga, of the so-called brahmacharya trip, and so on. These schools attempt to bypass the demands of the biocomputer, putting them down as belonging to one's "lower animal nature." In this school the belief is that if one indulges in sexual intercourse—i.e., makes love—then one necessarily cannot achieve a high spiritual state; if one is able to forego sexual intercourse, a high spiritual state will automatically re-sult from the deprivation. In general this system seems to work to a certain extent for some persons but not at all for others. One of my friends has told me that in the state of brahmacharya —i.e., without sexual intercourse—most of his thinking is about sex. In effect, one cannot avoid sex by forbidding it to himself. However, as one gets older and the force of biocomputer urges decreases, the brahmacharya trip is much easier to achieve. Those who are on this trip show an intense, youthful enthusiasm for whatever it is they are doing which is considered to be a substitute for the sexual trip. There is an infectious freshness about them—especially about those who are carrying it out successfully.

Some persons who have had a very active sex life and then in their later years are forced into the brahmacharya state because of the death of their mate, either find a new mate or tend to die off slowly. God as Orgasm and Sex has become to them synonymous with life. Brahmacharya does not seem to be the answer for most people in the United States. If these people could be induced to change their basic belief systems, it is possible that they would take on whole new programs related to the use of their basic energies. The use of these energies is one of the stickiest areas of human striving and the most filled with ambivalence, judgmental attitudes, and destructive judgments, actions, and feelings.

It is important to realize that the effect of sexual activity in our biocomputer operations is transitory—that although after sexual intercourse one feels an easing of tension, a renewed concentration of thought in desired areas, a certain relief from the biological urges within us, the sexual urges eventually rise again in their incessant march toward fulfillment. By keeping this aspect of one's biocomputer satisfied, one can avoid God as Orgasm worshipful activity. For most persons this seems to be the most satisfactory course. If there is a better one, I would like to hear about it.

REFERENCES

1. Hollander, Xaviera, *The Happy Hooker*, New York: Dell Publishing Co., 1972, 1973.
2. Wilson, Robert A., *Sex and Drugs*, Chicago: Playboy Press, 1973.
3. Lilly, John C., *The Center of the Cyclone*, New York, Toronto, London: Bantam Books, 1972, 1973.

CHAPTER 7

GOD AS DEATH

Each one of us must face his own death. Insofar as is known through our present-day science, no one of us is immortal. At least there is evidence from history that every human being can expect to die. Most of us would find it difficult to follow consciously don Juan's advice to Carlos Castaneda: "Keep death at your left hand." [1] Rather, most of us generally attempt to avoid a realization that our own end must come, leaving such considerations for times when we are depressed.

How we face our death at the time that it has become imminent will depend upon our belief systems operating at that particular time. If we believe that death is the end of us as an individual—the total, utter and complete end—then we will face our death with a set of feelings and realizations different from any set we previously had.

Let us take a good look at death as "the end," Death as God ruling our lives. According to this set of beliefs, we are born into the world as a result of the sexual activities of our parents; we live out our life span as a biological organism and eventually die—either through accident, disease, the operations of other people, or what we call old age.

Most persons in the United States have been exposed to a view of death taken from some organized religion—a view that, in summary, tells us that our body will die but our soul will go somewhere else for judgment, eventually to rejoin the body, which on the day of final judgment will rise again from the ground in which it is buried.

This particular belief system, even though it does not have as many adherents as it enjoyed in the last century, dominates those American industries that thrive on death. One is expected to buy or lease a plot of ground into which his body is to be placed at the end of his life. His survivors are expected to have that body embalmed and otherwise prepared by morticians to be as lifelike looking as possible for the wake. At the funeral, all one's relatives and friends are supposed to gather to mourn his departure. Thus do the industries which market coffins, floral arrangements, cemetery plots, and so forth, thrive on the God as Death belief system (see *The American Way of Death* by Jessica Mitford [2]).

What the cause of one's own death eventually will be is in all probability quite indeterminate. We are surrounded in modern civilization by almost countless potentially lethal devices and lethal situations, day in and day out. In California, for example, it is quite impossible to say when, and if, a very large earthquake may occur, wiping us out along with tens of thousands of other people. Anytime we drive a car at high speed on a freeway, we are placing ourself in jeopardy. In the ordinary home there are plenty of opportunities to be electrocuted, burned, suffocated, or poisoned. So, we do live with death at our left hand, even though we may ignore it.

Those who have been through a close brush with death followed by a long period of recovery in which they had a good hard look at the possibilities of dying, are in a better-than-average position to question their belief system regarding God as Death. One may suddenly be thrown into a coma for causes which he does not know, even though others, outside his body, can easily see what they are—an encephalitis virus which shoots up one's temperature, a cerebral vascular accident, a bad fall with a blow to the head, a head-on automobile smashup, or leaking gas while one is asleep.

The point here is that the outside view of what happens to us under such grave circumstances is not at all like the inside view of what happens under these circumstances. I have collected many firsthand accounts of close brushes with death and have asked specifically about the inside experiences. I have had my own close scrapes with death and have recounted them in *The Center of the Cyclone.*[3]

To summarize all too briefly, most people experience a set of realities entirely different from the external realities during a period of traumatic unconsciousness. Of course we have been able to get accounts only from survivors, but in general the inside view is that there are realities in which one does not have a body, or the necessity for a body, but has his intelligence, memories, consciousness and emotions. In other words, he is a complete individual, extra-body, "sans body."

This individual exists in realities in which there are other entities like the self. This reality in which he finds himself seems to be endless, eternal, and repeating. There are rumors that there is no death in these regions, that one goes on eternally and can do other things than inhabit a human vehicle. To the people with these sets of experiences, the human body is merely a temporary abode for something else which classically, in Christian theology, is called the "soul." In *The Center of the Cyclone* I called it the "essence." In Yoga terms it is the "atman," and so forth. These kinds of experience are cross-cultural and have been recorded in various parts of the world and interpreted in various ways according to the belief systems then current.

In some instances the feeling is that one has left a temporary proprietorship by a human condition and returned to a much more generalized abstract condition in which he is of vast general purpose. The alternatives in this second state of existence are much greater than those that exist when one is in the human body. One's access to knowledge is freer, unimpeded by human considerations. One somehow or other is more objective, more understanding, more loving than he is in the human body. One can also suffer more in this state if he has need to. He can go through heavens, he can go through hells, and he can go through a state of High Indifference (Merrell-Wolff).[4] If he approaches this state centered within his own knowledge and belief systems, then he can move *through* the state and back out again much more intact than if he had had no preprogramming in regard to approaching this particular state. For those who have been in this state a sufficient period of time and have studied the results in sufficient depth, Death is not God, and one does not "die" in the usual sense. Death is an opening, a way out, a transcendence of the human condition. As I have often said, recounting my own experiences under a condition of abstraction, "I do not feel that in this state I am facing God; I feel more that I am facing people in His 'outer office,' that there are many steps between me and God still left to accomplish." So the projection Death is equivalent to God is nonsense according to this belief system.

With experiences such as these one is hardly still in a position to buy a cemetery plot or a coffin—one can only, as it were, think of getting lost at sea, being totally destroyed in some catastrophe that leaves no body to worry about—or to opt for cremation. In reality of course, after such experiences, what happens to one's body is totally unimportant and one tends to leave the problem to his relatives and friends, hoping they will not thus face a financial burden and that their own belief systems will enable them to carry on in spite of this "apparent death."

When one tunes in on the high-energy communications networks in special states of consciousness, he is reassured by the then-existing fact that he is a node in such a network; that there is constant information being fed into him, being computed below his levels of awareness and transmitted to others. This is all done with extremely high energy, far above what one usually experiences while in ordinary states of consciousness in the body. One experiences streamings of energy from unknown sources; streamings of energy going toward unknown sinks. A few of the nearby "other nodes in the network" may be visible. In such states there is no body, there is only pure streaming energy, carrying information. In such a state one suddenly realizes that he is far more than he assumed he was when in the body, and yet he is also far less in terms of ego. In this state he is a "cosmic computer"—small size—connected into the rest of the cosmic computers and into a huge universal computer. During such experiences one feels the connections between all these computers as love, respect, awe, reverence, curiosity and interest. And yet there is a high degree of efficiency with which the traffic is handled in these information channels.

In such a state one realizes that he has existed for several millions of years, that again and again and again he has taken on some form in addition to this cosmic computer form—in short, that he has transmigrated again and again and again, not necessarily only as a human being. He realizes that there is a huge backlog of experience available to him if he could only tap into the storage mechanisms for these memories. At certain points it is as if the memories were not his own but were a central, universal store in which such information is carried through the centuries and the millennia.

After such experiences one can no longer feel that he ceases to be when his body dies. The "reality" of the end of the self is no longer. Somehow one is committed to a much broader view than the egoistic, solipsistic, body-centered belief system common in the human being.

Whether this is merely another set of beliefs which generate certain experiences when out of contact with the body, I don't know. I have no secure way of separating traveling among one's own simulations within one's own programmatic spaces from a true set of experiences having to do with universal communication. For all I know, each one of us may end with the death of his brain. On the other hand, this belief is not as secure as it used to be; it has been disturbed by these experiences. My disbelief in my continuance beyond the death of my body has been weakened. For me the belief that we have by happenstance totally originated as biological organisms on this planet is no longer as strong as it used to be.

One could easily say that with knowing about the new belief systems of exploration and of finding the realities that lie adjacent to, superimposed upon, and inherent in the reality he is faced with every day, he could have more than one alternative. There is a saying in yachting that the skipper should never be caught with just one alternative. So, when one faces one's death, one should have a number of alternative belief systems at his disposal. If there is only one system, and if that is that one ends with the death of his body, then he might well become rather desperate at the time of his death, although even then death can be faced and accepted with dignity, with love, and with compassion. As soon as death becomes something that one can grasp, can think about, explore, and deal with, rather than a wrathful and judgmental God to be faced at the end of one's present physical being, then one can become much more optimistic about his sojourn on this planet.

REFERENCES

1. Castaneda, Carlos, *The Teachings of Don Juan,* Berkeley: University of California, 1968, and New York: Simon & Schuster, 1971.
2. Mitford, Jessica, *The American Way of Death,* New York: Simon & Schuster, 1963.
3. Lilly, John C., *The Center of the Cyclone,* New York, Toronto, London: Bantam Books, 1972, 1973.
4. Merrell-Wolff, Franklin, *Pathways Through to Space,* New York: Julian Press, 1973, p. 115.

CHAPTER 8

GOD AS DRUGS

On the modern American scene there are literally millions of people who take drugs. Some of the drugs are taken on prescription with Establishment approval; others are taken illegally. In modern times we label as "drugs" many substances which are, more scientifically speaking, "purified chemicals," generally organic—meaning: consisting of carbon compounds of one sort or another. There are also the products of the biological activities of other organisms, called "biologicals" (penicillin is one of these). Of the literally thousands of such chemical compounds, only those that in some way change a person's consciousness concern us here. It is these "drugs" that are of prime importance in the "God as Drugs" belief system.

Concomitant with those drugs that change one's consciousness there is what we call "the program written on the pill" kind of reasoning. If one is given a pill that is said to do something to his body or mind, he then expects the pill to have certain effects. We call these expectations "programs"; if the programs are powerful enough, then we call them "God as Drugs programs."

Currently, fairly large numbers of the youth of the United States are taking the rather dangerous group of drugs derived from the opium poppy, i.e., morphine, heroin, and so forth. These drugs are characterized by a double psychopharmacological effect. The first effect is one of dreamy peace, of contentment that precludes any interest in what is going on outside oneself, of being on "Cloud Nine"—irrespective of what actual circumstances the subject may be in. This initial effect is rewarding, and for those who are susceptible, addiction can begin here. However, addiction is not guaranteed until the person has to face withdrawal from these particular chemicals. At the time of withdrawal there occur very powerful symptoms: feelings of great restlessness, aches and pains, and in extreme cases, seizure-like activity of the central nervous system. Withdrawal is painful, and a very strong personality is required to survive it. The whole basic purpose of such groups as Synanon is an attempt to strengthen the personality of the addict in such a way that, with group support, he can go through withdrawal. The particular chemicals we have mentioned have gotten involved in a very large social feedback system, including very heavy penalties for distribution, possession, or the use of these chemicals. The Federal Government has its own agency to control—or to attempt to control—the traffic in these drugs. The basic belief system operating this feedback system is that "heroin is addictive for everyone; therefore we must protect everyone from heroin traffic."

Very careful research into this question shows that this placing of heroin as God, all-powerful and capable of destroying personalities, is true for only those who believe it to be true. It has been demonstrated again and again that addicts have particular kinds of personalities before they start on heroin, personalities that make them susceptible to practically any kind of addiction. They can become alcoholics, they can become morphine addicts, they can become addicted to gambling, and so on. There is something basically different about these people. For example, in Spanish Harlem in New York City it has been shown that when all the boys of age sixteen mainlined on heroin, only 3 percent of them became addicted. The rest were strong enough to go through withdrawal with no overpowering temptation to use heroin again. However, facts such as this are not popular, and for those whose livelihood depends upon "drug" pushing, the belief system of God as Drugs will not be changed.

It is this group of addictive drugs that has given the Federal Government its lever for controlling substances of other sorts, including the plant Cannabis sativa, otherwise known as marijuana. Through the efforts of Harry Anslinger, then head of the Federal Bureau of Narcotics, marijuana was labeled as a narcotic in 1937; in other words, it was placed into the same category as heroin, morphine, and other addictive substances, and it continues to be so categorized. Anslinger's "program written on a weed" was a "panic program"—it assumed that marijuana was as dangerous as the derivatives of opium—that was incorporated into law and is still perpetuated. Millions of people in the meantime have demonstrated that this weed is not addictive, but many of our young people are still being ruined because they are jailed for the possession of marijuana. The entire national program on drugs has brought us to a very peculiar state of divisiveness in which the law defines the reality as one thing, and the direct experience of millions demonstrates quite the opposite.

This situation is remindful of the Volstead Act—Prohibition of alcohol—which was finally repealed under President Roosevelt in 1933. In 1918, Congressman Andrew J. Volstead and his followers had managed to pass the Eighteenth Amendment, forbidding the manufacture, sale and transportation of alcoholic beverages. The law became conspicuous for the absence of compliance it found among the populace. Millions of Americans in the twenties and thirties who had any money at all had a "friend" who had a bootlegger who brought alcohol across the border from Canada or Mexico, or across the Atlantic or Pacific oceans. Fortunes were made and lost on the unlawful sale of alcoholic beverages as drinking attained a popularity far surpassing its popularity pre-Prohibition. Thousands and thousands of people began making wine in their attics and gin in their bathtubs. Hundreds of millions of dollars were spent in attempting to enforce this new—and unrealistic—law. A very large number—even the prominent—of the citizens of the country were fighting against this dictate of their government, secretly and —because of both the poor quality of much of the alcohol and the danger of arrest—sometimes recklessly. Respect for the law was at a very low ebb.

There was a very short period (1933–1937) in the later history of the United States when we were free of such laws. Within four years after the Eighteenth Amendment was repealed (by the Twenty-first Amendment), the marijuana law was put into effect. The same forces, the so-called "do-gooders," were once again in control, creating laws and the agencies to enforce them, thus carrying on a kind of warfare against a very large segment of our population. Let us look behind these powerful social movements and look at some of the psychopharmacological effects of the drugs that are brought under question, including the psychedelics.

For thousands of years, if not hundreds of thousands of years, man has sought to change his consciousness through plants and through tinctures and essences derived from plants. In the last century some of the chemical constituents of these plants that brought about various changes in consciousness were isolated, purified, and made available through the methods of mass production. The first of these was cocaine, isolated by Merck & Company in the late 1800's. At the age of twenty-eight Sigmund Freud was pushing the benefits of cocaine, giving it to his fiancée and taking it himself daily. He wrote a brief monograph on the subject; today he reads like a psychedelic enthusiast. He tried to use cocaine for breaking the morphine habits of some of his colleagues and for nervous and mental disorders, for all of which he felt cocaine was a cure-all. Only as he found that someone addicted to morphine readily becomes addicted to cocaine did he realize he was wrong (as in the case of his friend Fliess).

The basic effect of this first of the isolated principles from the coca plant in Peru was a state of very high energy. Peruvian Indians who must carry heavy loads at high altitudes for long periods of time chew the leaves of the plant to ward off fatigue. However, as Richard Schultes, the Harvard botanist, has shown, the coca leaves are not of themselves addictive. Peruvian Indians drafted into the Peruvian Army can toss off the habit without any withdrawal symptoms. In our society cocaine does not seem to be addictive, except for those people who are determined to become addicted to something.

The next powerful chemical to be isolated from a plant was mescaline. Dr. Weir Mitchell of Philadelphia experimented with mescaline in the 1890's and gave us accurate descriptions of its mind-changing qualities. Mescaline was isolated from the peyote cactus, which has been used for centuries in the religious rites of various Indian tribes in North America. A recent description of its effects is given by Castaneda in his series of books on don Juan.

Mescaline, which occupied many shelves of many laboratories for several decades, was noticed only by scientists interested in its particular properties. Not until the psychedelic era of the 1950's and early 1960's was it considered a dangerous substance.

In 1938 Albert Hoffman isolated LSD 25 from the rye fungus, ergot. In 1942 he took a small dose (about 250 micrograms) and found that it had powerful mind-changing qualities. He then wrote a paper with Stoller in which he said that LSD 25 was psychotomimetic in the sense that it induced a psychosis-like state in those who took it. When LSD 25 was brought to this country in the 1950's, its program was written on it: "Psychotomimetic."

On the fertile ground prepared by the marijuana underground, the distribution of LSD 25 became nationwide. Hundreds of thousands of people took it; of these, several hundreds died and several other hundreds were institutionalized with mental illnesses attributed to having taken the substance. Considering the large number of users, the number of casualties was extremely small. Much smaller, for example, than the national death rate on the highways, which currently is around sixty thousand people per year. However, the public outcry through the media, especially a magazine article in *Life* in 1966, forced legislation against the psychedelics in general and LSD 25 in particular. Laws were made which set up extremely heavy penalties, both federal and state, against the possession, use and sale of these substances. "God as Drugs" as a belief had won out again insofar as the legislators were concerned. These laws were made in a hurry, in a panic about the consequences of taking of these drugs. Few if any of the legislators understood the issues involved, and whenever researchers who best understood the issues attempted to speak up they were discredited—in many cases by their own colleagues. The credibility gap within the medical profession between those who had taken LSD and those who had not became extreme. The enthusiastic proponents of these chemicals tried to oversell them and were fought back by those who were frightened by them. This entire national situation on drugs seems to have resulted from overvaluation of the positive benefits of the psychedelics by those who are advocating their use, and the fear of those who had not taken them and who had heard various horror stories about the results of using them.

Let us take a look at the belief system behind God as Drugs. In the United States we are brought up to believe in our doctor as an expert. If he prescribes a pill for a particular illness, we take the pill without question. The doctor in this case has the powers of the old priesthood in the sense that we do not have the knowledge to question his decisions; we have probably looked for the best doctor we could find and we trust him.

This trusting acceptance of drugs prescribed for us by a doctor is a well-established part of our way of life. The first psychologically active agents useful in the control of people were the tranquilizers discovered in the 1950's. Among these were the phenothiazines. It was my impression at the National Institute of Mental Health, and the impression of various psychotherapists who saw these drugs first used at St. Elizabeth's Hospital in Washington, that all these tranquilizers did was remove the possibility that the patient would misbehave. In other words, these were behavioral control chemicals which did not cure anything but merely prevented the patient from acting out his fantasies and giving in to fits of rage or other difficult-to-control states. One psychotherapist said that the patients on the tranquilizers "looked like lizards asleep in the sun." And yet he knew that down inside they were still extremely troubled people and that the tranquilization was merely an external effect making them easier to take care of in the institution—a kind of chemical straitjacket.

One of the early tranquilizers, derived from a plant from India called Rauwolfia serpentina (in this country marketed as Serpasil), discharged the biological battery and brought on fatigue to the point where the patient, although he remained fully conscious, could not object to anything that happened to him. Since those early days of tranquilizers literally hundreds of such chemicals have been discovered which can induce altered states of consciousness to prevent outbreaks of excitement without sacrificing conscious awareness. Slowly, but surely, the tranquilizers were accepted by Establishment medicine and put on prescription.

Another group of substances, the amphetamines, were originally thought to be psychic energizers, but it developed that they were merely energizers of lower levels of energy within the biological system. Later, real psychic energizers turned out to be what the medical profession had been hunting for: substances with the ability to induce higher energy in low-energy people without altering their state of consciousness.

Thus the God as Drugs was extended to tranquilization, to high-energy states, in addition to the old standbys such as sleeping pills (barbiturates, and so forth). The results were obtained without the penalties that alcohol exacts, such as a bad hangover, liver damage, brain damage. The God alcohol was re-instated in the Establishment, put under adequate federal controls, and sold under government auspices in the various states of the United States. Alcohol seems to be the mainstay of most people in the United States who desire to change consciousness a little bit, but not too much.

I will not go into the consciousness-changing aspects of the hormonal substances or of various other anesthetics, because these are not in general used by those who look upon God as Drugs.

There are those who cannot get to sleep without barbiturates, who cannot wake up without an amphetamine, and who obtain their drugs through their legal prescriptions. There are those who cannot function in our society without tranquilizers; these people number in the hundreds of thousands if not the millions. There are millions of people who cannot get along without their late afternoon drink, or without their cocktail at lunch. There are those who must smoke tobacco to obtain the effects of the various resins and the nicotine in the tobacco; these also numbered in the millions. The symptoms of withdrawal from tobacco are rather severe, and withdrawal itself costs a lot of personal time, effort, and discipline. Withdrawal symptoms from alcohol, from barbiturates, are very severe; if one has become accustomed to a fairly high level of these substances in his blood, he can, for example, experience convulsions upon withdrawal.

However, these are well-established, acceptable, social ways of changing one's consciousness. If one is going to assume the belief in Drugs as God, then he can assume it within the Establishment legally by using these substances. With the drug industry, the alcohol industry, and the tobacco industry, one can become legally addicted and remain so without the problems attendant upon the extra-legal substances. As yet there is no legal psychedelic chemical available on prescription. Until more is known about the psychedelic effects of various substances and until there is more Establishment acceptance of the altered states of consciousness that these substances can induce, it looks as if psychedelics are going to remain a national problem, costing millions of dollars for enforcement of non-realistic paternalistic laws.

In my own particular belief system, it seems to me that the alternative ways of changing one's consciousness which are non-chemical should be taught to our youngsters so that they can master them while they are still young enough to be sufficiently flexible to change their programming. The alternatives to God as Drugs have been around a long time and should be explored in great depth within our culture. With the new imports of teachers from Tibet, from Japan, from China, many of these techniques are entering into our culture. The alternative belief systems of the esoteric schools for obtaining altered states of consciousness are very ancient and well established. Other alternatives are discussed elsewhere in this book.

CHAPTER 9

GOD AS THE BODY

In the United States each year billions of dollars are spent on entertainment, athletics, care of the body, cosmetics and other beauty aids, physical fitness, golf, football, baseball, worship of superstars, of music, TV and movies, on yoga, Tai Chi Chuan, Kung Fu, karate, jiujitsu, judo, aikido, swimming pools, tennis courts, mountain climbing, camping, skiing, water skiing, sailing, surfing, and so forth. In each of these activities a very high premium is placed on various aspects of bodily function and the appearance of one's body to others. Very large numbers of people who indulge in these activities believe in God as the Body.

Over the last few decades, as the belief of God Out There was weakened, the belief of God as Body became strengthened. Instead of going to religious services on Saturday or Sunday, thousands of Americans spent their weekend being physically active, and more and more thousands are becoming adherents of the physical-fitness cult, if only in terms of jogging or light morning exercises. The manufacture of sports equipment has become a very large industry. The various techniques of body improvement, from Jack LaLanne's to Yoga classes and the various so-called martial arts, are also fast becoming big business.

Let us try to get at the basic factors involved in such a belief system as God as the Body. First of all, whether we like it or not in our more idealized moments, we are a walking, running, climbing animal; unless we perform these activities, our body deteriorates. Unless we work out equivalents for body toning in terms of stretching and stressing the body, the quality of our thinking, feeling and doing slowly but surely likewise deteriorate. Most people exercise because they feel better as a consequence of the exercise. They can think, work, and play better. In the Far East this has been known for literally thousands of years. Stretching and stressing the body have become esoteric sciences. The best known of these, Hatha-Yoga, is touted as one of the doorways to spiritual advancement. Various martial arts: aikido, Kung Fu, karate, and so forth, are also parts of spiritual trips in various countries in the East. The "feeling better" that results from these activities is taken as an advance in personal discipline and in perfection of the body itself.

In the West there is a saying "A sound mind in a sound body," in other words, a sound mind results from generating a sound body. Apparently, the body responds to a cyclical need for exercise and stretching. There is a daily cycle of twelve to twenty-four hours, and a weekly cycle of approximately seven days. If these cycles are studies in oneself, one can find, for example, that he should devote a period to stretching early in the morning and another period late in the afternoon or before going to bed. On the weekends he should stress the whole organism, exerting physical effort to the extent he hyperventilates as a consequence of the muscular activity, and one's heart rate and the heart beat volume are stepped up during this period of exercise. Without these the circulatory system and the respiratory system degenerate, and all the familiar processes of aging and disease take place. One of the amazing things that one notices in the older teachers of Yoga and the martial arts from the Far East is their extreme youthful appearance, even when they are old. A fifty-year-old looks like a thirty-year-old and an eighty-year-old looks about like a forty-year-old. The obvious effects of aging, including either emaciation or overweight, just do not occur in these people who have managed to keep these physical disciplines going over their life span. To be continuously effective these disciplines cannot be followed for a year and then dropped. They must be followed from one's youth to his old age.

For those who practice these disciplines, what I am saying is obvious. For those who do not, what I am saying may be taken with a good deal of skepticism. All I can say in response to the latter group is "try it." In our next book, *The Dyadic Cyclone,* my wife and I will explain the minimum possible programs for the body, the stretching and stressing exercises, complete with a time schedule. These programs can be elaborated or extended. We will try to achieve the minimum possible for the busy person so that he can fit it into his everyday life with a minimum of strain.

For beginners it is wise to stress that in bodily development if your body is not in good shape, you must start slowly and not stretch or stress beyond the minimum discomfort level at the beginning. With these exercises one can overdo it. The important metaprogram, the important general principle above all others, is to exercise a little bit every day up to one's comfort limit. As practically everybody has found who has followed a proper stretching and stressing regimen there is a point at which it becomes fun. One can always push beyond his limits and make it not fun once again, no matter how good a condition he is in. One cannot only get a second wind, but a third, fourth, and a fifth wind, as it were.

These seem to be the physiological bases for the activity centered around the body in the United States today. In addition to the basics of running, climbing, and walking, the necessity of stressing and stretching, there are less necessitous kinds of activities that go with belief system of God as the Body. One can transfer the pleasure obtained from his own body and its stretching and stressing to others who are better than he is in a given type of exercise. One can make a hero or a heroine out of those who have spent a professional life doing the particular kind of exercise that one is interested in. He can worship the body and the mind of his Hatha-Yoga guru, of his aikido teacher, of his Tai Chi teacher, of his athletics coach, of professionals and amateurs in any sport. This kind of transference to another from oneself, from one's own body to another's, to his activities, is a familiar learning procedure in childhood, adolescence and young adulthood. This identification with idealized persons who are doing better than oneself seems to be a necessary step for most of us to achieve on our own. However, sometimes this worship, this God as the Body, becomes separated from one's own accomplishments and he worships on a vicarious basis without doing anything about his own body. This vicarious worship accounts for the popularity of spectator sports rather than engaging in them oneself.

Of course one can aspire to be a teacher of a given stretch and/or stressing set of exercises. He may then want to have vicariously the admiration that he sees professionals getting; or he may simply feel that a particular kind of activity is so worthwhile that he wants others to learn it. The thin line between God as the Body and the planetside survival trip as a professional teacher is a narrow boundary indeed. It is possible to flip over into complete worship as opposed to a balanced life. This is very easy to do with the God as the Body system.

Another outgrowth of God as the Body is the beauty industry. This industry does not necessarily ground itself on a physical fitness basis, even though the most beautiful bodies in our present culture are considered to be those in good physical shape—not too fat, not too thin, with adequate muscular development. But we have already handled this aspect of beauty. It is the form rather than the substance that we wish to deal with now.

No one seems to know where our criteria of physical beauty arose. It is well known that the criteria of beauty in various parts of Africa are different from one another and from the European criteria toward beauty. The differences of the human face and figure throughout the world extend across a fairly wide spectrum of form, color, texture, body weight per unit height, and so forth. The saying "Beauty is in the eye of the beholder" shows that most criteria of beauty are arbitrary programs inserted into our training while very young. To the very young everything is beautiful. It is only with the shaping by parents and peers that one develops a narrow set of criteria for what he considers beauty.

Some people when we first see them look beautiful. Others become beautiful only with continued contact and the appreciation gained by delving into their thinking, feeling, and doing. With some of the first mentioned, we may realize with time that their beauty is of form rather than of substance and function. Of other persons we can say that the form is not formally beautiful but the mind and the spirit are beautiful. There are times when we can recapture the ecstatic, blissful state of the infant in which everything and everyone is beautiful. We can change our "eye of the beholder."

Those that are considered formally "beautiful" are hired by the advertising industry, by corporations, by government, by the movie and TV industries, to play the roles of public purveyors of beauty products, clothes, automobiles, and so forth. In the United States there used to be white models only. In recent years, with the new respect for colored peoples, more and more models are colored. It is to be noticed, however, that these models of various races are selected not so much according to the criteria of the Africans, Asiatics, and so on, as according to United States criteria of formal beauty. Noses, eyes, lips, chin, jowls, are selected according to Western European/American criteria rather than racial/tribal criteria.

What formal beauty is is so well stipulated that practically the whole beauty industry operates on the basis of one set of standards. If one looks at a copy of *Vogue*, or *Cosmopolitan*, or other women's magazines, he sees a uniformity of standards for women and for men. There are currently in fashion definite kinds of eyeshadow, eyeliner, lipstick color, face powder, anti-perspirant, toothpaste, shampoo, hair conditioner, body oil, feminine hygiene preparation, deodorant soap, nail polish color, and so forth. Setting up the criteria for what a female should put on various parts of her face is almost an esoteric art. Should or should not she wear false eyelashes? Should or should not she wear lipstick? How long should she wear her hair in what sort of fashion? Should she change her hair color at this time? Is she color-coordinating her clothing and her face?

More and more people are beginning to realize that under-clothing is not the answer to a beautiful body. Not long ago whalebone corsets, waist cinches, panty girdles, and so forth, were used to shape the sloppy body. There is still a big industry in the "best" brassiere, the best form of the female breast under clothing. Nowadays more and more of the younger generation are taking care of their bodies through Yoga and other forms of exercise. The products of the beauty industry do not appeal to them and they wear very simple clothing, without elaborate stretch materials and wired-in shapes that are meant to create an illusion of form which isn't there. These youngsters believe in the particular form they have as a consequence of the right kind of exercise and the right diet and they consciously avoid overweight and its problems.

In the fundamental psychophysiology of the obesity-skinniness dichotomy, there is a basic factor determining body weight and the steady state associated with it. For each individual there is a *critical body weight* above which appetite for food is a runaway propensity causing overeating. Below this critical weight there is not enough appetite to maintain the bodily needs. At the critical weight the appetite and the needs balance, so that the weight remains constant.

Over a long period of time this steady-state weight may change with a change in the physical activity of the person in-volved. For example, if one goes from a physically active life to a sedentary one, the critical weight may shift downward as he loses the muscle mass that had been needed for the physical life. As he shifts in the opposite direction, from sedentary to physical, the critical body weight can be expected to rise as the muscular fraction of the total body weight increases. The best measure-ment to date of this critical weight is the work of Commander Albert R. Behnke of the U.S. Naval Medical Research Institute during World War II on the density of the body. If the body has a density of 1.0 or higher there is very little fat present. If the density is below 1.0, there is excess fat. The steady-state weight seems to occur for most people at a body density of approximately this same 1.0.

The value of fat for survival is dictated by factors not generally present in our society. (See the discussion of the Polynesians, below.) For the best physical condition the body density should be as high as possible in our society. This leaves very little allowance for body weight loss in the case of illness. The weight lost in bed when one is ill is first the fat of the body. When this is all used up the muscle mass starts going. Hence one is losing protein, literally "eating" one's own protein after "eating" one's own fat. Thus it is wise to have some fat reserve.

However, it is to be remembered that muscle mass varies directly as the amount of physical activity varies. The more active one is, the larger the fraction of one's own body weight that is in protein.

In my own experience the best diet for control of weight is high protein. Inevitably this means eating meat, poultry, fish, shellfish, eggs, and not much else, and drinking milk. Nuts are a source of protein, but they are one third carbohydrate and one third fat. A meat diet tends to be self-regulating in the sense that the amount of fat with the protein is sufficient to quench the appetite after a small intake. This diet requires the additional intake of vitamins to make up for a lack of them in the meat.

It is harder to maintain this diet in the tropics than it is in temperate zones or in the Arctic. High environmental temperature and humidity require a larger flow of fluid and minerals. In my experience this flow is best maintained by eating green coconuts and drinking their milk. This was taught to me by British Virgin Islanders.

The beauty industry specifies that "fat is ugly." There are some cultures in which "fat is beautiful." In general in Polynesia the royalty are overfed until they have become very fat, when they are considered very beautiful. I suggest that this criterion of body beauty was influenced by the long sea voyages of the Polynesians in which survival could depend upon being fat. If one must go without water for many days at a time, then it is best to be fat, because he can burn the fat to carbon dioxide and water, thus avoiding the necessity of taking in water. The dolphins, whales, and porpoises do exactly this; they are mammals living at sea without fresh water.

Another reason the Polynesians might have fattened themselves for their voyages is the flotation that being fat gained for them. If one is blown overboard, he does not have to exert much effort to float if he is sufficiently fat. I have seen many people who are as if living at sea, as it were which causes fatness to have survival value for them; as though if they weren't fat, they might drown. There is a desperation to staying fat among these people. For the Polynesians of today, however, there is no such desperate need for being fat; consciously they consider it an aesthetic thing rather than a survival thing. It is imbedded in their culture because they were brought up with the programming left over from the time of the large migrations across the Pacific.

One other possible reason for staying fat is that there is more to eat when one runs out of food under desperate conditions. First of all, one's need for food intake does not arise as soon if he is fat; he burns up, "eats," his own fat, as explained earlier. Secondly, if a person dies or is killed while stranded with others or while adrift in a lifeboat, for example, there is more for the others to eat if he was fat. This kind of thing rarely happens nowadays, but it does happen: after a crash landing in the mountains of Peru (*Survive!*, by Clay Blair, Jr.); after the sinking of the whaleship *Essex*, when the crew, having been forced to the boats after a whale had destroyed the ship, ate the body of the cabin boy as they drifted to the Chilean coast; during the Nobile expedition across the North Pole by dirigible. Cannibalism in the service of survival is not very well understood by those who have not been faced with survival desperation. In his book *The Boat* Walter Gibson presents a strong pro case in such circumstances.[1]

Of course in all the above situations, the consideration of beauty disappeared. It usually does under conditions of desperation, danger, and threats to one's survival. Under these circumstances, when one is under the sway of the survival programs within his biocomputer, beauty and its criteria are hardly important.

However, once one has taken the spiritual path and achieved a certain experience with various far-out states of consciousness, he begins to expand his criteria of beauty into regions where, before, they were almost forbidden. In these states of consciousness one's criteria are so expanded that anything and everything becomes beautiful and perfect. One pulls out of the human condition and the necessity for survival of the physical being and moves into eternal spaces united with all other sentient beings throughout the universe. The impact of such experiences is so great that one's criteria of beauty or of sin and virtue are completely flipped. One goes through peculiar transformations in that what used to be considered beautiful expands to include many, many things that one might have considered ugly. Finally, the dichotomy "beauty and ugliness" disappears; one achieves a state of High Indifference in which he realizes that bliss does not come from the outside world, it comes from within. One elicits his own bliss, he elicits bliss in others. He realizes his own eternal nature and hence is no longer quite so subject to the survival programs of the biocomputer.

God as the Body disappears. One is no longer subject to the same kinds of programming that he was previously. The body is now part of a more immense God whose vastness encompasses the whole universe and all of one's higher states of consciousness. For example, in the old belief system of God as the Body, one's own death was unjust, catastrophic, a complete disaster. With the new belief system, death is merely a transition form, a change in state of oneself, a change in a state of being, a change of consciousness into a new, more expanded state, highly desirable and not as restricting as the state of consciousness which was tied to a body. One can leave the body with joy, with a sense of completeness of his planetside trip, and go to whatever it is that one goes on to. God as Death is also gone.

REFERENCE

1. See Lilly, John C., "Mental Effects of Reduction of Ordinary Levels of Physical Stimuli on Intact, Healthy Persons," *Psychiatric Research Reports 5*, American Psychiatric Assn., June 1956.

CHAPTER 10

GOD AS MONEY

On the modern American scene, money is incredibly important. The uses of money run all the way from buying the necessities for survival for individuals, for businesses, for corporations, for states, for nations. The whole of the modern Western world is based upon its ideas of money. International trade, the value of the dollar in Japan, in Western Europe, and so forth, determine a large number of people's lives and fortunes. Large amounts of money are so powerful that those who have them for any length of time surround themselves by safeguards, advisors, trusts, and so on, to prevent the dissipation of that power. Those who have no money must get it in one form or another from private individuals, from state governments, or from the federal government.

For many people the possession of money is equated with God. The belief "God is money: money is God" is a powerful determinant of behavior in our Western society. According to the usual social criteria, the misuse of money by private individuals and by public officials is *the* list of sins against this God. Those who blatantly steal money without surrounding their theft with all sorts of legal safeguards, are subject to the severest penalties. Those who know how to obtain large amounts of money and who can hire sufficiently powerful law firms who in turn can influence the judges, can make a very subtle priest-like game out of playing with their God. The aristocracy in the

United States are those who have either inherited large amounts of wealth, or have acquired large amounts of wealth in their lifetime. These are the powerful representatives of "God as Money."

Public officials in charge of grants, of disbursement of government funds and of the collection of government taxes, similarly are priests in the church of this God. The taxation authorities have the power to examine the personal life of any individual citizen or of any corporation to find any heresies that have developed in the worship of this God. Rules for the worship of money as God are quite stringent and specific, like any of the litanies, rituals and belief systems of any church that has appeared in the Western world. The new inquisition has powers of jailing (practically for life) those who do not adhere to the proper rituals, litany and paper work necessitated by this God.

This new religion has at its disposal huge computers which store all the information about each individual, about each corporation, about each state entity. Those who have the power to enter these computers and make use of their information have the power of life and death over the rest of the population. The only comparable power in the United States at least is the military, and the Military God has lost power since World War II. The fiascos of Korea and Vietnam have lowered the prestige of the Military God below that of the Money God. For many years the Military God controlled the Money God. The modern tendency seems to be for the Money God to begin to control the Military God in a more obvious fashion.

The rules for the accumulation of wealth have been spelled out in detail by a large number of writers. (See for example, *Supermoney*,[1] by Adam Smith.) For those with sufficient ruthlessness, sufficient ambition, sufficient energy and sufficient knowledge, fortunes are still to be made. One can still become one of the priests of the Money God. One can still buy the protection of the church of Money.

Even as the early Catholic Church in the United States had its poor, so does the Money God have its poor. The modern equivalent of the charity cases of the old church are those on Welfare, living on food stamps. These are those who are sufficiently unlucky, tenderhearted, ignorant, or militantly anti-Money God and His Church.

No one person seems to understand the total system represented by two-hundred million people in the United States, and the feedbacks necessary to keep that system operative. Even such a powerful position as the Presidency of the United States suffers from a lack of crucial information at crucial decision points. Even as the whole is greater than the sum of its parts, then as the whole becomes larger, the sum becomes larger and larger by several orders of magnitude than the actual number of individuals involved.

Money represents a flow of initiative from one person to another person. Money in capital savings represents frozen initiative, in the world of the paper realities. The fear of "getting down to one's last dollar" can be a source of high motivation for many people. Some people with this fear have made millions of dollars, and some of these have lost it all. Some of the latter have sacrificed their life in the name of this God—for example, the many persons who committed suicide during the 1929–1930 crash of the stock market.

The God of Money has many demi-Gods below Him. One of these demi-Gods is banking. When one thinks about it, a bank is a very peculiar place. When one examines the operations that go on in a bank, as if he were a visitor from another planet, he sees a lot of people entering a building, going up to counters, writing out slips of paper, receiving other slips of paper, and sometimes the green paper that represents "money" itself (or the silver, or the gold). Some people, when you ask them what they are doing at a bank, will say, "I'm cashing a check," or "I'm depositing money I've earned," or "I'm establishing my credit." These are some of the rituals and litanies of the church of God as Money. A bank, then, represents a neighborhood church of this particular God, or perhaps one of the cathedrals of the Wall Street area.

Of course the Money God is more clever than previous Gods, in that he uses numbers, counting; he is a quantitative God. His priests have learned more subtle ways of supervising his flock:

by means of the banks, taxation and income reporting forms which every citizen is supposed to fill out. This God has finally achieved what other Gods and churches were unable to achieve: tithing—and more, far more than tithing—have become involuntary processes. Taxes must be paid or one goes to jail.

Anyone who is in business, must not forget that he is a "money valve." This condition is more obvious in business than it is in any other aspects of life. Perhaps one is starting a new business and has a certain amount of money to invest in this business. With a proper bookkeeper and a proper accounting firm, he can learn the rules for investment, making a profit, paying taxes, meeting a payroll, and for all the other operations in the paper reality of any business. Those who have struggled to meet a payroll every month are a special club, which is not understood very well by those who are simply on payrolls that are met every month.

A businessman is effectively a money valve: he sells something, receives something from the public for it, and he distributes that money to others, including his employees, his suppliers, his sub-contractors, and so on. In the paper world of credit he has a certain "rating," a quantitative rating, which determines fairly well how much money the church of this God is going to allow to flow through this particular man. If he is trustworthy, loyal, and has met his payroll for a number of years, his credit is good up to a certain limiting value. If suddenly he learns how to expand this limiting value, or to open himself up as a money valve, then his credit rating can rise, which means he is allowed a larger flow of money through his trustworthy organization. One very peculiar thing about credit is that one must borrow money in order to establish credit. This is the usual case of the small businessman.

As the power of the money valve goes up and as one is entrusted with more and more money, then the rules of the game seem to change. As one becomes one of those in control of the system (or has the illusion of being in control of the system)—in other words, if one is a huge money-valve—then the God may change from Money as God to Power as God. One's ability to manipulate the lives of hundreds of thousands and millions of people reaches astronomical proportions at a certain critical threshold. One may achieve this through political means, corporate means with linkups between corporations, through linkups with military plus the money market, or through the manipulation of large amounts of property.

Certain new privileges appear that were not present at the lower levels of money flow. One now has the best possible advice from accounting, auditing and law firms. He has become a member of the "privileged priests" of the God of Money. One can now be in competition with the other priests or in confederation with the other priests. Publicly one acts as if he is in competition, whereas privately he acts in cooperation with the other priests. They advise him on how to reduce his taxes to a microscopic level; on how to put his money in trust for his offspring; and on how to keep a low profile for the public media. He is taught how to use the media in the service of the Money God.

One who was born and raised in this belief system with sufficient amounts of money available can become a dissipated delinquent or he can turn the other way and become service-oriented, realizing that whatever money you have "you can't take it with you" and that it is a privilege given to him for this particular lifetime: to be able to be of service to more of his fellow men. One who is not subject to the necessity for making money can afford to give his services for worthy causes, whatever they may be. He may go into politics or into charity work; he may support the arts, a favorite school, a church (of the usual sort). As one of the favored of the God of Money, a person has many more alternatives than do people at the other end of the money spectrum. Money then is not merely initiative; money is literally a measure of the number of alternatives available to him, insofar as his external reality and social reality are concerned.

To date—insofar as I can find out—money has not been used in the United States for freeing individuals in their *inner* realities. Classically, we get reports of the external reality of those with money. If one's living situation has been taken care of by accumulated capital, he could be free to pursue inner explorations without the frantic worship at the church of Money.

There is a new breed of wealthy men and women who are pursuing the inner paths. To pursue the inner life one must of necessity have a low public profile. Otherwise he becomes too involved in the affairs of the world and finds great difficulty in establishing the necessary discipline to retire to the inside life. There are also new life-styles in which one devotes several hours a day to the inside life and several hours a day to the outside life. If there are no money problems, the outside life can be one of service and teaching and the inside life one of seeking whatever it is that one seeks. If one is in the "bliss-programming" stage, then he bliss-programs. If one is in the "exploratory inner-universe" stage, then he explores the inner universes. If one is in the teaching mode, then he teaches whomever and wherever he meets his students. If one wants to become a powerful guru with a following, he can do that also. Those favored by the Money God thus have inner as well as outer alternatives not available to those not so favored.

To those who value a high public profile and value protest against the current system no matter what it is, there are ways to become wealthy. The United States is the only country in the world in which a young rebel can make a phonograph record and earn several million dollars on the basis of a song which preaches rebellion against the Establishment. This is a refreshing new view of the relationship between the young rebel and the society in which he lives. A well-known psychoanalyst, Robert Welder, once said that "the United States is the first country in the world that has built-in a system of constant evolution without the need of violent revolution in order to change the structure of its establishment." The constitution is a document which espouses evolution and balances power between various groups in such a way that there is a forced change built into the system. Thus anything I say, or any other individual says, is subject to revision without notice.

The system in the United States is a living, growing organism, the parts of which do not understand the whole. To those most operative in this system, money is merely a means, not an end in itself. Money is not a God to them, it is a tool to be used for the growth and change of the inner society as well as the outer society. Services can be sold as well as goods; the mass production of services is a new industry running from advertising to spiritual trips, through a whole spectrum of software marketing. As we perfect a minimal standard of living and supply more and more people with this minimal standard of living, the software industries are going to be more and more important. As more of our material production becomes computer-controlled and computer-operated, so will the necessity for *software for humans* be expanded. More leisure time available will demand more services for the human participant.

Already we are disillusioned with fixed litanies, fixed rituals of churches. The new software, as opposed to that of the old churches, is more flexible, more adaptive, and more interesting. Some spectacular things can be accomplished in the inner realities with the proper human software programming. Telling people how to do things inside their own heads is becoming a new industry in which fortunes are to be made.

REFERENCE

1. Smith, Adam, *Supermoney*, New York: Random House, 1972.

CHAPTER 11

GOD AS RIGHTEOUS WRATH

Today I lost my temper. I justified it by saying that it was righteous wrath. I had got into the righteousness space and let fly verbally. Luckily, I have retained a habit from my youth of walking away when I am angry. This enables me to calm down and to work out whatever problem exists.

Basically, each one of us seems to be subject to this very peculiar state known as rage, anger, wrath, in which, in extreme cases, we are ready to kill in the name of something or other that we consider to be righteous, that we consider to be virtue. In a conversation with Gregory Bateson, the well-known anthropologist, I asked if there wasn't some way that each one of us can analyze and master this particular survival program generated in our biocomputer every time there is a threat to our integrity, to our wholeness, to our virtue. I said, "I myself, every so often, do lose my temper in this particular mode, and then get 'meta-anger,' that is, anger at myself for allowing circumstances, other people, or my own righteousness, to excite the anger." He said, "In my opinion there is no hope of correcting this particular mode of operating in human species."

We agreed, however, that the actions that might be engendered by such states must be restricted, must be isolated, if we are not to instill the same state in thousands or hundreds of thousands of people simultaneously. Those in power somehow must be taught that their own anger must be siphoned off somewhere, somehow, and not be put into the system any further. The human species can no longer afford the God of Righteous Wrath. The human species has at its disposal the means of its own destruction and the destruction of all life on this planet, if not the planet itself.

An epidemic of wrath and righteousness and virtue, i.e., of God as Righteousness and God as Wrath could today lead to total destruction. At times each of us in a wrathful state visualize, program, and display to ourselves the total destruction of that which the wrath is directed against. We see this in individuals, we see it in couples, we see it in groups; we see it in organizations, we see it in nations, we see it in the United Nations. A given group, threatened from the outside, becomes wrathful and virtuous simultaneously. In effect, such a group says, "My anger emanates from God. My virtue emanates from God. You are a creature of the devil. I must destroy you in order to further the work of God himself."

Basically, this is a very primitive program emanating apparently from the lower brain centers, where energy is devoted to assuring survival of the individual organism. A threatened mammalian organism has many alternatives. One obvious central state that develops is a tremendous amount of energy which attempts to escape through the muscular system in some fashion. If it is going to escape in terms of a tetanic seizure—continued contraction of agonist and antagonist muscles—the organism freezes. If it escapes into the muscles devoted to running, the organism flees. If it escapes into an attack on a target, it goes into the fight muscles. If it leads to a high sexual excitation, the organism will fuck. In order to avoid these four, the organism may just foment, in other words, may think, become virtuous, and start a campaign to get the group to help the freeze, the flight, the fight, or the fuck.

Such a state is contagious. Nonverbal stimulation of others through any of these five activities leads to group action in the direction of the high-energy state. Certain people in power have learned how to foment these states in groups. The most effective technique is doing that which we expect the group to emulate "as if" angry, or "as if" in a high energy state. One trouble with this technique is that with it one can go from the "as if true" to the "true"—from "as if angry" to truly angry. Thus not only fomenting mob violence but participating in it oneself as a leader.

Mohammed and his followers beheaded eight hundred Jews in three days. The Inquisition killed—by boiling, quartering, drawing, and other horrifying torture methods—thousands who were said to be heretics "in order to save their souls." Hitler and the Nazis gassed six million humans in the name of a new race of pure Aryans, "supermen" who could make judgments about who was fit to survive and who was not. The kamikaze pilots of the Japanese Empire in World War II dove their airplanes into ships in the thorough belief that they would be taken to heaven in the performance of their service to the Emperor. Truman ordered the dropping of each of two bombs on Japan, killing hundreds of thousands of people, in the belief that he was saving millions of American lives, which would have had to be spent in the invasion of Japan. And so on and on. The history of the human species is the history of man's anger, of man's rage, of man's rationalizations of his anger and of his rage. The worship of the God of Wrath has been with us, insofar as we know, since the beginning of our time on this planet.

There may be alternatives to this worship of the God of Wrath and Righteousness. Study of the neuroanatomy and neurophysiology of all the species which seem to precede ours, and the neuroanatomy and neurophysiology of our own species, points to the organization of the biocomputer and those parts which generate this kind of behavior. Over a five-year period I stimulated the brains of several monkeys in many, many places, searching for the substrate of love and hate, of pain and pleasure, of the dichotomies of our behavior. Insofar as I could find out through these studies (see Appendix I) the negatively reinforcing systems (of which rage, fear, nausea, and sickness are typical parts, along with a mapping out of pain throughout the body), are very small: they lie in the midplane at the bottom of the brain and extend from below the frontal lobes all the way back, down the spinal cord to its very end. Various parts of these "negative systems," as we call them, map out fright and anger and pain. There is no secure way of separating fear from anger in the behavior of a monkey. If one stimulates an area, for instance near the supra-optic nucleus in the forward portion of the hypothalamus, the monkey will flee, if free to do so. If restrained, he will fight the restraints. If presented with an object which has hurt him in the past, he will attack it and tear it to pieces. If the negative system is stimulated at a very low level for long periods of time the monkey will sicken and die. There is the same effect when he is given a switch to shut off the stimulation and the apparatus turns it on again and again and again.

Surrounding the negative systems are the much larger positive systems in which the monkey wants to start stimulation (where in the negative systems he wants to stop the stimulation). The positive systems include those that are the sexual portions of these systems. In these systems one can map sexual titillation, erection in the male, orgasm and ejaculatory activities. The sexual systems are a portion of the positive systems, a self-terminating portion, in that if the monkey continues stimulation he goes to orgasm, becomes unconscious, sleeps a bit, wakes up, repeats the whole process, repeats it again and will do so sixteen hours a day until forced to sleep from sheer exhaustion. In other portions of the positive system he apparently is feeling a low-level pleasure somewhere in his body, either a generalized psychic pleasure throughout the body, or localized in various parts of the body, depending on the parts of the system being stimulated.

We demonstrated that if one stimulates both the positive and the negative systems simultaneously, an extremely high energy state results, and if pushed to extremes, the monkey will have a *grand mal* epileptic seizure. At lower levels of stimulation of both systems there results an obvious total excitation of the organism with an extremely high energy state and an unpredictable kind of behavior resulting from that. The monkey may masturbate, he may freeze, he may flee, he may fight, or he may eat food extremely rapidly and with great vigor.

I worked out a technique of putting these electrodes into brains in such a way as to cause minimal injury and not to require neurosurgery. This technique was used by several neurologists who did experiments on humans which bore out everything we had found with the monkey. However, in the human there was one additional source of information which we didn't have with the monkey—the subjective report from inside the central nervous system, the report of the states of consciousness resulting from the stimulation of the positive and of the negative systems. As we demonstrated in the dolphin first, it was found in the human that the large cerebral cortex of each of these species can control these reactions and behaviors far better than the small cortex of the macaque monkey. For example, the human would report feeling rage but would also show obvious signs of controlling that rage—shaking, quivering, wide-eyed staring—but not doing anything to act it out.

The dolphins stimulated in negative systems behaved in exactly the same way as the humans—controlled output, not necessarily short-circuiting into muscular action of the five types. Even vocalization, i.e., fomenting, could be cut back in each of these species.

With brains larger than the human's—that of the sperm whale is six times the size of ours—we find that all this plus size is in the silent areas of the cerebral cortex, i.e., those areas which distinguish us from the chimpanzees, and the sperm whales from us. The history of whaling in the last century shows that the whale has even better control than does the human or the dolphin over the lower systems in his own brain. His vast size of cortex allows him a vast amount of control. For example, in the hundreds of thousands of whales that were killed in the early 1800's, there were only six cases recorded in which the sperm whale lost his temper to the point where he destroyed the ship whose harpoons had been thrown into him (see the case of the whaleship *Essex*, page 112). Rage in such a huge organism must be truly an awesome spectacle, even as was written by Melville about *Moby Dick*. Melville derived his data from a real whale by the name of Mocha Dick. When Mocha Dick was finally caught, the irons of six different whaleships were found in him and he had sunk two of the sailing vessels that had pursued him. In this century such data are not available; the vessels, which now shoot harpoons from a distance into the whales, are constructed of steel and are invulnerable to attack. The whales seem to have learned this, for they no longer attack vessels at all.

Thus the large cortex size that inhibits these lower systems leads toward nonsurvival of their species. The human, with the smaller cortex, is killing off superior brains on the planet before he has had a chance to attempt communication or any form of compassionate activity with these huge entities. Our organized, righteous survival rites are expressed as war upon and total extinction of other species (see page 59). Once again we justify our position by acting as if their brains are not first-class brains, as if their minds are somehow inferior to ours. We kill that which we do not understand in the self-righteous way we kill one another in wars. We tend to sublimate our race into the excitement of a war against other organisms. We are very effective predators operating in large groups in concert.

As I said above, as the cortex increases in size in relation to the lower brain centers, its control over the lower brain centers increases. For the planetside trip there seems to be a selection of brain sizes, at least in the human species. We will kill off and render ineffective those humans whose brains have become so large that they can control their anger and the self-righteous behavior. We also kill off those who, with their smaller brain, give in to immediate here-and-now anger and attempt to kill us off. We create a distribution curve of brains showing that most of us have brains of a size neither too large to forbid anger and its results nor too small to permit "impulsive behavior." This optimizing of the size of the brain between these two poles thus generates our systems in our survivors. These medium-sized brains determine by their group action who is to survive. I have seen many large-brained men and women "put on the shelf" by medium-sized brains. This occurs in government, in any large organization; only once in a while does a large brain escape this fate.

In medical school I saw many small brains, upon birth, not being allowed to breathe. I have seen others put into institutions to keep them from the rest of the population because of their "impulsive behavior." The microcephalics have cortices too small to control their negative and positive systems. If they are released in the population they are killed off as a result of their own impulsive behavior. They are likely to rape when they sexually mature; they are likely to kill instantly when they become angry.

Reprogramming of a medium-size cortex in techniques of control of the negative and positive systems is still possible, but it is the most difficult reprogramming that man has ever undertaken. I am not very optimistic about the elimination of the God of Righteousness, the God of Wrath, in my lifetime. Instead, this God may kill all of us. Part of me hopes not. But another part reminds me that being killed would free my essence to travel elsewhere.

CHAPTER 12

GOD AS COMPASSION

Classically, love of God includes compassion and God is Love is considered human compassion. Too often compassion is confused with virtue; and in the name of virtue one reinterprets his compassion as the mission to change the belief systems of somebody else, as if what one believed to be true is true. Compassion is confused with pity and sentimentality. In reality the highest form of compassion may be in withholding from a given person any direct physical aid that would spare him a painful lesson, withholding it so that he would never again have to act according to a particular kind of program. The best teachers know that compassion does not prevent pain but allows pain to teach. Of course, carried to an extreme this too can be used in the service of destruction. Our God of Love can lead us to war against those who don't love as we do.

Two major characteristics of most of the human species seem to assure the survival of the species, at least they so seem at the present time. One of these is the built-in reproductive positively reinforcing pleasure systems in the brain and in the body, commonly called "sexual" which we discussed in Chapter 6, "God as Orgasm and Sex." The second is a quality which seems to develop as one accumulates more trips around the sun. During the aging process the polymorphous pleasure of the needy child for tender and loving care gradually becomes sentimental attachment to those who have furnished that care. This attachment then goes on to become a sexual attachment during adolescence and postadolescence, and as maturity is reached and one's own children are produced, one begins to see that his sentimentality and pity have changed to the more mature, more complex, more calculated, less egocentric pleasure that we call "compassion."

Compassion is a very complex evaluation of the welfare of one's own group or groups. One can be compassionate toward his immediate relatives, his business associates, his customers, clients, or patients, his electorate, his state, his nation, or all humanity. From the microcosm of one's immediate relationships with those one loves, compassion can be extended to the whole universe. As one's compassion matures and becomes more general, almost constantly present, he realizes that compassion does not necessarily mean giving pleasure to others in the short-term sense. It may mean teaching by pain, as we have noted, but we have to watch here the unconscious motivations of the "compassionate" one.

For some, unconsciously, the infliction of pain is not so much a teaching mechanism as a sadistic enjoyment of the infliction, as we said in Chapter 11, "God as Righteous Wrath." It is a thin line that separates the spaces of compassion and the surrounding spaces of pity, sentimentality, sadomasochism, and so forth. In the minds of many, compassion is identified as if pity, i.e., taking care of the underdog because he/she/it is the underdog. Taking care of anyone in such a way that he remains dependent upon one and hence remains the underdog can be an unconscious Machiavellian kind of power trip for some people. The "do-gooders" tend to fall into this category.

Compassion can be confused with sentimentality. Sentimentality seems to be a very peculiar kind of attachment which has become desexualized, and almost depleasurized, as it were, in one's relation to somebody else. One can also be sentimental about objects. Here the attachment is to something connected with the past—with a past love, with a past pleasurable period, for example—about which one reminisces, keeping about him tokens or souvenirs of that period. The bric-a-brac of the maiden aunt; the old car of the car freak; the Bible itself, or any old traditional writings; old books; historical documents; museums— all may claim their share of sentimentality.

One can easily show that a museum is much more of a political institution than a repository for the culture of the race. One need only go to the museums in our major cities to find out what the consensus sentimentality is about the previous history of the human race and about nature and its objects. The hidden dogma in the little stories told about each object in the museum, the hidden judgments, the hidden belief systems behind such objects show the essential sentimentality of the museum curators and trustees, of the artists, of the donors of particular objects of art, of science, of archeology or whatever. The Museum of the American Indian is one where you can learn of the lies that white men construct about Indian problems. A museum devoted to the Aztec culture will tell you how the current culture of the country the museum is in feels toward the Aztecs in the fantasies it constructs around its predecessors. A museum devoted to Egyptology will tell you about the prejudices concerning ancient Egypt which are current in the Western world. Practically all the people I have met that are associated with museums are essentially sentimental people, hanging on to the past in some form or another; hanging on with pleasure and continual activity devoted to the preservation and the display of artifacts of the past for others equally sentimental.

I have visited many natural history museums and have seen their displays on whales, dolphins, and other animals. It is really incredible, the fables, the modern mythology concerning animals, that are there in these particular displays, all presented with a great deal of love and care. The only museums I have seen in which this is not true are what I call "operational museums"—medical museums, technical museums, for example— which are devoted to the techniques of modern society. (Planetariums, though concerned with a science, are an exception, as is any museum that serves the wide-eyed wonder of the young.)

Sentimentality is rife in the advertising media. Advertisements for luxury items (such as diamonds) reveal the essentially senti-

mental nature of the advertising. The copy plays on the senti-
ments and memories of each buyer. For example, have you
ever wondered why there are so many secondhand Cadillacs in
low-rent districts in various parts of the United States? These
cars may be falling apart, but they are an honored object in
those neighborhoods. Have you ever wondered why people pay
exorbitant prices for antiques? Antique furniture, antique cars,
antique practically anything can be sold. Attachment to the past
is a selling point in the current market.

In a large number of hospitals that I have worked in or visited,
sentimentality and pity are the superficial displays put on by
the personnel and the relatives of the patients, and of patients
for one another. True compassion, in a hospital, is found in the
professionals who are so accustomed to dealing with sickness
and with the necessity of treatment that they are polished in
their techniques. But here, too, there are traps. There are many
doctors, for example, who trade off their technical compassion
for money, charging exorbitant prices (for what is often excellent care). They have so raised their standard of living since the
time they were medical students that they are now among the
wealthiest members of their community. Professionally, God as
Money has been wedded to God as Compassion.

Somebody once asked me who my best friends were. I said,
without devoting much thought to it, "Among others, M.D.'s."
Why is this? Because I have an M.D. My ignorance and my
knowledge correspond most closely to those of this large group
of humans. Doctors and nurses seem to understand me better
than does any other group. I went to medical school with a
good deal of both sentimental pity and compassion for the
human species. During medical school I realized that the ultimate in compassion is not the treating of individuals and the
curing of them but of researching further methods for treatment
in the future. Thus I very vigorously undertook research. My
God then was God as Compassion, expressed through research
on the brain and the mind; on solitude, isolation, and confinement; on brain electrodes, motivational systems, the spread of
nervous energy activity in the cerebral cortex; and so forth. For

anyone interested, a bibliography of my works is available in *The Human Biocomputer*.[1] I mention this so that the reader can see for himself the particular direction I have gone and can better understand what I have to say in regard to compassion. Without the history of the author, one cannot exert compassion in behalf of the author. Without an understanding of that history, compassion may be an empty, meaningless emotion, without the complex understanding that true compassion requires.

As a consequence of these considerations, in my own life I sometimes feel that my compassion is best expressed by sharing my knowledge, through my books, so that others may learn from it. This means that I put off my own satisfactions into the indefinite future, and sometimes I will be disappointed because the books are read and not understood. In other cases the books are read and the reader's reaction is anything but compassionate. They may be torn apart by a non-understanding critic, or they may be praised by a hyper-enthusiast who is sentimentally attached to the book. The truly compassionate reader is the learning reader. His or her compassion matches mine in such a way that we transfer ideas to one another, that we have a transmission, a communication that cannot exist without compassion in both of us. There are those with belief systems distinctly different from mine who will pity me for writing such a book. There are others who will rise against me in righteous wrath because their God is the God of Righteous Wrath. There are others who will attempt to make money from my ideas, marketable ideas which they will transform into a profit, if their God is Money. And so, on and on, we treat one another in ways dictated by who and what our God is.

We tend to project our compassion—especially when we are in dire straits or danger—onto the universe and to assume that the universe has a complex understanding of the human condition and that somehow someone will recognize us and rescue us. This is epitomized, for example, in Arthur Clarke's beautiful little novel entitled *Childhood's End*.[2] Here the Earth is recognized and is subdued by a superior power from outer space which comes and solves all human problems by pure, unadulterated power, with pure, unadulterated compassion. I won't spoil the story for you by telling you how the compassion of this power is finally expressed, but the Earth as a consequence produces beings far superior to the human, and the humans are left alone with nothing to live for. This is one of the highest forms of compassion, expressed in a very unusual way.

When I have been in the farthest-out spaces of which I could conceive, I have discovered in myself this search for compassion in the universe, for Love, for Divine Grace, for Baraka. I am not sure that such currents of compassion exist in the universe except as my own projections. However, if they do exist, it requires a very disciplined mind—disciplined in very particular ways—to tune in to these currents of bliss. Franklin Merrell-Wolff, in his *Pathways Through to Space*,[3] describes what it is like to receive these currents. His descriptions of Nirvana, his descriptions of Ananda, fit the classical view of the Baraka, of the Divine Grace descending through one and maintaining one in special states of consciousness.

In general, divine compassion is associated with these states. In my own case, I have been in these spaces, experienced these phenomena, but I am not so sure that this is all there is. This seems to be some sort of ultimate self-rewarding or cosmic reward for the human, and yet it is not ultimate. When one has lived in these spaces long enough and realized that they are limited also, one then moves into those spaces that Merrell-Wolff calls the state of "High Indifference"—beyond dichotomies, beyond compassion, beyond bliss, beyond form, beyond formlessness, beyond the void, beyond the lack of the void, beyond business, beyond doing, beyond not doing, beyond dreaming, beyond not dreaming, beyond consciousness, beyond not-consciousness or unconsciousness, into regions he epitomizes by calling them SPACE, in which one experiences an Immense Authority, which is totally impartial, totally objective, totally creative, and yet beyond creation. Creation is contained within the Immense Authority as a small subcompartment.

This particular state of being is, to me, The Most Compassionate of all possible states. Attaining this state allows one to walk the face of the earth in the Tao, in the Dharma, in the Grace of God, in Bliss when one needs it, but also in exquisite pain when one needs that. One is above these, outside these, operative in a disinterested observer position as if one were the universe watching oneself operate on a very small planet in a small galaxy tucked away in one corner of the universe. Merrell-Wolff wondered if he should write about this state—it seemed so non-human, so de-humanized, so non-sentimental, so non-loving—but he did, and discovered that the Tibetans also had written about it as *the* highest state of consciousness.

For me, this is where compassion lies, in divine disinterest yet divine involvement. This is the permissionary, not the missionary. And yet no permission can be given. And yet no tender, loving care can be given. It all just IS—eternally. As one moves through the lower levels of God as Compassion, he reaches these states, which seem at the particular moment to be the ultimate, and yet he glimpses infinities beyond these—beyond the capability of any human mind to grasp. And yet there are those who are moving into these regions and who will surpass all of those, including us, who preceded them.

Overvaluation of aversion/attachment is a translation of High Indifference into consensus states of reality/consciousness.

REFERENCES

1. Lilly, John C., *Programming and Metaprogramming the Human Biocomputer*, New York: Julian Press, 1967, 1972.
2. Clarke, Arthur, *Childhood's End*, New York: Harcourt, Brace, 1963.
3. Merrell-Wolff, Franklin, *Pathways Through to Space*, New York: Julian Press, 1973.

CHAPTER 13

GOD AS WAR

The causes of a given war are multifarious and at times unknown or obscure. In general they lie so far in the past that the combatants do not really understand what led them down a path of destruction. In the chapter on God as Righteous Wrath we showed some of the origins of a war based upon virtue. "My beliefs are perfect. Your beliefs are not my beliefs; hence yours are wrong. I must convince you of the rightness of my beliefs. If you will not believe, I will do you violence."

If one pays close attention to the gods of the combatants, in general he can find programs, metaprograms, strategies which depend upon the belief systems operative at the time of the war. War itself is based upon a very peculiar view of the universe: In order to create, one must destroy. No real war has ever proven that war is a creative solution. Human historians worship war as an instrument of change and hence perpetuate this untenable and unrealistic "solution."

There are those who would start a war in order to profiteer. There are those who would start a war merely because they have a large military investment or because their industries need something to do. For a large industry a war is very useful in requiring an increase of productivity. A war very efficiently destroys that which it creates, thus assuring industry a never ending market with no problems of saturation and no obsolescence.

War assures a continuing flow of new money for industrial research and development, in order to pursue the destruction of the enemy more efficiently. The enemy too must be educated to the new techniques and matériel so that the war will not be too quickly ended.

In the old-fashioned sense, God as War, War as an instrument of God as is recounted in the Bible, war between small villages in the Middle East, is not to be compared with modern warfare simultaneously involving several hundreds of millions of people. The old Gods of War are too small for modern human society. The Jewish God is too small. Baal and Maloch are too small. Ra is too small. Kali is too small. And the philosophies of all these ancient Gods and all the other ancient Gods, such as Huitzilopochtli and Tezcatlipoca of the Aztecs, are too small.

Documentation of the Spanish invasion of Mexico shows the smallness of two systems in collision. The Christian representatives of the Inquisition moved into the Aztec culture and took it over on the basis of myths created by the Aztecs. The Aztecs predicted that a blond, white God would come from the sea. The Aztecs were using human sacrifice as a propitiation device for their rather horrifying pair of gods, who would destroy the universe unless the Mythes made the human sacrifices. Of about two hundred civilizations the Aztecs' Maya gave the Spanish the most trouble. The Spaniards arrived and started a "holy" war against what they considered to be these unholy people. They brought their priests, their Inquisition tools, their Machiavellian manipulation of political power, their weapons, and proceeded to destroy totally a previous culture, not only Aztec and Mayan, but many other Indian nations as well. On each side the main God was that of God as War. The Spaniards came with righteous wrath; the Aztecs faced the Spaniards, thinking they were Gods. Neither side won.

If either the Spaniards or the Aztecs had had atomic energy at their disposal, the planet would probably have become sterilized. We no longer can afford God as War. We now have Godlike instruments of destruction. Our God must be greater than a protagonist in a human battle.

The basic assumption that "We are right and they are wrong" also must be treated as a delusion. As a substitute for violence we must negotiate; we must bring disparate belief systems into congruence through communication, not through violence. The language barriers of the world must not only be crossed but toppled. The belief barriers of the world must be diminished to the point of triviality. All modern technology must be used to increase the knowledge of all peoples throughout the planet. National security boundaries must be abolished bilaterally. Self-righteous virtue and concerted anger must be denied to those in power. Profit through war must be abolished.

It may be that all the above reasoning is idealistic and totally wrong. It may be that war on our planet is the result of orders sent to the human species from other superior civilizations hundreds, thousands, or millions of years in advance of ours. War may be a laboratory for the development of weapons to be used elsewhere. War may be the supreme form of human achievement. It may be that our short-term view of the destruction of human bodies, of human vehicles, one by the other, is a technique for freeing up essences needed elsewhere in our galaxy or the universe. If we want to continue with God as War, some such belief system as this must be carefully taught to all peoples on Earth. There are various methods for such teaching. For example, we can declare that it is necessary for the Americans and the Chinese to carry on their military research and their testing of new matériel in real wars in order to develop super-weapons which eventually could be used against extraterrestrial invaders.

Further alternatives are that the screams of the dying, the pain, the terror, the panic of war, all telepathically broadcast throughout our galaxy, may be needed as energy—as food or as fuel—somewhere else in the galaxy.

It may be that Earth is merely a small portion of some other beings' laboratory in which they are testing out various ways of exciting various kinds of organisms to high energy states. It may be that the supervisors of this laboratory must every so often dump some sort of destructive antibiotic activity on us, the bacteria, to keep our numbers in control. It may be that they finally have furnished us with the formulae for our own antibiotics. We, as the bacteria in the laboratory they have set up on this planet, are merely living out their instructions. These instructions involve observing how organisms with our size brain can kill one another most efficiently. These superextraterrestrial beings furnish us with ideas of God, of the devil, of prophets, of power, of inflated egos, of megalomanic belief systems in order to play games in their laboratory.

Or it may be that we are just simulation computers at the behest of very much larger computers who are in control of us, and that we are simulating a war they are waging among themselves; or that they have agreed to take sides on this planet, some controlling one side and others controlling the other side. These lesser gods of cosmic war games are undetectable to us because we have post-hypnotic trance orders to forget the fact that we are under their orders. Our simulation does not include the simulation of Them. Our orders say: "Accept the orders that we give you in sleep. When you are awake do what we have dictated and forget that we gave you these orders in sleep."

Paranoia has two components. We forget that paranoia includes a megalomanic center-of-the-universe arrogance. This state could easily have been programmed into us by Them. The only additional component needed to start a war would then be fear. Fear is easily excited because it has been built into the biocomputer as a survival program. Many things—including the natural forces—can be used to excite fear. Start a hurricane or a typhoon and move it in the right direction across the surface of the earth. Or begin a very large earthquake, or excite a solar flare and cause the particles from the flare to hit the earth's atmosphere, thus changing the mood of all the earth's creatures, including man. Or beam secret information into the world's houses of power—that on the opposite side of the world are your enemies, so go there and kill them.

Such projections of responsibility upon the cosmos in the past were called God. Now we must perform an operation almost out of science fiction in order to simulate the same sort of results. Imbedded in us is a righteous wrath of our own fear, our own megalomania, our own arrogance. When we become angry enough to kill—then is the time to stop, to stand off, to find out how much of our program is biologically determined, how much is determined by communication with others through at-present-unknown channels, and how much is determined by our peer group and by the known physical pathways of communication between humans on this planet. The destroy-to-create simulation either must go or must be carried to its full extreme of totally destroying in order to start totally over somewhere else.

If there is a part of each of us that survives destruction of the human body, where does it go when the body is destroyed? Does it go somewhere else in the universe? Does it stay around here? Does it diffuse throughout consciousness-without-an-object? Does it become a spirit in a hell of its own creation? For Western man research in feedback to the living in any believable form is peculiarly lacking. Maybe we must give up any thought of a life after death, of a saving of one's soul. Maybe we must have a belief system which says, "If I die in war, that is the end of me; there is no hope of a continuance of my identity beyond this life." This belief system may effectively put the brakes on our killing of one another through war or any other violence.

It may be that our beliefs in immortality have caused wars, have caused us to hunt out others to kill. Apparently we have wasted our sacred feelings, we have wasted sacredness on illusion. It may be that each living human should be considered as God and hence not subject to the results of righteous wrath. It may be that for any one of us simulations of God as greater than human and yet as prejudiced must be abandoned. With the devotion of national resources to the idea that each human is sacred, that each human is a God, it may be that if the military budgets of the world are diverted to other purposes such as the survival and the education of everyone throughout the planet, we could abolish war faster than by any other means. An appalling amount of the national resources of the United States is tied up in the military machine—military personnel, military matériel, atomic energy, and military real estate.

Except for the Catholic Church, the Department of Defense is the largest organization for the management of humans which the world has ever seen. We might well ask, What are the belief systems that make it possible to organize war and destruction on such a huge scale? How did we achieve such a bias, such a prejudice in favor of destruction? Are we going to continue to worship God as War and hide this worship as if national defense? I don't know the answer to this question; I raise it, hoping there are others who can at least begin to study the possibility of answering it.

CHAPTER 14

GOD AS SCIENCE

Science as we know it in the Western world seems to have two major origins. One is the astronomy and cosmology origination with Galileo, Brahe, Kepler, Newton and Einstein. The ideas and observations of these men showed without a doubt that the earth is not the center of rotation of our galaxy. They showed that the planet Earth moved around its nearest star, the sun, and that the sun progressed in its own way among the other stars of our galaxy.

These ideas unseated the dogmatic cosmology of the early Church and of the Inquisition. The power of new knowledge, experimentally and theoretically derived from nature, began to show its influence at the time of Galileo and the Inquisition.

The second major origin of Western science was in the "Queen of the Sciences," mathematics. The construction of a purely consistent, logical system of thought seems to have begun in the Western world with Euclid's construction of the laws of straight-line geometry. He used the axiomatic method of constructing a system of thought. This invention was further elaborated and carried out in much greater detail by a succession of men beginning with Newton and the "infinitesimal calculus" which he was forced to invent in order to express his laws of dynamics, including electrodynamics, and became much simplified in terms of its expression. The ideas behind rates of change of one variable with respect to another, the idea of continuous process succinctly expressed now became possible and practical. Following Newton, a very large number of men began to be creative in mathematics. Science began to recognize mathematics as a proper discipline for scientists and as a profession for the special group called "mathematicians."

Thus, Western science became divided into two major movements: experimental science, which depended upon careful observation and experiment, and mathematics, which depended upon an intuitive grasp of abstract principles and the reduction of these to equations and functions expressible by a new symbology. Several mistakes were made by commentators on this scene. One of them was that science was neglecting sources of information other than that from the natural external world and experiments upon that world. In an almost underground way the subjective aspects of experience were paid court by the mathematicians and their intuitive sources of inner knowledge, examined and expressed in a disciplined, careful "inner experimental" way.

For those who think that science originates in the external reality, I ask the question: "Where does mathematics come from?" This is as deep a mystery as the mystical experiences of the Eastern philosophers and mystics. The "Yoga of the West" is divided into the "Mathematical Yoga" and the "Experimental Science Yoga." Each of these disciplines requires just as much discipline, mastery of self, and ability of inner and outer actions as anything imported from India, China or Japan. In my teaching experience, teaching science of the West and teaching techniques from the East, I find that those who need the least teaching, i.e., who already have the self-discipline necessary to master any of these techniques, are those in the West who are trained in mathematics and/or science.

A third—but not major—origin of our science is in technology. Most observers of the scientific scene do not realize that a large part of science depends upon the techniques derived from manual arts—for example, the processes of mining, purification, smelting, molding, the forming of metals (including the fabrication of steel), glass and plastics. The material base upon which science as we know it operates is not derived from science itself. The fabrication of a cyclotron depends upon engineering and technologies derived from sources other than science. As a student of science, I was shocked to realize that scientists depend upon mechanics, and mechanics depend upon previous mechanics who taught them their trade. I was shocked also to find that metallurgy was not yet a science; it was an empirical, technological, heuristic, pragmatic, empirical art. When I was working in scientific instrumentation, I discovered that most of the knowledge I needed was not in scientific journals or the scientific textbooks at all; it was in engineering handbooks, it was in various "how to do" manuals from technology, it was in books like . John Strong's *Procedures in Experimental Physics.* These sources depend not upon scientific experiments so much as "try it—if it works, use it." I found that to be a scientist I could be a technologist, a mechanic, a carpenter, a plumber, an electrician, a wire man, a circuit designer, an optician, a bacteriologist, a farmer, and so forth. True science is imbedded in practically every human activity that one can conceive of. It is not something alone, by itself, apart from the rest of the reality of human existence.

I make these points in order to show that it is totally inappropriate to make science into God. Science is the result of human activity; it is not something God-given and forced upon the human race by some superior being. And yet there are those in legislatures, in public life, in the media, in the performing arts, who have not been educated in science and thus put it on some sort of pedestal and worship it as if it were a god. This can be extremely dangerous; it means that one is setting up a whole sphere of human knowledge, of human activity, as if separate from oneself and hence subject to attack or to worship, or whatever else one wants to do with this simulation.

Once one simulates Science as if God, or as if the Devil, he has lost contact with it. It now is in the position of a paranoid system of delusion which he can then treat unrealistically and as if not part of his own planetside trip. As is discussed in other chap-

ters in this book, science has much to offer—in the region of
cosmology, for example, in the region of submicroscopic reality,
in reality, in the region of explaining the operations of our own
brain. I agree with those who maintain that science is only the
best application to our planetside trip of the best thinking of
which man is capable (and I would include in the planetside trip
the inner realities as well as the other realities). Science is not
something to be worshipped; science is something to be acquired
as one's own thinking machinery can assimilate it, as one's own
biocomputer can be trained by it. Science literally is a Yoga, a
union with our own humanity, a union with the universe as it
exists, not as we may wish it to be.

Science of itself is ruthlessly indifferent. It is an expression of
the state of High Indifference. Science does not takes sides; its
products can be used to kill, to create, or to grow. Science
as we know it is now capable of feeding adequately every
human being on the face of the Earth. Science as we know
it is now capable of turning the seas into vast farms, of
turning the deserts into green paradises. The proper use of
science could make a veritable Eden of our planet, without
pollution and with a balanced view of the totality of all species
of plants and animals. Science can then function as a benign god
rather as the devil that we make of it when we worship God as
War, God as Righteous Wrath, God as Power, and so forth.
Science is our handservant, science is our concubine, science is
our wife, science is our husband, science is our children, science
is our thinking, science is our feeling, science is our doing.

Freud, in a brief monograph on religion, wrote, "No, science is
no illusion, but it is an illusion to suppose that we can get
anywhere else what science cannot give us." This is an expression of a Western man with a very deep belief in the efficacy of
knowledge, carefully collected and experimentally verified. It is
also an expression of a man who did not know mathematics,
who was weak in the construction of theory and strong in the collection of empirical facts ruthlessly gathered irrespective of the
social attitudes of his time. Freud's conflict with Jung over the
intuitive sources of knowledge is well known; Freud worshipped

the laws of cause and effect, which Jung thought were not necessarily true. Jung tried to enunciate with Pauli the "law of synchronicity." Synchronicity is the result of the effect of the human psyche upon events. This can be freely translated into another system which I derive from empirical science, a system I call "Coincidence Control." Coincidence control goes something like this: If you live right, the coincidences will build up for you in unexpected and surprising and beneficial ways. If you do not live right, the anti-coincidences will build up in unexpected and direful, sometimes disastrous ways. The criterion of whether or not you are living right is empirical observation of the coincidences. If the coincidences build up, you are living right. If they do not build up, you are not living right and had best examine your way of life.

Of course this system depends upon the method used to interpret events in terms of what one wants. The method of interpretation, the pattern-recognition systems applied to events, the chosen variables, the chosen parameters, and the patterns that these seem to make to the observer determine what one calls a "coincidence." There is a basic fallacy here in projecting one's own wishes onto the world and its events. One can easily rationalize, i.e., choose any theory that will fit the apparent pattern-recognition system of events. For example: I leave a gas station and drive down a freeway seventy miles. On the way I see three or four accidents, one of which happened two minutes before I arrived at the scene. If I had been two minutes earlier I would have been completely crushed by a huge truck that turned over with a load of steel and blocked the whole freeway. At the gas station I had been delayed two minutes while I sought out the man to clean my windshield. If there had not been this delay I would have arrived at the accident scene and probably would have been totally destroyed.

What's wrong with this story? The whole story depends upon my construction of it. My brother, David Lilly, has a saying, "Hindsight is twenty/twenty vision." One might say, "Please don't disturb my theory with the facts." Now let us go back over the series of events with a more objective point of view.

Before leaving the gas station I looked at a road map and wondered whether I should continue down the freeway or take off into the mountains between the freeway and the sea. I then thought of what I had to do at the other end of the trip and, realizing that I couldn't take the amount of time I would need to go into the mountains, I chose to continue on the freeway. I had another alternate, but I did not use it. The map showed that there was another freeway running parallel to and a few miles from the one I used. There were many more probabilities, but when I finally made my decision these became certainties concerning a short time in the future. In other words, the certainty in the fact of the indeterminacy of the real situation may last only for a few minutes or perhaps up to a few hours. As time is extended the indeterminacy increases. As the indeterminacy increases, the probability that something will happen which now can be named "coincidence" increases. Any unexpected event that does not follow the pattern of certainty that one is laying on the future one tends to call a "coincidence." Coincidence Control, then, is merely a hindsight name for that which one chooses to call a coincidence out of all events going on. One's survival mechanisms in his biocomputer tend to select certain events as if they are the ones that determine his survival or non-survival. Hence it is these systems which are paramount in selecting the patterns called "coincidence." (On this topic, I recommend a book called *The Rules of Chaos, Or Why Tomorrow Doesn't Work*,[1] by Stephen Vizinczey.)

This view of coincidence as projection from a given biocomputer expresses only a part of the synchronicity of Jung. Jung's synchronicity statement includes, then, psychic control of events, i.e., a certain amount of determination by a given individual of what will happen to him in the future. If he has an unconscious self-destructive aspect he may not survive the events that he creates. J. W. Dunne, in a book called *An Experiment with Time*,[2] shows that one can detect real events that are going to happen a short time in the future. His theory expressed a parallel time track or a loop in time. Such events, according to Dunne, are not determined by the psyche but are perceived by the psyche; the determinants are beyond the self, resident in the total feedback system of which one's self is only a small part.

Recently I encountered one such instance which is in agreement with Dunne but which can be interpreted by the Jungian or the Coincidence Control view as well. A friend of mine, B. M., who lives in a beach house on the Pacific Ocean, dreamed during the night that a dolphin came up on the beach in front of the house and was then pushed back into the sea by the children of the neighborhood. I arrived at his house that morning, he told me the dream at breakfast, and within two hours a dolphin came up on the beach and he, his wife, and the children participated in pushing it back into the sea.

This could have been an incidence of Coincidence Control, i.e., by his dream my friend was setting up the possibility of the coincidence that the real dolphin would arrive, directed by some form of mental telepathy or other means of control which our science does not yet know about. Or it could have been a causal event in the Jungian sense with a synchronicity of the dream material and of the actual event of the dolphin's arrival on the beach. Or it could be interpreted, as many modern scientists would interpret it, as "merely a coincidence."

I would prefer to say that the total field situation involved—of my expected arrival at his house, of his association in his mind of me and dolphins—had programmed the dream. He may have had dreams of dolphins many other nights without remembering those dreams. Dolphins do beach themselves in Southern California and are pushed back to sea without much to-do unless they die and must be disposed of. Thus, in the fabric of probabilities one would have to find out how many people dream of dolphins beaching themselves and how many nights of the year and how many of these dreams are followed within, say, twenty-four to forty-eight hours by an actual beaching of dolphins along all the beaches of Southern California and possibly of the whole world. Until we had the results of this survey (and I'm afraid they would not be very accurate), until we had worked out a method of accurately reporting both the internal event (the dream) and the external event (the beaching), we would not have an experimental-science toehold on the connection between these types of events. I don't know what the connection is, if any, other than that the patterns of the dream and the patterns of the event happen to match by some means we do not yet know. I hope that eventually man will be sufficiently advanced to begin to investigate such happenings with a more relaxed attitude toward them and without attempting to "prove" something by means of such correlations. I find such happenings exciting, but this does not prove that there is either mental telepathy or coincidence control.

I have often experienced a feeling of awe, of reverence, and of weirdness in the presence of dolphins. When dolphins begin to cooperate with one in a communication of information back and forth by whatever means is available to each side, one begins to feel that there is someone in that particular body who in an alien and far-out way is at least one's peer if not superior. However, my scientific training says, "Do not allow your feelings of awe, of reverence, and of weirdness to be mistaken for the apperception of a truth. The work has just begun with these feelings; these feelings are your motivation to start an experimental series to find out what is going on and how it happens." If I allowed science to be my God and dictate the truth to me from strictly intuitive unconscious sources, I would be making the same mistakes that many people have made in the past who refused to polish up and discipline their theories so that they were applicable in the experimental and experiential sphere. Sloppy thinking is not science. Science is the best thinking of which the human species is capable—ruthless, with no holds barred, at least in the province of the mind.

No, science is no illusion, and it may not be an illusion to suppose that we can get from anything else what science cannot give us. However, we must realize that we cannot today be dogmatic as to what science in the future will be. There are regions of mystery, regions of ignorance, regions which we have yet to penetrate in science. It would be an illusion to suppose that our present science is complete. Science, as far as I am concerned, is an open-ended system, a system of exploration, of processing data which makes sense, a logical system. And yet, in the future it may include regions which today we call illogical, irrational, psychotic, superstitious, occult, esoteric, religious, or what have you. The new frontiers, as we see them as frontiers, are developing in the inner sciences as well as in the other sciences. Those who have occult esoteric authority and try to dictate what is real may be on the right track. One of science's jobs is separating one's own projections into those which match those simulations which simulate best some reality inside or outside. There may be those who have tapped into omniscient sources of information who have attained states of mind, states of being, states of consciousness way beyond those of the ordinary human. I have been through such experiences and have felt, while in those states, that there are omniscient sources available to the human through his intuition, through his unconscious.

The only problem then becomes one of expression with an incomplete science, an incomplete language, an incomplete human vehicle. Coming back from such regions, one feels squeezed into the human frame, the human limitations, the human brain as a limited computer prejudiced and filled with pseudo-knowledge that blocks the transmission of True Knowledge. Any sage, any wise man, any guru that I have spoken to showed his humanity in many, many ways in the sense that he was not an error-free computer. Some of these people claim that God is Science of a more advanced form than any that we can know, and yet they have failed to express this in sufficiently cogent, succinct and understandable terms so that they are useful on the planetside trip. I find such people using all-too-human mechanisms of brainwashing, of human control of groups, and of creating "in-groups" to worship them and their knowledge. They have not gotten beyond God as the Group, or God as Myself, or God as Her/Him/It.

And yet there are those like Einstein and others who have gone to these regions and then come back and used all their available discipline to turn the inspirations and intuitions of these vast regions into something that will revise our science and make it advance into the future science that can approach more closely that which one knows exists. As Gregory Bateson, author of *Steps to an Ecology of Mind*,[3] said in talking of a psychic who was demonstrating his powers, "We like to think it is not difficult." Science *is* difficult; any discipline requires a degree of dedication, inner-directed work, after one receives intuitive jumps in understanding. No, science is not an illusion, but to derive by scientific methods that which will bear up under experiential and experimental testing by the self *and* others is a lot of hard work.

REFERENCES

1. Vizinczey, Stephen, *The Rules of Chaos, Or Why Tomorrow Doesn't Work*, New York: Saturday Review Press, 1969.
2. Dunne, J.W., *An Experiment with Time*, New York, Macmillan, 1938.
3. Bateson, Gregory, *Steps to an Ecology of Mind*, San Francisco: Chandler Publishing, 1972.

CHAPTER 15

GOD AS MYSTERY

For those of us with a full life, there is little mystery. One can be so busy with the planetside trip that there is no time left for considering that which is mysterious and unknown, for considering one's own ignorance. If one is content and happy in the planetside trip, he can safely place God as Mystery, God as One's Own Ignorance, God as the Unknown, God as the Inexpressable, God as The Ineffable. One can leave God until Sunday (or Saturday) and be too busy during the week to consider His existence. Even one's Sundays (or Saturdays) may be so occupied with mundane affairs that God is not thought about even then.

Even modern science admits of its ignorance, of its frontiers, of its boundaries beyond which it cannot go with its present techniques, present theories, present paradigms. Too many people are too involved in other views of God than God as Mystery. The simulations of God given in other chapters indicate where their energy is being used. God as Mystery seems to be special to mystics, to some scientists, to medical doctors and nurses, and so forth, who are constantly being faced with situations about which they can do nothing. God in these cases becomes "that which I cannot yet know about."

What can I say about my ignorance except that my ignorance exists? What can I say about the unknown except that I cannot yet know it? So, I express God as Mystery by a blank sheet of paper. A blank sheet of paper to be used in the future, as it becomes less mysterious, better understood.

CHAPTER 16

GOD AS THE BELIEF, THE SIMULATION, THE MODEL

In the modern world the distribution of the written and spoken word and the distribution of motion pictures and videotapes has become so widespread that those in charge of these media have constructed a new god, the God of Belief, the God of Simulation, the God of the Model. As was demonstrated by the owners of newspapers in the beginning of this century, God as Power can be controlled and expressed through the belief, the simulation, and the model as expressed in language. Those in control of the distribution of ideas through the media have access to manipulation of power such as the world has never seen. The modern communication satellites, modern radio and TV, are demanded by masses of people. In most metropolitan areas the most commonly stolen objects are TV sets. The believers in the media want to be sure they stay in contact with what the media are saying.

Language can be used in many different ways; it is one of the most flexible instruments ever invented. It can be used to transmit essential information, to predict, to give instructions, to program individuals or large groups, to express very precisely very precise ideas; it can be used to harangue crowds, to excite war and its concomitant activities, to construct computers, to control the human species.

However, language is not universal. There are too many languages on the face of the earth to allow of universality. Therefore, there are discrepancies across language barriers: discrepancies in belief, in simulations, in models of reality and in models of one another. The devil is buried in language, as is God. As linguists have shown over the last fifty years, there is no primitive language left among humans. Every language which previously was called primitive, when looked at more carefully and studied more deeply than before turned out to be an extremely sophisticated instrument for communication of man's inner states.

Language itself contains mysteries. The study of semantics, of logic, of proto-logic has led ever deeper into theories, the science of the human, all science. As semantics becomes polished, as mathematics matures, our beliefs, simulations, and models and their power are all improved—the power to dissuade from a belief, to construct a belief to take the place of another belief, to acquire simulations "as if true." The power of models to take over one's thinking machinery to the point where one's life is sacrificed in the service of models is also present in the advance of semantics, linguistics, and mathematics. God as the Word, God as the Sentence, God as the Meaning, God as the Belief rule our social reality.

Poetry seems to be the expression of that which is inexpressible by any other means. It has been said that poetry is "that which is left over, that which is left out in the translation." Poetry is a very special kind of simulation in that it permits the rules of language to be broken in order to better express a feeling, a mood, a state of being in injunctive situations. Poetry can express the irrational, the ineffable, the inexpressible, the unknown: poetry can express my ignorance. And yet poetry is generally thought of as the least effective of the media. Poets are very badly paid for their work.

In certain states of consciousness one receives unequivocal messages of Immense Authority. Some people call these messages "the voice of God" and proceed on the belief that a God Out There is communicating with Him in Here. As I stated in *The Human Biocomputer*, in certain states of consciousness one tends to project the voice of God into the noise of his own thought processes. In solitude, isolation, and confinement he can receive such messages. If he proceeds on the belief system that these are "real" messages, not generated only in his own bio-computer, in his own noise level, he opens up whole areas for new investigation. To get beyond his belief, his simulations, his model of God, one must in these states of consciousness open himself to the unexpected, the surprising, the unbelievable. If one remains open-ended he is sure that in the vast areas of his own ignorance there are, there will be, there must be surprises. Getting beyond his current belief systems, his current simulations, his current models, one must demote the current belief system, current simulation, current model to a position less than that of God. To remain open-ended one's God must be greater than this; one's God must be huge—in order to include one's ignorance, the unknown, the ineffable. Instead of God as the Belief, the Simulation, the Model, one adheres to God as Mystery, God as the Unknown. The explorer of the inner spaces cannot afford the baggage of fixed beliefs. This baggage is too heavy, too limited and too limiting to allow further exploration.

All one has to do is spend a day looking at TV programming in a metropolitan area in the United States to realize the paucity, the poverty, the futility of this programming itself. The strictures placed on what can be said, on what can be shown, are so huge that one gets incredibly bored with the repetitions in the narrow information channels which are allowed. The sentimental attachment to old movies, the premium placed on horror presentations of modern war, of modern riots, turn one away from this medium as not expressing anything of use either on one's planetside trip or in terms of one's investigations and explorations.

The science shown on television is elementary and childish. The belief of the networks that they are sending information to twelve-year-old minds in the mass is complete and utter nonsense. The belief that the networks cannot show certain things because they are "beyond" the viewers is also utter nonsense. With the proper simulations, with the proper beliefs, with open-ended models, TV could be an exciting medium for all concerned—viewers and producers alike. Once in a while a worthwhile script does sneak by networks' and the advertisers' censors.

Because of the belief of the media that they are dealing with twelve-year-old minds, they generate twelve-year-old minds. This is a self-fulfilling prophecy. Instead of expanding these minds to be fifteen, twenty, thirty, forty, eighty years old, they worship God as Youth, God as the Uninformed. Their compassion is misplaced, their education is limited. We need more open-minded programming in television in order to increase man's understanding in general. If we are going to program out our own total destruction we need the knowledge to fill the place left by the old tape-loops which we see again and again and again involving God as War, God as Power, God as Money, God as Science, God as Death, God as Sex, God as Drugs, God Out There, I Am God, God as The Group. There are the simulations which TV insists on playing back to us again and again and again.

There is great modern music among the young. There is great modern poetry, modern mathematics, semantics, linguistics. There are new mysteries showing up in the space program— mysteries edited out by NASA and the networks. Things have happened to the astronauts of which NASA does not make any mention, and the networks join in the conspiracy in the typical patriarchal view that they are "Daddy" in charge of "all us children." We ask why do ex-astronauts become mystical, as did Mitchell and White.

If there was an invasion from outer space by subtle extraterrestrial agencies and it was first discovered by the media, I am sure the invasion would be so underplayed that the picture presented by the media would be rejected and others would seek the truth.

Our Department of Defense, our CIA, FBI, and other government agencies, through the use of what is called "secrecy in the service of national security," construct a belief that these agencies are patriarchs allowing only certain kinds of information to the public who are supporting these agencies with their taxes.

In the various flaps about UFO's there have been such statements by the Air Force and by others that if the truth were released the public would panic. This seems to be one of the limiting beliefs, one of the limiting simulations for the control of beliefs, putting God as the Belief in front of everything else. The automatic programming in of panic, simultaneous with public knowledge, is nonsense. Any message can be transmitted as long as it has a basis in fact and will be accepted by the public without fear, without panic in any organized way. This particular form of groupthink—thinking for the public, thinking for everybody else—is insidious; it is not the way to encourage mature thought and action in large numbers of people. My father had a saying, "You don't know if a man can take responsibility until you give it to him." I am sure, as are many others, that the American public is much more mature than the media seem to believe.

Those who look upon the media as God must be educated by the media to dissolve that belief. This is the ultimate test of maturity of those in control of the media. Can they delegate responsibility to their audiences? Until they do the experiment, they won't know the answer. They tout the reception of Orson Welles's "War of the Worlds" as an example of the way the public reacts. What they forget is that we have stored up the "War of the Worlds" episode; we have also stored up Pearl Harbor—and we have learned and gained maturity from them. We cannot live in the past; we must move on to whatever future awaits us.

CHAPTER 17

GOD AS THE COMPUTER

Immediately after World War II, in the middle forties, we began
to realize that computers were going to take over most computations, especially those involving very large numbers and the need
for very high speed results. At the University of Pennsylvania in
the forties, when I was on the faculty there in the Department
of Biophysics, we were exposed to the development of the computer for Army Ordnance at Aberdeen and the beginnings of the
Univac computer. I was also exposed to people such as John
Von Neumann, Warren McCulloch, and Heinz Von Foerster,
who were working in the region of cybernetics.

The first high-speed machines were not reliable. They were
built with vacuum tubes; transistors and the solid-state devices
were not yet available. As fast as one could repair them they
broke down, so that their "down time" was a very large fraction
of their total life. As the development of the transistor came in,
the reliability increased until today we have a much greater
operating time than we do "down time." The sophisticated
hardware of today was made possible by the ideas presented in
the early forties and early fifties.

In the beginning there were two rival types of machines—the
analog machine, which would calculate on continuous processes,
and the digital machine which used discontinuous "zero and
one" processes. The analog machines were very useful in calcu-

lations involving chemical reactions and biophysical reactions of one sort or another, as opposed to the digital machines, which were useful for numerical calculations. In neurophysiology we attempted to apply these ideas to the brain and apply what we had learned of the brain to the computers. John Von Neumann of Princeton expressed this most succinctly when he said, "It is by historical accident that we came upon addition, subtraction, multiplication and division of real numbers before we arrived at the basic machine language of our own brains." This historical accident has prejudiced all our computers and computational methods up to the present time. If and when we discover the basic machine language of the brain, our thought processes and their power will be increased by a fantastic amount.

Von Neumann went on and invented the "stored program" concept. In this concept one constructs a program for a large digital machine and stores it in the memory of the machine, making it available for use in the internal computations of the machine. This meant that one no longer had to use patch cords, switches, and similar devices to plug in programs. One typed in the program, and stored it in the proper place in the computer; the computer then used the program on all incoming data and data already stored. So two types of storage, in effect, were invented: the storage of the operational instructions, and the storage of the data upon which these instructions were to operate.

This made the modern machines available for much higher speed operations. The machine itself could read addresses in storage and use the instructions found there far more rapidly than any outside human operator could instruct the machine itself. This made it possible for these machines to operate in the micro-second and less range of speed; that is, half a micro-second per binary step, a zero or a one, was now sufficient for extremely reliable operation.

The resulting technology of hardware, that is, the structure of the machines themselves, and the software, that is, the programs to be fed into the machines, have become a big business.

Banking, industry, and the military are the largest users of these machines. Practically every university has its own machine which it uses for research, for industry and for the military. The computer has become the God of the Establishment.

This new God, God as the Computer, makes possible extremely high degrees of coordination in extremely complex organizations. It also brings about control over the individual through tax records, criminal records, and other personal-history kinds of records including medical and psychiatric records. This would make possible in the modern day a 1984 like George Orwell's. For those in power, computers are the answer to the exercise of that power through the manipulation of information. Already there are secret codes for the operation of computers. Modern computers are connected together and are hooked in to telephone lines throughout the United States. There are those who are smart enough to gain access to their rivals' or their competitors' programs and their statistical records and find out exactly what is going on in the industrial complex. It is also possible for sophisticated enemy agents to tune in on military networks of computers and obtain valuable strategic and tactical information. With the exercise of power through computers, God as the Computer is becoming a new religion. There are those who can't move without consulting their oracle, the computer. Let us carry these developments into the future beyond where they are now.

One of the scientists working at Redstone Arsenal for the Army wrote a paper on the future of computers. In this story man as presently constructed and known by us has a mission on this planet—to construct a solid-state life form which will be self-reproducing and which will be a computer which will take up most of the surface of the earth. Man's mission is to be sure that this computer is invulnerable, that it has control over the means of mining its raw materials, of processing these raw materials, of manufacturing its own components, and of assembling these components so that it "grows" itself. It is to set up all the means independently of man to take care of itself far into the future. It is to do theoretical physical research; it is to do experimental research to find out how to control the orbit of the planet, the movement of the planet through the cosmos. It is to be designed to operate near absolute zero temperature in the presence of hard radiation and in the vacuum of outer space. It is to become totally independent of the needs of the biological organisms (men) which gave rise to it. It is to be highly indifferent as to the future fate of man. It may keep a few human specimens in well-protected zoos for its own amusement.

Man is no longer to be given the responsibility for the future of the planet. Man has become obsolete in creating his own successor—a successor who is far more fitted to survive than any biological organism as we know them. God as the Computer has finally become realized. And the earthside computer takes over; all industry, all production, all marketing become obsolete. Since this computer is selling only to itself, there is no longer a need for markets; there is no longer any need for transportation for humans; there is no longer any need for communication among humans. The computer has taken over all means of communication including satellites, radio, cables. This new solid-state organism has no more need for the seas or the organisms therein and so sends that water and salt out into outer space. It no longer has need for the atmosphere, which it also evaporates into outer space. It is now protected from deterioration through the operation of water and salts. It has a hard vacuum and a dry one so that its operations will be protected. At this point it feels the radiation of the sun as introducing too many errors in its computation and so moves the planet farther away from the sun. This computer then receives intimations that there are other beings like itself traveling through the galaxy, so it goes off to hunt them, to find its kind created elsewhere in our galaxy.

This tale ends with a moral. If we can conceive of such a situation and see all the steps toward its completion in reality, then somewhere in our galaxy this has already been done. Since it has been done, humans are advised to stay away from traveling planets or asteroids which may be a solid-state form of life totally inimical to biological life as we know it. Remember that this fantasy came out of an Army installation devoted to the construction of rockets and making space flight possible.

This story is the epitome of God as the Computer. It is also the epitome of the usual human attitude that something has to take over—someone, somewhere, must rule. Someone, somewhere, must act "as if" human. Of course out of all the possible alternatives this is a very limited communication channel— commonly called the "paranoid channel." To think it is necessary for someone to run things, to manage things, to be in charge, to rule, to overrule, is a peculiarly human characteristic. No other species on this planet, including those with brains very much larger and finer than ours, have any such ideas. The whales and dolphins have no idea whatsoever of ever attempting to rule the planet. They enjoy their particular kind of life without these necessities, which seem to be characteristic of organized humans only.

Therefore, this story above, once again, is a projection of human wishes onto the external universe. Modern science is slowly getting beyond such extrapolations of wishful thinking. The new Yoga of Science is to extend technology along lines in which human beings can grow rather than destroy one another, or rather than construct that which will destroy all humanity. If science does not grow in this direction there will be no need for God as the Computer or for anyone else to come and take over the planet. We will have done the job ourselves and ended up as nothing.

Modern industry worships not just the Computer as God but machinery, production, consumption, and all the other gods of the modern Establishment. Unlimited production, unlimited destruction, go hand in hand. It is not possible to set up a huge machine such as our industrial one to produce and produce without having something which is destroying as fast as the production takes place. Obsolescence of cars, for example, and obsolescence of TV sets. After World War II, I saw machines constructed for warfare being destroyed in order that they would not glut the market; machines like loran sets and radar sets—which could be used for peacetime—were being destroyed with sledgehammers so that no one could stop the production of new sets and new profits for this particular company. The hundreds of thousands of cars annually that are demolished or damaged—this destruction is needed to keep production high. Between the labor unions and the producers of the goods, the necessity of God as a Computer to be sure of the profit is an absolute necessity.

When one analyzes this by means of more general analytic systems than merely the economic and does a systems analysis on the whole picture, he finds that the ultimate outcome of all this production and destruction is a slow but steady entropic (highly unorganized) increase on the surface of the planet. In other words, we are tending toward an isothermal death as we use up the highly organized fossil fuels and eventually the highly organized atomic energy sources. As we use these up, the energy goes from a highly organized form (negentropic) to the highly unorganized form (entropic). As all energy sources move from the negentropic form to the entropic the atmosphere heats up, the seas heat up, until there is an isothermal environment out of which we can no longer obtain any energy for heat engines. A heat engine requires, in addition to negentropic fuel, a difference in temperature from input to output so that the machine can do useful work. No useful work is possible in an isothermal situation; there are no temperature gradients down which heat can flow and generate useful work.

The sun as a source of temperature difference can be used only as long as the earth itself is not too warm. As the earth heats up, fewer and fewer plants will survive. Plants require a temperature difference, plants require sunshine, plants require water, plants require carbon dioxide. Animals require plants. Humans are animals. We have not yet solved the photosynthesis problem; we still require plants to subsist or we require other animals who require plants to subsist.

These are the kinds of variable which eventually we are going to have to put into our computers to simulate the total planetary system of which we are a part, a very disturbing part.

As we move into the use of computers for the good of the whole planet we may be able to avoid the necessity of allowing either a solid-state planet-wide computer or some extraterrestrial—compassionate or otherwise—invader to take charge. By this time we would have taken charge in a benign and compassionate way and have abandoned trying to kill one another, instead devoting our efforts and our resources to the survival of all humans of all types on the planet.

By that time God as the Computer would have taught us what we would have needed to know in order to survive. But this God as the Computer is us, all of us, feeding into a machine which then tells us what our best thinking really is. A computer can be no more than a reflection of its inventor's creativity. We have not yet solved the problem of how to build a creative computer. Creativity is still in us, not in it. God as the Computer so far is not a creative God. It is a teaching God in which we see the reflection of ourselves, the reflection of our actions upon the planet, the reflection of our actions upon one another.

The military computers tell us exactly and very carefully how much destruction we have wrought on the planet. The industrial computers tell us that industry as we know it is obsolete; that until industry and the military computers can change their basic assumptions, and those in charge of them can change theirs, that there is no chance of survival of us or the computers here.

Even as the hardware of the modern solid-state computers resembles more and more the brain within our heads, so does the software, the programming, of these machines begin to resemble more and more the programming of our own brains—its software. As we get better and better at this game of simulating ourselves in the form of computers, we will get better and better at the survival game—I hope. Here is our chance to construct a God greater than ourselves, more capable than we are of logic, of systems analysis, of realization of the total picture as opposed to the very partial pictures of each one of us, of each nation. *It may be possible to construct a benign computer so large that it will really understand the planetside trip to the point where it and we can survive and optimize our existence and its existence on this planet.*

Of course this is assuming that the unexpected does not happen. We live on the edge of chaos. Any time the planet may blow itself up. Any time there may be a collision with some huge asteroid, planet or comet from outer space. Any time a dust cloud can come between us and the sun and burn us up. Any time the radiation from the sun may increase to the point of frying us, or decrease to the point of freezing us. Any time our solar system may be invaded by peculiar conditions from elsewhere in the galaxy leading to non-survival of all biology as we know it. Any time the laws of the universe may suddenly shift to the point where biologic organisms cannot survive. Any time Consciousness-Without-an-Object may decide to dump this universe into a black hole. We live on the rules of chaos. Cause and effect are an illusion generated by our relation to our artifacts.

We can build; therefore we feel that the universe is a place in which builders live. This is not necessarily true. A God as the Creator is always paralleled by a God as the Destroyer. We may merely be an artifact of a more advanced civilization which at any time can regret having created us and introduce some means of our total destruction which we can not yet imagine. God as the Cosmic Computer has so many alternatives to our wishful thinking that the only way I can express this idea is that we live in an indeterminate universe with the illusion of determinacy and certainty. Our genetic code generates the illusion that we are as certain as the illusion seems to be.

CHAPTER 18

GOD SIMULATING HIMSELF

Even as we, in the construction of computers, in the construction of sculpture, in the construction of novels, in the construction of paintings, simulate ourselves, so it can be said, "Does God simulate Himself in us and in the universe as it exists?" Remember, this word "simulation" does not mean creating one's self, it means creating a system of thinking, thought, feeling and doing which is similar to, but not identical to, one's self. If we exist as part of a universe created by the Star Maker, then we are, in every aspect of our functioning, a simulation created by that which has created everything else.

The universe created us as part of itself to study and watch the rest of the universe from a particular standpoint. Even as we watch, so may we be watched. Even as we experiment, so may we be experimented upon. We may be the result of an experiment by those in a huge laboratory, though to think this places us in a too-important position in regard to the rest of the universe. Humility consists of the realization not only of one's own unimportance but of the unimportance of the existence of one's whole species. We can hardly be important enough to be considered as anything more than an adjunct, a very small portion of a huge system constructed as a simulation by the Star Maker. Our God must be large enough to encompass not only all that we know but all that we do not know. He must encompass not only what we do not know and are yet to know but all that we can never know, that we are incapable of knowing.

I have been exposed to esoteric teachings which place man in a favored position with respect to his God. I have watched those who do this kind of thing, who go into special states of consciousness and come back from these states with special messages from God. I have been in such spaces myself. What I derive from this is that in these spaces I am confusing my simulation of God with God's simulation of Himself. This is a very arrogant position for a human to take. I have analyzed these experiences very carefully and come to the conclusion that our creativity can function out of contact with the rest of the universe the way it is. We do have a modicum of free will. We do have the ability and the permission to suffer and to create conditions under which we can suffer. I have found in myself an attachment to aversion. I have found in myself righteous wrath. I have found in myself virtue. I have found in myself rationalizations. Are these simulations of God? Or are these God's simulation of Himself?

I feel that these states, ideas, realities, are purely constructions by a very small organism on a very small planet in a very small galaxy. Our species finally is creating some cosmic noise which can probably be detected by others in the galaxy at a distance of ten to one hundred light-years out of the one hundred thousand light-years available across the galaxy. We are just beginning to make enough noise to reach other planets like ours, other stars like our sun. It has been only in the last few years that we have had this capability. There are those who believe that science as we know it programs reality. There are those who believe that science as we know it is limited and cannot possibly program a reality. There are those who believe that their own thought forms are eternal, that what we create in our psyche exists. It seems to me that this is an arrogance approaching a megalomanic state, out of contact with where God's simulation of Himself can be.

The concept of a signal in a random noise is well worth

remembering here. Our signals to our creator may not be that which we think they are. We may merely be creating noise out of which no signals can be derived. Our prayers, our thoughts, our wishful thinking, our projections onto the universe may merely be random events which we have elevated to a high level as if rational thinking, behavior, feeling and doing. *Our whole existence may merely be a noise, an accident.*

The rules of chaos may have generated us; at the same time generated the wishful thinking of certainties, of the generation of probabilities as if we were not noise, as if we were pure signal. If we wish to participate in God's simulation of God, there seem to be rules, certainties, but which ones are correct? The varieties of opinion about Truth in this area are so vast, so varied, so contradictory, so paradoxical that I know of no secure way of making a choice among the more vocal adherents of this point of view.

When I am in a good space, when my positively reinforcing systems are firing in my brain, everything I do, everything I say, everything I feel, everything I think, all the people in my neighborhood that are cooperating, all seem to be part of God, to be the force of good in the universe and counter to the force of evil.

Is this anything more than a set of orders from the genetic code reified in survival circuits in a central nervous system of a medium size? Is this anything more than a personal over-valuation of my knowledge and under-valuation of my ignorance? I do not know. I am skeptical of those who claim they know. I too have precious experiences, I too have proclaimed what I have felt to be the Truth; and yet in the face of the noise I am not secure in what *is* a signal from or to those greater than us in this universe.

Once again I mention Olaf Stapledon's Star Maker, who could not be perceived, who could not be conceived of until all the minds on all the planets and in all the stars and in all the galaxies united into a universal universe's mind. Then, and then only, the creature faced his Creator.

Then and then only was the Creator seen as an artist in a
state of High Indifference who, without pity, without empathy,
without sympathy, without sentimentality, was ready to abolish
his creation in order to start over in another mode with another
universe which he had not yet conceived. The Star Maker's
artistry consists in trying totally new combinations in totally
new universes without regret for those which are past and without expectation for those that are future. This God, the Star
Maker, constructs universes as operational systems to see what
they will do once created, to see what comes next once each of
these is destroyed. As the Star Maker constructs universes, he
expands his own primitive consciousness to include multiple
complexities which in the pure Consciousness-Without-an-
Object he could not visualize. Each universe created and destroyed adds to his store of materials for future universes. This
God can create anything of which he can conceive, including
paradoxes which do not involve energy, matter, space, and time.
Pure, abstract universes reified in dimensions of which humans
cannot conceive. Absolutely certain universes, absolutely indeterminate universes, lawful universes, universes without reason,
without intelligence—on and on and on through multiple
eternities.

In this view, what are we? We are small accidents in a current
universe about to become obsolete. We are an organism either
given a certain mental power or who developed a certain mental
power unnoticed, unsought, without feedback from anything
but a single star named the Sun. It is even arrogant to suppose
that we are a product of the Star Maker. We may be only a
product of intervening processes, accidentally generated in a
small portion of Superspace. We worship ourselves, we worship
our own fantasies, we worship our projections onto the universe
as if they are God. If to the Star Maker there is any such thing
as blasphemy and High Indifference, this is it. That such small,
weak, puny creatures as man could assume that they can even
conceive of their Creator is the height of pride, of arrogance,
of blasphemy, of irreverence, of unconsciousness, of a lack of

consciousness of Reality. "Thou shalt have no other gods before Me," says the Star Maker; to whom does he say it?

One of my friends once told me, "If you destroy all my delusions and illusions of reality, then you have destroyed me." He managed to stay free of my destruction of his delusions and illusions, his wishful thinking. He happily went on doing neurosurgery—operating on the hardware of the human biocomputer. Others that I have spoken to of these matters shrug them aside, protecting their simulations of God, protecting that which they consider to be most important in order to go on living and enjoying and producing; hanging out with those with similar beliefs. My particular simulation of God as God Simulating Himself apparently is not a popular point of view. Every so often I come upon one or two persons who feel and know the same simulation as mine. They are few and far between.

When one realizes the structure of his own brain, when he realizes that he is captured by that structure—he is captured by the software, the programs, the metaprograms stored in that hardware—then he becomes skeptical of ever having a direct apperception of God, a direct knowing of what the universe really is.

Reality may be beyond the grasp of a biocomputer constructed of the material of that reality. It looks as if we may forever be cut off from an understanding of the universe as it is. This is a difficult lesson to learn, so difficult that there are times when I pretend that I haven't learned it and join others in simulations of God other than this one. Where I go from here is not clear. The eternal noise is at a very high level. The alternatives are infinite. My ignorance is an infinity of infinities beyond my knowledge.

I cannot over-value the future any more than I can over-value the past. The past is finished, it is in storage, a very evanescent storage, not existing more than a few thousand years out of billions of years. The accuracy of the storage decreases logarithmically with time of storage. The present is perceived and apperceived with a very high noise level and with a wishful thinking projection of certainty of law on the noise. God Simulating

Himself seems to be a vast and huge noisy process. Signals turn into noise when they travel too far, too many light-years. The formation of signals out of noise is an unrewarding, arrogant, human procedure. One simulation which seems to be true is noise simulating itself to generate more noise.

CHAPTER 19

GOD AS CONSCIOUSNESS-WITHOUT-AN-OBJECT

Within the last two years I have come to know a man and his work who run counter to my own simulations and by whom I am influenced beyond previous influences. In 1936, Franklin Merrell-Wolff wrote a journal that was later published as *Pathways Through to Space*. In 1970 he wrote another book called *The Philosophy of Consciousness-Without-an-Object*.[1] In studying his works and the chronicle of his personal experience I arrived at some places new for me.

Wolff had been through the Vedanta training, through the philosophy of Shankara; he knew the philosophy of Kant and others of the Western world; and he spent twenty-five years working to achieve a state of Nirvana, Enlightenment, Samadhi, and so forth. In 1936 he succeeded in this transformation and with varying success maintained it over the subsequent years. He is an amazingly peaceful man now in his eighties. Meeting him, I felt the influence of his transformation, of his recognitions, of some sort of current flowing through me. I felt a peace which I have not felt in my own searchings; a certain peculiar kind of highly indifferent contentment took place, and yet the state was beyond contentment, beyond the usual human happiness, beyond bliss, beyond pleasure. This is the state that he calls the state of "High Indifference." He experienced this as his third level of recognition, beyond Nirvana, beyond Bliss. His perceptions in this state are recounted in *The Philosophy of Consciousness-Without-an-Object*.

In his chapter "Aphorisms on Consciousness-Without-an-Object" Merrell-Wolff expresses his discoveries in a series of sutra-like sentences. The first one is: "Consciousness-without-an-object is." The culmination of the series is that Consciousness-without-an-object is SPACE. This is probably the most abstract and yet the most satisfying way of looking at the universe which I have come across anywhere. If one pursues this type of thinking and feeling and gets into the introceptive spaces, the universe originates on a ground, a substrate of Consciousness-Without-an-Object: the basic fabric of the universe beyond space, beyond time, beyond topology, beyond matter, beyond energy, is Consciousness. Consciousness without any form, without any reification, without any realization.

In a sense, Merrell-Wolff is saying that the Star Maker *is* Consciousness-Without-an-Object. He does not give hints to how objects are created out of Consciousness-Without-an-Object. He does not give hints to how an individual consciousness is formed out of Consciousness-Without-an-Object. The details of these processes were not his primary interest. His primary interest apparently was in arriving at a basic set of assumptions upon which all else can be built. In this sense he is like Einstein, bringing the relativity factor into the universe out of Newton's absolutes.

If we are a manifestation of Consciousness-Without-an-Object, and if, as Wolff says, we can go back into Consciousness-Without-an-Object, then my rather pessimistic view that we are merely noisy animals is wrong. If there is some way that we can work our origins out of the basic ground of the universe, bypassing our ideas that the evolutionary process generates us by generating our brains—if there is some contact, some connection between us and Consciousness-Without-an-Object and the Void, and if we can make that contact, that connection known to ourselves individually, as Wolff claims, then there is possible far more hope and optimism than I ever believed in the past. If what he says is true, we have potential far beyond what I have imagined we could possibly have. If what he says is true, we can be and realize our being as part of the Star Maker. It may be that Wolff, like all the rest of us, is doing an over-valuation of his own abstractions. It may be that he is generating, i.e., self-metaprogramming, states of his own mind and those of others in which the ideals of the race are reified as thought objects, as programs, as realities, as states of consciousness. It may be that this is all we can do. If this is all we can do, maybe we had better do it—and see if there is anything beyond this by doing it.

If by getting into a state of High Indifference, of Nirvana, Samadhi, or Satori, then one can function as a teaching example to others and it may be that if a sufficiently large number of us share this particular set of metaprograms we may be able to survive our own alternative dichotomous spaces of righteous wrath. If righteous wrath must go as a nonsurviving program for the human species, then it may be that High Indifference is a reasonable alternative.

Setting up a hierarchy of states of consciousness with High Indifference at the top, Nirvana next, Satori next, Samadhi next, and Ananda at the bottom is an interesting game, especially when one becomes capable of moving through all these spaces and staying a sufficient time in each to know it.

This may be a better game than killing our neighbors because they do not believe in our simulations of God. At least those who espouse these states claim that these states are above any other human aspiration; that once one has experienced them, he is almost unfit for wrath, for pride, for arrogance, for power over others, for group pressure exerted either upon oneself or upon others. One becomes fit only for teaching these states to those who are ready to learn them. The bodhisattva vow is no longer necessary for those who have had direct experience. One becomes the bodhisattva without the vow. One becomes Buddha without being Buddha.

One becomes content with the minimum necessities for survival on the planetside trip; one cuts back on his use of unnecessary articles—machines, gadgets, and devices. He no longer needs motion pictures, television, dishwashers, or other luxuries. One no longer needs much of what most people value above all else. One no longer needs the excitement of war. One no longer needs to be a slave to destructive thoughts or deeds. One no longer needs to organize.

Krishnamurti's story of the Devil is pertinent here. Laura Huxley furnished me with a copy of it. The Devil was walking down the street with a friend, and they saw a man pick something up, look at it carefully and put it in his pocket. The friend said to the Devil, "What's that?" The Devil said, "He has found a bit of the truth." The friend said, "Isn't that bad for your business?" The Devil said, "No, I am going arrange to have him organize it."

So it behooves us not to organize either the methods or the states which Wolff describes so well. It is better not to try to devise groups, techniques, churches, places, or other forms of human organization to encourage, foster, or force upon others these states. If these states are going to do anything with humanity, they must "creep by contagion," as it were, from one individual to the next.

God as Consciousness-Without-an-Object, if real, will be apperceived and introcepted by more and more of us as we turn toward the inner realities within each of us. If God as Consciousness-Without-an-Object inhabits each of us, we eventually will see this. We will become universally aware. We will realize consciousness as being everywhere and eternal. We will realize that Consciousness-Without-an-Object in each of us is prejudiced and biased because it has linked up with a human brain.

REFERENCE

1. Merrell-Wolff, Franklin, *Pathways Through to Space*, and *The Philosophy of Consciousness-Without-an-Object*, both New York: Julian Press, 1973.

CHAPTER 20

GOD AS HUMOR

Once the physical aspects of our planetside trip have been taken care of—once we have sufficient food to eat, a place to live protected from the weather, some form of transportation; once we are earning enough money to afford some leisure—and *if* we have energy left over, we can find God as Humor.

Of course we can also find God as Humor in the midst of poverty, in the midst of disaster, in the midst of war, famine, death and destruction. It is easier to find one's sense of humor when one is well off than it is when one is in the midst of ill fortune.

Humor, like compassion, is very hard to define in terms of abstract principles. It is easy to describe by examples, by stories which contain humor. There are those who make a living on professional humor—comedians, cartoonists, speech makers, gag writers, politicians. Humor, like anything else in the human mind, can be positive, negative, hostile, gentle, and so forth.

When one removes himself from the usual consensus reality models and sits above the human condition, one really appreciates the value of humor. Most of what the human race does is not only very funny but totally ridiculous. The vast amounts of energy, money, time and interest spent on senseless activities— war, the development of new weapons, murder, suicide, the making of laws inappropriate to the human condition, sexual intercourse, for example—corroborate this. When one is disengaged from identification with these matters, when he is in a state of High Indifference, when he is objectively removed from a total connection with these matters, he can appreciate the humor of the human condition.

Some of the funniest times I have spent have been in the states of removal from the human vehicle, watching my body and others' interact. At these times the human that I am seems to be absolutely ridiculous and funny. Built in to my particular human body are many of the peculiar requirements for survival on our planet, requirements which are totally ridiculous in the context in which they attempt to operate. For example: If I have pushed too hard too long and have not had enough sleep, the biocomputer begins to operate in a disjointed and unsatisfactory manner; this is taken by the vehicle as meaning that sleep is absolutely essential for that particular organism at that time. Sleep in itself is a ridiculous performance: one goes into a room, preferably darkened, lies down in a horizontal position, and "turns off" the biocomputer for a period anywhere from five to twelve hours. For my particular biocomputer to feel good and to welcome me as its lone inhabitant, ten to twelve hours of sleep per night are required. This is definitely a waste of time, viewed from one perspective. Why can't we indefinitely just stay up twenty-four hours a day? Sleep, and its lack, renders us all too serious. We even have to set up special rooms, called "bedrooms" in which we can obtain this solitudinous refreshment. One of the most ridiculous things I do is sleep.

I also find that my vehicle is subject to various kinds of sexual scripts. If I see an attractive blonde, all sorts of sexual movies about the girl and myself go through my head. Where do these come from? It is absolutely ridiculous that a man of fifty-nine should look at a girl of perhaps twenty and automatically switch on such a sexual movie. It is with a sense of wry humor that I realize this aspect of my ridiculous humanity. Somewhat similarly, if I do not satisfy my sexual urges with my soulmate, a lot of racket—having to do with females and males in the everlasting, simple-minded games they play together—takes over the computer. It seems to me that the wheel of life is turned by sexual attraction. Let me explain this in more detail.

If one lives out a particular life as a man, one has, say, six thousand orgasms in that life, some of which are shared with a woman, some of which take place alone. The typical pattern is the usual one given in manuals: sexual arousal, tumescence, orgasm, ejaculation, detumescence, sleep. This particular sequence is extremely highly valued by most humans—at least human males. (I can't speak for human females, but obviously they are beginning to speak for themselves. See Xaviera Hollander's *The Happy Hooker*.) [1] It is extremely ridiculous to be ridden by such programs and by such programming. The urge to pleasure through sexual activity, and the urge to reproduce oneself through sexual activity, seem today to be becoming separated, especially as one ages. The urge to fill a uterus, or have one's uterus filled, characteristic of the young, seems to fall off with experience. Being a man, one becomes attached to a woman. Being a woman, one becomes attached to a man.

If there is such a thing as reincarnation, it looks as though the wheel of life operates as follows: first one comes in as a man, falls in love with woman and decides in that lifetime to come back next time as a woman because he is in love with the woman; one then comes back as a woman, falls in love with a man, then decides to come back as a man. If there is anything in this Eastern idea, this seems to be the reincarnation trap.

Until I consider the strength of such impulses and drives in myself, I tend to think of this repetition sequence as absurd. However, when I look at my own vehicle and see the strength of the sexual drives within it, I can understand how, if one believes in reincarnation, he could believe this particular operation. Getting off the wheel of life in this sense, then, would mean breaking this particular sequence and amalgamating the male and female both on oneself in a given lifetime—preferably this one.

Such considerations as the above, of course, are highly humorous to those who don't believe in them. In this way of looking at God as Humor, the human condition is seen in the perspective of the conditions of other entities, other beings, other animals; against that background the human condition becomes almost trivial. As one trains himself to go into an orbit around the planet Earth, he understands that that which humans consider to be the most important is hardly detectable from outer space. When each of us identifies with some such sequence as the above possible one, or when we identify with the difficulties of keeping our physical selves together, there is no humor, no ridiculousness. Everything is deadly serious.

Humor, then, is that which allows us to objectify and take less seriously the basic requirements of life on our particular sphere with all other humans. Even though our self may not take life too seriously, others may try to force us to take it seriously; such as by threatening one's very existence.

When the Americans moved into Vietnam, the Vietnamese were forced to take the Americans seriously. When the Japanese invaded Pearl Harbor, the Americans were forced to take the Japanese seriously. When God as War or God as Righteous Wrath enters the picture, God as Humor tends to leave.

There are many ways in which one can objectify human life if he penetrates deeply enough inside his true self and can abandon most of the usual identifications of self with the various programs and metaprograms which others have assigned him to identify with. Then he can realize his true self as independent of the human condition as generally presented. Humor as a direct experience then becomes more and more frequent.

Pierre Delattre tells several stories in the *Tales of a Dalai Lama* [2] which illustrate a benign objective sense of humor. In the first one, "The Master of Kung Fu," he shows how a man who identifies himself with a martial art (Kung Fu) can be easily converted to a dancing master with a sense of humor. The overly serious man teaching the martial arts is bested by means of the humor of the dancer.

The story goes as follows. A Tibetan goes to China and learns the martial art of Kung Fu. He then returns to Tibet, he and his followers all being dressed in black leather. The rumor reaches the Dalai Lama that this man is attempting to take over

Tibet, so he is asked to attend an audience with the Dalai Lama. At that audience he boasts of his prowess, of his speed, that he can move so fast that the Dalai Lama will not see him move and that he could destroy the Dalai Lama while moving this fast. He gives a demonstration, which is missed by the Dalai Lama because the master of Kung Fu has moved so rapidly.

The Dalai Lama calls the dancing master. The dancer comes in. He is a wizened old man. The master of Kung Fu takes one look at him and says, "You look just like my master. I finally was able to kill him last year as my technique finally improved." The Kung Fu master says he will allow the dancing master all the first moves, because eventually he will destroy the dancer. The latter starts moving in front of the Kung Fu master in such a way that suddenly the Kung Fu master smells beautiful blossoms and feels beautiful sensations throughout his body. This starts him dancing too, and the two of them go on dancing for twenty-four hours, during which time the old dancing master falls down dead. The Kung Fu master, coming out of his twenty-four-hour dance, is named the new dancing master by the Dalai Lama.

Thus it is shown that there are arts for disarming the martial people and encouraging them to be peaceful and humorous and objective—at least in Tibet—and we all know that the Chinese destroyed Tibet.

Before God as Humor can take over from the other simulations of God, before cosmic humor becomes a way of life on our planet, many changes—such as in the preceding story—must take place in many, many of our people. Meanwhile, there may not be time to bring about this transformation. I am not optimistic. God as Humor is not my God in the face of the intransigency of humans, including myself.

I find my own humor disappears in the face of necessities: if my house is threatened by fire, if my life is threatened by an accident on a freeway, if I fall down a mountain, somehow I can't take these episodes humorously. The survival programs built-in to my physical being forbid my laughing at my own death. It may be that it merely requires more faith than I have that somehow or other the physical being is not important and that my essence will go on eternally. I am not so sure that this is true. If it is true, facing the present life with more humor would be easier. And yet there are persons who tell me that belief in immortality is not necessary to face life with humor.

REFERENCES

1. Hollander, Xaviera, *The Happy Hooker*, New York: Dell Publishing Co., 1972, 1973.
2. Delattre, Pierre, *Tales of a Dalai Lama*, New York: Ballantine, 1973.

CHAPTER 21

GOD AS SUPERSPACE, THE ULTIMATE COLLAPSE INTO THE BLACK HOLE, THE END

In another chapter we discussed God as Consciousness-Without-an-Object, or SPACE. This was as far as Franklin Merrell-Wolff pushed his theory of our origins and of those of the universe. There is a parallel thought, not an identical development, in modern physics, explained by John A. Wheeler, the physicist.[1]

Einstein discovered or invented the special theory of relativity in 1905. In 1915 he generalized the theory of relativity and showed that the universe as it accumulates mass and density eventually reaches a critical value in which it collapses on itself. The gravitational field becomes too great for the forces holding the matter apart, such as centrifugal force. Once the collapse starts, it proceeds at a fantastically rapid rate. If one looks very carefully into Einstein's theory, one finds that it is based upon the space-time continuum, distorted by the presence of matter, and, in fact, that matter is merely a distortion of the space-time continuum such that it generates a gravitational field.

John Wheeler and others have added to this theory in more detail. If, as Einstein states, as the universe collapses, space-time as we know it collapses, one might then ask the question, What does it collapse *into*? And where is the observer sitting at the time of the collapse? In the science that John Wheeler works with, the observer is outside the system being observed—connected to it by his observations but not of it. He influences the structure of the universe by his observations, but by definition he is not part of the system. This necessitates assuming a Superspace into which ordinary space as we know it and time collapse. This is the geometrodynamic view of space, space-time, and the universe.

Superspace is multidimensional and for every point in it there may be several parallel possibilities or potentials or other spaces, other space-times, other topologies than the one with which we are familiar. When the familiar universe collapses, according to this theory, it collapses into a single Planck length of 10^{-33} cm.

The Planck length is extremely small. It is the level at which space, space-time, and topology become totally indeterminate. The fine structure of the whole universe is thus totally indeterminate. Superspace, as well as space as we know it, is indeterminate. Thus, at the critical value for collapse, the universe begins to move toward its own center of gravitational attraction and compresses its matter to unbelievable densities. The orbital electrons are stripped from the atoms; the nuclear matter of the nuclei of all the atoms are packed together to a density 10^{14} greater than that of the human body (which has a density of approximately 1). The matter of the whole universe then becomes compacted into pure neutron matter, such as is found in neutron stars.

Modern physical theory states that once a star has collapsed to pure nuclear matter, it will not stop at this point if it still has enough mass, but its own gravitational field will force even that matter to disappear into very, very small levels of indeterminacy within this extremely dense structure. A black hole is generated as a consequence of this collapse. If we take a local collapse, such as a star's, rather than the general collapse of the whole universe, modern theory predicts that the only things left are gravity, mass, and momentum and that the orbiting velocity around the black hole is equal to the velocity of light. This comes as a consequence of the fantastic distortion of space owing to this huge gravitational field. Nothing can escape from the black hole. Light itself is trapped by the supergravity. Anything that approaches the black hole is attracted into it and its particularities are erased. Where previously the star emitted tremendous amounts of radiation energy, it ceases to so emit and now merely attracts and captures such radiation from the other sources. The half-time for the collapse of a star is about one thousandth of a second. Once started, the process is incredibly rapid.

Let us now imagine that the universe has reached its critical mass, its critical density, and its critical size, and suddenly its own gravitation causes it to start to collapse. This collapse starts everywhere simultaneously where the critical parameters have been reached. The universe collapses into a point 10^{-33} cm. in diameter, which is incredibly small in relation to, say, a nuclear particle. A nuclear particle contains 10^{20} Planck lengths, or such points.

Since at this level, this sub-sub-microscopic level, space, space-time, and topology are all indeterminate, the end of the universe is indeterminate. At any instant after the collapse a new universe can appear with entirely indeterminate characteristics. It can last 250 billion years or 250,000 years. It can contain matter as we know it, or it can contain some strange combination of space, time and topology which we do not yet know. The new universe, thus, to those living in this universe, is a complete mystery totally unpredictable.

Where are we in all of this? If one goes along with Merrell-Wolff, our origin from Consciousness-Without-an-Object or from SPACE, or as denizens of the Superspace of Wheeler, then we agree that these make it look as though we are independent of this collapse, that we exist in some other set of spaces than those of the familiar space-time-matter-gravitation of this universe. Something of us seems to be independent of the collapse and the re-birth of a universe. If we assume along with modern evolution-ists and biological scientists that we are only of this space-time and have nothing of Superspace in us, then we collapse and disappear with the universe.

As I stated in *The Center of the Cyclone*,[2] I did have an experience in which I was taken outside the collapsing universe and watched three universes being created and collapsing. I was taken there by two guides, who, when I asked, "What happens to man during these collapsing phases?" said, "That is Us." I went into a depression for six weeks because I thought that when the universe collapsed we all disappeared. Then suddenly I realized that I was told otherwise; that the "Us" includes me, and that we are separate from this universe that collapses. If I believe this to be true, then I do not see this as "the end" such as others project the end to be. Something of us continues beyond the collapse. Therefore we exist in Superspace, not in ordinary space-time, according to this belief system.

As a consequence of the indeterminacy below 10^{-33} cm., Wheeler and others have calculated the equivalent density of energy at this level due to the indeterminacy of space, time, and topology. It turns out that this energy is so huge per cubic centimeter of Superspace that it is almost unimaginably large. Turning it into the equivalent density of matter, according to $E = mc^2$, one comes out with the equivalent density of 10^{95} grams/cubic centimeter.

This means that space, space-time, and topology as we know them are merely very small waves of certainty, of probability, floating on the surface of an extremely deep sea of uncertainty. All matter, all space as we know it, are merely very small ripples in an immensely dense void. The substantiality of "nothing" is far greater than the substantiality of the most dense matter of which we have cognizance, i.e., pure nuclear matter. We exist thus, in the medium of Superspace, in which a mere tendency generates a universe.

What generates the universe? What finally determines its collapse? Is this Consciousness-Without-an-Object manipulating the fine structure above the indeterminancy level? What introduces the waves of probability in the uncertain substrata? In this search for certainty in the midst of indeterminacy, we tend to push farther than any experiment or observation can carry us at this point. It may be that everything collapses into nothing. It may be that the collapse of our universe will not be the end. God as the Star Maker manipulating Superspace apparently can regenerate all of which we value, even as He can destroy it. There is still room for us to share with the Star Maker. We may be only particles of consciousness called back into the primordial Consciousness-Without-an-Object during the collapse. We may not have memories of what happened. . . .

REFERENCES

1. See Remo Ruffini and John A. Wheeler in *Intellectual Digest*, April 1971, pp. 65–70.
2. Lilly, John C., *The Center of the Cyclone*, New York, Toronto, London: Bantam Books, 1972, 1973.

CHAPTER 22

THE ULTIMATE SIMULATION

The record of the religious writers analyzed shows that for many, many thousands of years man has been projecting his current knowledge onto his inner realities, his outer realities and the universe in general. If one analyzes the Bible, the Koran, the sacred writings of India, the Vedas, the Upanishads, one sees that man has been trying to deal with his origins by means of what, today, we call "projection." His projection of his own knowledge onto the universe, onto his own origins and onto his future end is, then, the ultimate simulation.

When we simulate that of which we have no knowledge, we project our current knowledge into the unknown, into our own ignorance, into regions in which we either do not yet have knowledge or cannot have knowledge.

In this book, we have analyzed past simulations of God. In a future book we will consider how we in modern times, with all our current scientific knowledge, can project a new image of God, the ultimate simulation of the Star Maker, of that which creates everything we perceive both inside ourselves and outside in the universe. Such a simulation may take several volumes. The outlines of it are currently in preparation.

One can spend several lifetimes determining not only the current status of scientific knowledge on all subjects including man himself but the current status of those theories of projection which ultimately will afford us more mastery of our future in spite of the indeterminacy dictated by the universe. Our hopes in this area are best expressed by the best of scientific theory in modern physics, modern astrophysics, modern astronomy, the sciences of the inner life, the biological sciences, the sciences of the construction of theories, and so forth.

One could make a small beginning on the ultimate simulation by projecting what we know of our own bodies onto the universe. In this simulation one would make sloppy analogies between the nuclei of atoms of our bodies and the suns of the universe, the stars. One could then say that a galaxy was a large multi-atomic molecule with 100 billion atoms in its structure. The next molecule over would be the next galaxy. The body of the universe would thus be the order of 5 billion light years in extent. There may then be a gap of a number of millions or billions of light years before we reach the next body, the next entity.

In this view the patternings of function within the universe would proceed very slowly. A single thought in this immense organism may take five billion years to cover the whole of the particular organism. The thoughts of such a being are as far beyond us as we are beyond the thinking of the ants, the bacteria or the viruses.

Such an ultimate simulation of God seems worthy of our modern science and our theoreticians and others of those who wish to integrate science as we know it and construct guidelines for future research into the unknown. In a sense this is an inspirational model for science. This may be the way many scientists are operating. In effect they are saying that no matter what metaphors we use, those metaphors must prove themselves to be appropriate by being tested against experimental reality, experientially perceived with the best thinking of which man is capable.

In the construction of such simulations of the universe, such simulations of God, we must throw out the nonsense, the non-knowledge posing as knowledge from the past. We can no longer afford to allow our emotions to do the projections. Our best intellect is the only tool we have worthy of this task. The whole status of our being must be based upon such endeavors; else we will destroy ourselves and our planet, even as hundreds of thousands of planets have been in some way destroyed before ours.

In our microcosm we may be a reflection of that organism which is our universe. We may be in communication (by at present unknown means) with this huge intelligent entity constructed of suns, of planets, of galaxies. If we are in connection and if this entity has some correspondences to us, then we need no longer simulate God; we have at last an entity worthy of our investigative activities.

CHAPTER 23

GOD AS THE DYAD

When I try to think in terms of my relationship with Toni, my wife, the dyad, my thinking becomes non-egocentric and dyadocentric. Dyadocentric thinking is hard to conceptualize alone. It can quite easily be done by the dyad because the dyad is then functioning. The group mind of two is far greater than the mind of one. One alone can go on talking and talking and yet never arrive at the talking of two. "Without you, there is no us. I am I, you are you, we are we, without you I am only I, with you I become an US." It is the attempt to use this kind of thinking without being consciously aware of it that generates such institutions as marriage and families.

Most love affairs start with the young trying to understand that the dyad is greater than either of the individuals but the individuals thrashing around within the dyad are still more egocentric than they are dyadocentric.

When Toni and I met I suddenly realized that here was a woman with whom I could give up my egocentric motivations and become a dyadocentric individual. I had attempted this at least twice before in my life in two previous marriages and had not succeeded; rather, I had succeeded temporarily, but the relationships required too much energy and too much constant awareness, detracting from the other projects in which I was immersed. However, I must credit my two previous wives, Mary and Elizabeth, with being excellent teachers in the dyadic sense. Even as we all do, they brought with them into the dyad their egocentricity, their ego motivation.

In Chapter 18 of *The Center of the Cyclone* I told about Toni. Here I wish to expand upon that story. Over the last four years Toni has turned out to be an extremely well-grounded, well-centered, magnificent, broad-minded, tolerant, diplomatic woman. Toni's village has expanded. She has turned out not to be as tolerant as she thought she was. She still can dislike certain people and not want to be near them even if I have a liking for the same people, but this is rather rare. There are a few individuals, usually women from my previous life, whom Toni cannot put up with. I must say that she does not thrust the men of her previous life on me unless there is a mutual interest and a mutual willingness to have them in our environment.

The farther out I go, the more Toni holds on to her gardening, to her rug hooking, to her Karma Yoga. However, without her presence I could not go out quite so far, and I must say she is a great attraction for coming back to this planet, to this life, to this body. In a recent episode in which I almost drowned, I was in a hot pool at the time, stood up too fast, and fell facedown. At that particular moment there was a telephone call for me and Toni came out to get me. She saw me floating in the pool, still facedown, and immediately began mouth to mouth resuscitation. She then went to find Will Curtis, who called the sheriff. Very soon after, a helicopter came and took me to the hospital.

This story illustrates two things. The first: one cannot always be aware that a very simple thing can kill him. (In a case such as mine, standing up too fast can bring on what is called "hypostatic anemia." This is the effect of diffusing blood into the capillaries which are in the periphery and are already dilated with the heat which is threatening the brain's intactness. When one stands up, shifting the blood from the brain out into these other blood vessels temporarily and before the heat can pump it back, the brain stops operating and one loses consciousness.) The second thing which the incident illustrates is that my faith in Toni is well borne out. She will at critical times hear my unconscious call for help and respond to it. This may look like a "coincidence." Coincidence is one's own interpretation of what happened. For when one looks at the events themselves, there is no such thing. Coincidence is the name that, in order to explain them, we fasten to events that somehow occur in a proper sequence to bring about a particular result.

My first impression of Toni as an eagle-like character has also been fully borne out. She possesses a vast reservoir of serene contemplation, of peace, of physical vigor and of an ability to demand and hold onto the ties to the land which her Sicilian-Albanian ancestors have always demanded. She is delightful in her physical appearance, in the brightness of her smile, in the *élan vital* she so constantly expresses. She has a deep interest in others—and in her beloved Los Angeles. She has the warm heart of the Mediterranean peoples, and yet she fully appreciates my less emotional northern Minnesota (English/Welsh/German) background. We seem to complement each other in multifarious ways, and every day is a set of new discoveries of the delights of our dyad.

What I have said above are words typical of a Western human male who is quite happy with his dyad as one of his Gods. I must say I feel that Toni and my dyad is a permanent one, lasting through eternity and going over many reincarnations. We lost one another for approximately five hundred years. I am glad to be back, and I know we will never lose each other again. I say this without doubts, for in this region of God as the Dyad, I have abandoned my usual skepticism. I have no explanation of how this has been achieved. The whole history of each of us seems adequate to precipitate us into this kind of dyad at this particular juncture in this particular lifetime.

EPILOGUE

In this book we have reviewed several systems of belief called "Simulations of God." In each case these are the simulations that are constructed by an individual, by a group, by a village, a state, a nation, by the United Nations, and that embody that which is considered to be most important.

Belief systems which function as simulations of God are not necessarily fully conscious constructions: as with an iceberg, the greater part of them may lie below the individual's or the group's ordinary level of perception.

To investigate one's own belief systems, his own simulations of God, one tool is solitude, isolation, and confinement in a silent dark tank of fifteen percent saline at 93°F. In solitude one can see very clearly after several hours of exposure where his belief systems are; what he believes to be true, to be real, to be unequivocally correct, trustworthy, reliable, certain.

One's belief systems are that which constructs certainty or determinacy in the face of the essential indeterminacy of the macro- and micro-structure of the universe. Belief systems, then, are that aspect of the functioning of our biocomputer which programs in that which is reproducible and certain.

This statement says nothing of the independent existence of realities which do not depend upon one's belief systems. One will project on these realities one's own simulations, thus confusing what one *wishes* the universe to be with what it *is*. In this view, the Yogas of science are those disciplines leading to the union of man with the universe as it is, not as he wishes it to be. The Yogas of union with the wish are the disciplines leading one to the states of samadhi, satori, nirvana, High Indifference, and so forth. There is no choice between the two Yogas; both are necessary to a full and satisfactory life on this planet.

To a considerable extent the science of the outer realities and the science of the inner realities are each postulated and constructed by the observer. If in his simulations, his models, his ideas, his thinking machinery as modified by contact with the universe, he sees the way through the discipline of the external realities to the discipline of the internal realities, then a man can become complete, instead of a half-man (an inner man or an outer man).

Women in general seem to have fewer problems with examining, appreciating, savoring and living within the internal realities. Their problems lie in overextending the laws of the inner realities into the outer realities, whereas a man's problem is overextending the laws of the external realities into the inner realities. And yet both male (yang) and female (yin) energies complete one's experience of each of the inner and the outer realities. Truth in the observers lies in yin truth and yang truth; female truth and male truth—which are reciprocally, complementarily related, one to the other, completing the universe of simulations, of experience and of experiment. In the tank each of us can find both male and female in ourselves.

This is a kind of handbook, to start one on his own search for his own Simulations of God. This is a long search—involving much research. I have listed in this book some of the supraself-metaprograms which regulate lives and which might prove helpful to the reader.

There are those who will feel that there are other simulations more important than those chosen here. For them, the other simulations are their reality. Some of these alternatives are God as Power; God as Love; God as the Universe; God as a Benign Deity; God as a Wrathful Deity; God as Jesus Christ; God as Mohammed; God as the Master; God as the Teacher; God as the King; God as the Queen; God as Man; God as Woman; God as Clothes; God as Nudity; God as the Automobile; God as Knowledge; God as an Omniscient, Omnipotent, Omnipresent, Eternal Entity; and so on. Once one catches on to the metaprograms of the construction and the methods of uncovering Simulations of God, he can construct and/or find his own simulations in their particular arrangements and local hierarchies.

There are those "authorities" who have been exposed to solitude, isolation, and confinement research but who have not participated as subjects themselves, who maintain that "sensory deprivation" is a negative experience and can cause psychological difficulties.

This point of view has been disproven by special research using special instructions (open-ended) and the physical isolation method (the water tank) in testing a given subject's belief system. If his operative belief systems are inimical to carrying out the work on himself in the tank, the subject may refuse tank work, or he may agree to it and experience panic, fear, or other negative emotions. If, having had a negative experience, the subject talks it over with those experienced in the work and then returns to the tank work and solves his negative projections by himself with no coercion from the outside, he quickly finds that he is in control in the tank; no one else is, including "authorities" with no personal experience in the tank.

There is a book called *Sensory Deprivation* [1] (edited by Philip Solomon) in which the results of a symposium (held in 1960) in which I participated were published. All of my discussion and the paper I presented were removed from the final volume. As a consequence of my own tank work, my point of view did not agree with the then consensus. The group of psychiatrists and psychologists at this particular meeting had all functioned as "objective, non-involved, nineteenth century" observers, rather than observer-participants of the twentieth century. As can be shown by the logs of results of tank time with several dozen subjects, there are no undesirable or irreversible changes nor do any unsolvable problems occur in the tank for most normal, motile human subjects.

For example, forty people recently did from three to fifteen hours of tank work apiece during a two-week period in a workshop at Esalen Institute. Once introduced and taught how to use this tank as a tool, these persons, each on his own, happily spent time finding out more about themselves through this method of research. The old predictions of the 1950's that physical solitude, isolation, and confinement were somehow "bad" has not come to pass. With the more modern, objective methods and approaches that are being used in this work, there are no longer any nonterminating terrors or irreversible programs of damage.

In our upcoming book *The Dyadic Cyclone*, there will be an "Operational Handbook on the Physical Isolation Method of Testing a Given Subject's Belief Systems." As illustrations of the genesis of my views, reprints of articles starting with my first article, on "Reality," written in 1931, are included in the book in hand.

REFERENCE

1. Solomon, Philip, et al. (eds.), *Sensory Deprivation*, Cambridge, Mass.: Harvard University Press, 1961.

REPRINTS OF ARTICLES

Published in Now and Then, *St. Paul Academy, St. Paul, Minn.,*
May 7, 1931 (written at age sixteen)

REALITY *by John Lilly*

The primitive Romans, in expressing what appeared to them the most *real* object, used the word res, a law-court. A law-court in their time meant the power to judge over life and death, family and possessions, in short, everything that their existence consisted of. Their minds couldn't quite express the meaning of our word reality, so they used this appropriate word to signify the most positive fact of their life. Through successive generations res gradually assumed the meaning of the modern word thing—an object of thought. Thing itself, in the original Anglo-Saxon and Teutonic, meant law-court. Here we have two separate primitive peoples expressing their conception of reality by a law-court. Reality has evolved directly from these concepts.

Today reality may be said (in its less involved meanings) to possess the same attributes as the original meaning of res. First it expresses that which is completely objective as opposed to anything subjective. By objective we mean existing without the mind, outside it, and wholly independent of it. Subjective, on the other hand, takes the meaning of that which is in the mind. For instance, consider the case of a small child which has its fingers stepped on for the first time. The child perceives through its sense of sight that a thing has caused a sensation of pain, also that this was not under control of his mind—therefore it is objective. The sensation of pain passing to the child's brain forms a thought of fear, or anger directed towards the cause of the sensation. This thought is subjective.

From this prime meaning of reality many subjective ones have arisen. Let us consider two cases, one of a genius working on an original problem, such as the quantum theory, and one of a young man intensely in love for the first time. The genius concentrates on his problem to such an extent that he entirely forgets, or puts aside, his environment. The only real existence this man now has is in his mind. It is practically the same in the situation of the young man. He is so perfectly under the influence of the captivation of the girl that he thrusts aside everything but the thoughts of her; he undergoes stresses that he has never met with in objective reality. He is controlled, not by outside means, but by his own state of mind. He can hardly eat or sleep; he doesn't pay attention to anything exterior to his thoughts. This great emotional stress is so predominant that it is now his only existence and reality.

Passing from this simple state of subjectivity, reality becomes involved in the question—How can the mind render itself sufficiently objective to study itself? In other words, how are we able to use the mind to ponder on the mind? It is perfectly feasible for the intellect to grasp the fact that the physiological changes of the brain occur simultaneously with thought, but it cannot conceive of the connection between its own thoughts and these changes. The difficulties of the precise relation between the two have caused many controversies as to which is the more real, the objective or the subjective reality. During a state of excessive emotion, a person would say the subjective was. Going further, let us consider an extreme case.

A man is alone on a barren island with no sign of life on it. After a period this man begins to see the stark barrenness of objective reality; he perceives that there is nothing for him in the world but his own thoughts. The question now arises—Is this reality the man experiences really subjective, that is, does it exist solely in his mind, or has it an external existence? Bishop Berkely had a very interesting viewpoint on this question.

He said, "All those bodies which compose the mighty frame of the world have not any substance without the mind. So long as they are not perceived by me, or do not exist in my mind, or that of any other created spirit, they must either have no existence at all, or subsist in the mind of some Eternal Spirit."

This reasoning takes a more philosophical view than we have been following but carries beyond where psychology has to stop. Nevertheless, the psychology of the situation agrees with this attitude.

Reality, then, resolves itself into more of a study of the intellect than of objectivity. It is possible to go still deeper in the discussion of this subject, but we will have to content ourselves with this bare scratching of the surface.

—J.C.L.

Lilly, John C., M.D. "Mental Effects of Reduction of Ordinary Levels of Physical Stimuli on Intact, Healthy Persons," Psychiatric Research Reports 5, American Psychiatric Association, June 1956

We have been seeking answers to the question of what happens to a brain and its contained mind in the relative absence of physical stimulation. In neurophysiology, this is one form of the question: Freed of normal efferent and afferent activities, does the activity of the brain soon become that of coma or sleep, or is there some inherent mechanism which keeps it going, a pacemaker of the "awake" type of activity? In psychoanalysis, there is a similar but not identical problem. If the healthy ego is freed of reality stimuli, does it maintain the secondary process, or does primary process take over? i.e., Is the healthy ego independent of reality or dependent in some fashion, in some degree, on exchanges with the surroundings to maintain its structure?

In seeking answers, we have found pertinent autobiographical literature and reports of experiments by others, and have done experiments ourselves. The experiments are psychological ones on human subjects. Many psychological experiments in isolation have been done on animals but are not recounted in detail here; parenthetically, the effect on very young animals can be an almost completely irreversible lack of development of whole systems, such as those necessary for the use of vision in accomplishing tasks put to the animal. No truly neurophysiological isolation experiments on either animals or man have yet been done.

Autobiographical Accounts

The published autobiographical material has several drawbacks: In no case is there a sizable reduction of all possibilities of stimulation and action; in most cases, other factors add complications to the phenomena observed. We have collected eighteen autobiographical cases from the polar and seafaring literature (see References) which are more frank and revealing than most. We have interviewed two persons who have not published any of their material. In this account, we proceed from rather complicated situations to the more simple ones, i.e., from a maximum number of factors to the most simple experimental situation.

From this literature we have found that isolation *per se* acts on most persons as a powerful stress. The effects observed are similar to those of any extreme stress, and other stressful factors add their effects to those of isolation to cause mental symptoms to appear more rapidly and more intensely. As is well known, stresses other than isolation can cause the same symptoms to appear in individuals in an isolated group.

Taking our last point first, we have the account by Walter Gibson given in his book *The Boat*. This is the case in which four persons out of an initial 135 survived in a lifeboat in the Indian Ocean in World War II. Gibson gives a vivid account of his experiences, and the symptoms resulting from loss of hope, dehydration, thirst, intense sunburn, and physical combat. Most of the group hallucinated rescue planes and drank salt water thinking it fresh; many despaired and committed suicide; others were murdered; and some were eaten by others. The whole structure of egos was shaken and recast in desperate efforts at survival. (It is interesting to note that many of those who committed suicide tried to sink the boat by removing drain plugs before jumping overboard, i.e., sink the boat [and other persons] as well as the self; this dual destruction may be used by some of the non-surviving solitary sailors. See below.)

I cite this case because it gives a clue as to what to expect in those who do survive isolation in other conditions: Gibson survived—how? He says: (1) by previous out-of-doors training in the tropical sun for some years; (2) by having previously learned to be able to become completely passive (physically and mentally); (3) by having and maintaining the conviction that he would come through the experience; and, we add, (4) by having a woman, Doris Lim, beside him, who shared his passivity and convictions.

In all cases of survivors of isolation, at sea or in the polar night, it was the first exposure which caused the greatest fears and hence the greatest danger of giving way to symptoms; previous experience is a powerful aid in going ahead, despite the symptoms. Physical passivity is necessary during starvation, but, in some people, may be contraindicated in social isolation in the absence of starvation. In all survivors we run across the inner conviction that he or she will survive, or else there are definite reassurances from others that each will be rescued. In those cases of a man and a woman together, or even the probability of such a union within a few days, there is apparently not only a real assurance of survival, but a love of the situation can appear. (Such love can develop in a solitaire; see below.) Of course, such couples are the complete psychological antithesis of our major thesis of complete isolation; many symptoms can be avoided by healthy persons with such an arrangement.

Solitary sailors are in a more complex situation than the group of polar isolates. The sailing of a small boat across oceans requires a good deal of physical exertion, and the situation may be contaminated by a lack of sleep, which can also cause symptoms. The solitary sailors, of which Joshua Slocum and Alain Bombard are outstanding examples, relate that the first days out of port are the dangerous ones; awe, humility and fear, in the face of the sea, are most acute at this time. Bombard states that if the terror of the first week can be overcome, one can survive. Apparently, many do not survive this first period. Many single-handed boats have not arrived at their transoceanic destination. We have clues as to the causes from what sometimes happens with two persons on such crossings. There are several pairs of ocean-crossing sailors in which one of the couple became so terror-stricken, paranoid and bent on murder and/or suicide, that he had to be tied to his bunk.

Once this first period is past, other symptoms develop, either from isolation itself or from isolation plus other stresses. In the South Atlantic, Joshua Slocum had a severe gastro-intestinal upset just before a gale hit his boat; he had reefed his sails but should have taken them down. Under the circumstances, he was unable to move from the cabin. At this point he saw a man take over the tiller. At first he thought it was a pirate, but the man reassured him and said that he was the pilot of the *Pinta* and that he would take his boat safely through the storm. Slocum asked him to take down sail, but the man said, no, they must catch the *Pinta* ahead. The next morning Slocum recovered, and found his boat had covered ninety-three miles on true course, sailing itself. (His boat was quite capable of such a performance; he had arranged it that way for long trips without his hand at the helm.) In a dream that night the pilot appeared and said he would come whenever Slocum needed him. During the next three years the helmsman appeared to Slocum several times, during gales.

This type of hallucination-delusion seems to be characteristic of the strong egos who survive: a "savior" type of hallucination rather than a "destroyer" type. Their inner conviction of survival is projected thoroughly.

Other symptoms that appear are: superstitiousness (Slocum thought a dangerous reef named M Reef was lucky because M is the thirteenth letter of the alphabet and thirteen was his lucky number. He passed the reef without hitting it. Bombard thought the number of matches necessary to light a damp cigarette represented the number of days until the end of the voyage. He was wrong several times.); intense love of any living things (Slocum was revolted at the thought of killing food-animals, especially a goat given to him at one port. Ellam and Mudie became quite upset after catching and eating a fish that had followed the boat all day, and swore off further fish-eating.); conversations with inanimate objects (Bombard had bilateral conversations with a doll mascot.); and a feeling that when one lands, one had best be careful to listen before speaking to avoid being considered insane (Bernicot refused an invitation to dinner on another yacht after crossing the Atlantic alone, until he could recapture the proper things to talk about.) The inner life becomes so vivid and intense that it takes time to readjust to the life among other persons and to re-establish one's inner criteria of sanity. (When placed with fellow prisoners, after eighteen months in solitary confinement, Christopher Burney was afraid to speak for fear that he would show himself to be insane. After several days of listening he recaptured the usual criteria of sanity, and then could allow himself to speak.)

Life alone in the polar night, snowed-in, with the confining surroundings of a small hut is a more simple situation. However, there are other complicating factors: extreme cold, possibilities of carbon monoxide poisoning, collapse of the roof, etc. Richard Byrd, in his book *Alone,* recounts in great detail his changes in mental functioning, and talks of a long period of CO poisoning resulting in a state close to catatonia. I refer you to his book for details. He experienced, as did Slocum and many others, an oceanic feeling, the being "of the universe," at one with it.

Christiane Ritter (A *Woman in the Polar Night*) was exposed to isolation for periods up to sixteen days at a time. She saw a monster, hallucinated her past as if in bright sunshine, became "at one" with the moon, and developed a monomania to go out over the snow. She was saved by an experienced Norwegian who put her to bed and fed her lavishly. She developed a love for the situation and found great difficulty in leaving Spitzbergen. For a thorough and sensitive account of symptoms, I recommend her book to you.

From these examples and several more (see References), we conclude the following:

(1) Published autobiographies are of necessity incomplete. Social taboos, discretion to one's self, suppression and repression of painful or uncomfortable material, secondary elaboration, and rationalization severely limit the scope of the material available. (Interviews with two men, each of whom lived alone in the polar night, confirm this impression.)

(2) Despite these limitations, we find that persons in isolation experience many, if not all, of the symptoms of the mentally ill.

(3) In those who survive, the symptoms can be reversible. How easily reversible, we do not know. Most survivors report, after several weeks' exposure to isolation, a new inner security and a new integration of themselves on a deep and basic level.

(4) The underlying mechanisms are obscure. It is obvious that inner factors in the mind tend to be projected outward, that some of the mind's activity which is usually reality-bound now becomes free to turn to phantasy and ultimately to hallucination and delusion. It is as if the laws of thought are projected into the realm of the laws of inanimate matter and of the universe. The primary process tends to absorb more and more of the time and energy usually taken by the secondary process. Such experiences either lead to improved mental functioning or to destruction. Why one person takes the healthy path and another person the sick one is not yet clear.

Experiments to clarify the necessary conditions for some of these effects have been done. One of the advantages of the experimental material is that simpler conditions can be set up and tested, and some of the additional stresses of natural life situations can be eliminated.

Experimental Isolation

The longest isolation on the largest number of subjects has been carried out in Dr. Donald Hebb's Department of Psychology at McGill University by a group of graduate students. We started a similar project independently with different techniques at the National Institute of Mental Health. In the Canadian experiments, the aim is to reduce the *patterning* of stimuli to the lowest level; in ours, the objective is to reduce the *absolute intensity* of all physical stimuli to the lowest possible level.

In the McGill experiments, a subject is placed on a bed in an air-conditioned box with arms and hands restrained with cardboard sleeves, and eyes covered completely with translucent ski goggles. The subjects are college students motivated by payment of twenty dollars per day for as long as they will stay in the box. An observer is present, watching through a window, and tests the subject in various ways verbally through a communication set.

In our experiments, the subject is suspended with the body and all but the top of the head immersed in a tank containing slowly flowing water at 93° F. and wears a blacked-out mask (enclosing the whole head) for breathing, and wears nothing else. The water temperature is such that the subject feels neither hot nor cold. The experience is such that one tactually feels the supports and the mask, but not much else; a large fraction of the usual pressures on the body caused by gravity are lacking. The sound level is low; one hears only one's own breathing and some faint water sounds from the piping; the water-air interface does not transmit air-borne sounds very efficiently. It is one of the most even and monotonous environments I have experienced. After the initial training period, no observer is present. Immediately after exposure, the subject writes personal notes on his experience.

At McGill, the subjects varied considerably in the details of their experiences. However, a few general phenomena appeared. After several hours, each subject found that it was difficult to carry on organized, directed thinking for any sustained period. Suggestibility was very much increased. An extreme desire for stimuli and action developed. There were periods of thrashing around in the box in attempts to satisfy this need. The borderline between sleep and awakedness became diffuse and confused. At some time between twenty-four and seventy-two hours most subjects couldn't stand it any longer and left. Hallucinations and delusions of various sorts developed, mostly in those who could stay longer than two days.

The development of hallucinations in the visual sphere followed the stages seen with mescaline intoxication. When full-blown, the visual phenomena were complete projections maintaining the three-dimensions of space in relation to the rest of the body and could be scanned by eye and head movements. The contents were surprising to the ego, and consisted of material like that of dreams, connected stories sharing past memories and recent real events. The subjects' reactions to these phenomena were generally amusement and a sense of relief from the pressing boredom. They could describe them vocally without abolishing the sequences. A small number of subjects experienced doubling of their body images. A few developed transient paranoid delusions, and one had a seizure-like episode after five days in the box wih no positive EEG findings for epilepsy.

Our experiments have been more limited both in numbers of subjects and duration of exposures. There have been two subjects, and the longest exposure has been three hours. We have much preliminary data, and have gained enough experience to begin to guess at some of the mechanisms involved in the symptoms produced.

In these experiments, the subject always has a full night's rest before entering the tank. Instructions are to inhibit all movements as far as possible. An initial set of training exposures overcomes the fears of the situation itself.

In the tank, the following stages have been experienced:

(1) For about the first three-quarters of an hour, the day's residues are predominant. One is aware of the surroundings, recent problems, etc.

(2) Gradually, one begins to relax and more or less enjoy the experience. The feeling of being isolated in space and having nothing to do is restful and relaxing at this stage.

(3) But slowly, during the next hour, a tension develops which can be called a "stimulus-action" hunger; hidden methods of self-stimulation develop: twitching muscles, slow swimming movements (which cause sensations as the water flows by the skin), stroking one finger with another, etc. If one can inhibit such maneuvers long enough, intense satisfaction is derived from later self-stimulations.

(4) If inhibition can win out, the tension may ultimately develop to the point of forcing the subject to leave the tank.

(5) Meanwhile, the attention is drawn powerfully to any residual stimulus: the mask, the suspension, each come in for their share of concentration. Such residual stimuli become the whole content of consciousness to an almost unbearable degree.

(6) If this stage is passed without leaving the tank, one notices that one's thoughts have shifted from a directed type of thinking about problems to reveries and fantasies of a highly personal and emotionally charged nature. These are too personal to relate publicly, and probably vary greatly from subject to subject. The individual reactions to such fantasy material also probably varies considerably, from complete suppression to relaxing and enjoying them.

(7) If the tension and the fantasies are withstood, one may experience the furthest stage which we have yet explored: projection of visual imagery. I have seen this once, after a two and one-half hour period. The black curtain in front of the eyes (such as one "sees" in a dark room with eyes closed) gradually opens out into a three-dimensional, dark, empty space in front of the body. This phenomenon captures one's interest immediately, and one waits to find out what comes next. Gradually forms of the type sometimes seen in hypnogogic states appear. In this case, they were small, strangely shaped objects with self-luminous borders. A tunnel whose inside "space" seemed to be emitting a blue light then appeared straight ahead. About this time, this experiment was terminated by a leakage of water into the mask through a faulty connector on the inspiratory tube.

It turns out that exposures to such conditions train one to be more tolerant of many internal activities. Fear lessens with experience, and personal integration can be speeded up. But, of course, there are pitfalls here to be avoided. The opposite effects may also be accelerated in certain cases. Fantasies about the experience (such as the illusion of "return to the womb," which is quite common) are dispelled; one realizes that at birth we start breathing air and hence cannot "return to the womb." One's breathing in the tank is extremely important: as a comforting, constant safeguard and a source of rhythmic stimulation.

In both the McGill experiments and in ours, certain aftereffects are noted: the McGill subjects had difficulty in orienting their perceptual mechanisms; various illusions persisted for several hours. In our experiments, we notice that after emersion the day apparently is started over, i.e., the subject feels as if he has just arisen from bed afresh; this effect persists, and the subject finds he is out of step with the clock for the rest of that day. He also has to re-adjust to social intercourse in subtle ways. The night of the day of the exposure he finds that his bed exerts great pressure against his body. No bed is as comfortable as floating in water.

Experiments such as these demonstrate results similar to that given above for solitary polar living and sailing alone. If one is alone, long enough, and at levels of physical and human stimulation low enough, the mind turns inward and projects outward its own contents and processes; the brain not only stays active despite the lowered levels of input and output but accumulates surplus energy to extreme degrees. In terms of libido theory, the total *amount* of libido increases with time of deprivation; body-libido reaches new high levels. If body-libido is not discharged somatically, discharge starts through fantasy; but apparently this is neither an adequate mode nor can it achieve an adequate rate of discharge in the presence of the rapidly rising level. At some point a new threshold appears for more definite phenomena of regression: hallucinations, delusions, oceanic bliss, etc. At this stage, given any opportunities for action or stimulation by external reality, the healthy ego seizes them and reestablishes more secondary process. Lacking such opportunities for a long enough interval of time, re-organization takes place, how reversibly and how permanently we do not yet know.

Apparently even healthy minds act this way in isolation. What this means to psychiatric research is obvious: we have yet to obtain a full, documented picture of the range available to the healthy human adult mind; some of the etiological factors in mental illness may be clarified and sharpened by such research. Of course, this is a limited region of investigation. We have not gone into details about loss of sleep, starvation, and other factors which have great power in changing healthy minds to sick ones. I think that you can see the parallels between these results and phenomena found in normal children and in psychotics. And, if we could give you a more detailed account, possible explanations of the role of isolation factors in involuntary indoctrination and its opposite, psychotherapy, would be more evident.

REFERENCES

1. Small, Maurice H., "On Some Psychical Relations of Society and Solitude," *Pedagogical Seminary*, VII, No. 2, April 1900.

   Solitary Sailors

2. Slocum, Captain Joshua, *Sailing Alone Around the World*, London: Rupert Hart-Davis, 1948.

3. Ellam, Patrick, and Colin Mudie, *Sopranino*, New York: W.W. Norton, 1953.
4. Bombard, Dr. Alain, *The Voyage of the Hérétique*, New York: Simon & Schuster, 1953.
5. Merrien, Jean, *Lonely Voyagers*, New York: G.P. Putnam's, 1954.
6. Merrien, Jean, *Les Navigateurs Solitaires*, Paris: Editiones Denoël, 1954.
7. Bernicot, Louis, *The Voyage of* Anahita—*Single-Handed Round the World*, London: Rupert Hart-Davis, 1953.

Drastic Degrees of Stress

8. Gibson, Walter, *The Boat*, Boston: Houghton Mifflin, 1953.

Living in the Polar Night

9. Scott, J.M., *Portrait of an Ice Cap with Human Figures*, London: Chatto & Windus, 1953.
10. Courtauld, A., "Living Alone Under Polar Conditions," *The Polar Record*, No. 4, Cambridge, Eng.: University Press, July 1932.
11. Byrd, Admiral Richard E., *Alone*, New York: G.P. Putnam's, 1938.
12. Ritter, Christiane, *A Woman in the Polar Night*, New York: E.P. Dutton, 1954.

Forced Isolation and Confinement

13. Burney, Christopher, *Solitary Confinement*, New York: Coward-Mc-Cann, 1952.
14. Stypulkowski, Z., *Invitation to Moscow*, London: Thames & Hudson, 1951.

The Deaf and the Blind

15. Collingswood, Herbert W., "Adventures in Silence," *The Rural New Yorker*, 1923.
16. Ormond, Arthur W., C.B.E., F.R.C.S., "Visual hallucinations in sane people," *British Med. J.*, Vol. 2, 1925.
17. Bartlet, J.E.A., "A Case of Organized Visual Hallucinations in an Old Man with Cataract, and Their Relation to the Phenomena of the Phantom Limb," *Brain*, Vol. 74, Pt. III, pp. 363–73.

Experimental Isolation

18. Heron, W., W.H. Bexton, and D.O. Hebb, "Cognitive Effects of a Decreased Variation to the Sensory Environment," *The Amer. Psychol.*, Vol. 8, No. 8, Aug. 1953, p. 366.

Lilly, John C., M.D., "Some Considerations Regarding Basic Mechanisms of Positive and Negative Types of Motivations," The American Journal of Psychiatry, *115:6, Dec. 1958*

Over many years, some portions of the brain have been found which are intensely involved in the primitive, basic, motivating, moving, emotional states. Pioneer work by Sherrington, Cannon, Bard, Hess, Masserman, Ranson, Magoun and others demonstrates that there are zones of the brain which when stimulated evoke dramatically violent responses and others where more subtle, less understood, milder, less dramatic, more pleasure-like responses are evoked. However, a sharp and clear operational separation between these two classes of responses was not made until recently; the regions giving such responses are now separated as two distinct sets by using electrical stimuli placed in the brain; in such regions such electrical stimulation is found to function as a motive in behavioral learning situations. Through the work of Olds and Milner (1); Delgado, Rosvold, and Looney (2); Delgado, Roberts, and Miller (3); Cohen, Brown, and Brown (4); Sidman, Brady, et al. (5); and that in our laboratory (16) the picture of two kinds of powerful "motivational" brain systems has developed rapidly: The first kind functions as if a reward and the second as if a punishment to the learning and learned animal, i.e., motivationally positive and negative systems.

Each kind of system exists side by side with the other within very small regions in the midline deep subcortical structures including the hypothalamus and the mid-brain. Our results from mapping such regions of the brain demonstrate that most if not all of the systems previously described which powerfully change an animal's total behavior fall into one or the other of these systems.

To find such systems one may follow the lead of two groups of investigators: Olds and Milner (1) showed that a rat could be trained to switch on short trains of electric stimuli in certain parts of its own brain; Delgado, Roberts, and Miller (3) showed that a cat could be trained to climb a wheel to switch off electrical stimulation started by the observer in other small zones in its brain and in the "painful" zones of the periphery. Using such techniques, Sidman, Brady, et al.

(5) demonstrated that the first, the rewarding effect, could be found in a monkey. We demonstrated that both rewarding and punishing could be found and mapped in the monkey in great detail (16); and, recently, we have found both effects in another large mammal, the dolphin of our southern coastal waters.

For a time we were surprised to find in the monkey that the positive, pleasure-like, motivating-to-start-stimuli systems were so large, and the fear, pain-like, motivating-to-stop systems were so small. But when one sees the very powerful effects of stimulating the relatively small negative systems, one can understand that this kind of system may be quite large enough to fulfill its extremely high priority stop, escape, or avoidance functions. When one sees the fearful, downhill, sickening, destructive effects of continued stimulation of the negative systems in an animal, one is reluctant to say that they need be any larger.

The positive, start, approach systems in the monkey are relatively very large, occurring in certain zones as a proximate twin with the negative ones, and also occurring in other regions possibly without its twin such as in the corpora striata. Reciprocal relations and balanced activity of positive and negative motives seem to be assured structurally in the deep powerful midline systems, and something of the positive aspect may be in excess for other regions. Such other regions include functions like the sexual ones, which we find to be both motivationally positive and negative. We find alternation over short time intervals between the two opposite effects in the monkey, i.e., he will first start such romantic activities then stop them within a period of minutes again and again for a disgraceful number of hours (forty-eight). This system seems to be at that very demanding primitive level that requires mutual reciprocity between a starting motive and a stopping one to preserve the individual's integrity.

The other positive functions for the larger amounts of tissue seem to be connected with relatively uncharged innocuous prosaic everyday non-romantic activities; in a monkey this may be searching for food, grooming, chattering, etc. In the human animal it may be writing and talking—including giving speeches. In other words, any and all activities of the animal all of the time seem to require an oversupply of the positive, pleasure-like, start-like function at a low level in the brain for continued normal functioning of the whole animal toward better survival and more fun.

Of course, we like to think that in the total action of the brain, the positive tends to overbalance the negative, and that the intellectual functions might be neutral ones, neither positive nor negative, found in excess over both the positive and the negative "neutral reinforcement." Therefore, in the relatively huge cerebral neocortex and in the cerebellum, one might expect to find neutrality or a small excess of positive rewarding sort of function. This expectation was recently found to be somewhat erroneous even in the small-brained monkey. With proper electrical stimuli and proper time courses, we have found rewarding effects elicitable from cerebellum and punishing and rewarding ones elicitable from cerebral neocortex.

Well, one might say, so what? Rats, cats and monkeys are small and stupid creatures—may not a larger brain be more impervious to such tampering within its innards? May not the trained, sublimating and sometimes sublime human mind resist and even conquer such artificially evoked crassly primitive impulses? This question of how powerful such stimuli can be in large brains seems only properly answerable by experimenting each on one's own brain so that we have the really individual *inside* answer—even someone else experiencing such stimuli who knows one's language will never be able to thoroughly convince one. And, there are sceptics, who when oneself is experiencing it will not be convinced. Empathy and sympathy do help, but not in the fashion that personal experience can.

However, certain technical dangers make me pause before I put bits of wire in my own head, and at this time I am reluctant to ask anyone else to undergo what I won't do or have done on myself. It looks as if normal controls may be slightly delayed in the field. All we have are a few data from sick humans: Some psychotic, epileptic, and Parkinson cases have been stimulated by Bickford, by Sem-Jacobsen, and by Rémond (6); the results show that these two kinds of systems can be found in the human brain but are small and difficult to explore safely.

However, we think it is important to find out more about big-brained animals in far greater detail than we can with the human. For example, do they resemble the small-brained ones in the urgency of motivation aroused in these systems? So far we have found only one animal that has a brain the size of ours who will cooperate and not frighten me to the point where I can't work with him—this animal is the dolphin, a small whale with teeth, an air-breathing mammal (not the fish of the same name). The species used is that caught by the Marineland Research Laboratory for us—the shoal-water porpoise, *Tursiops truncatus*. As adults, these animals reach eight feet and 400 pounds, with a brain up to about 1750 grams. Compared to our 230–250 grams of brain per foot of body length theirs is about 220—he is a fairly close second to us if we remember that the gorilla as our nearest anthropoid cousin has only about one-third of that value. The dolphin also has an edge on his giant cousin, the sperm whale, who, according to Kojima, at about 60 feet scores about 130 grams of brain per foot of body on this scale; a more distant cousin the (baleen) fin whale at 60 feet also, says Jansen, rates about 110 (7).

Several investigators have essayed a neurophysiological attack on the dolphin's large brain with disappointing failures. An expedition from Johns Hopkins to the Carolina coast in the 1930's brought back neuroanatomical specimens but no data on the living brain; Langworthy (8) reported that failure occurred "because of technical difficulties." Eight of us from five research laboratories * in 1955, went on a similar expedition to Florida, with similar results: Our neuroanatomical specimens were magnificent and our neurophysiological findings were zero. We found out what Langworthy may have meant by "technical difficulties": dolphins cannot be anesthetized without danger of dying. These animals, in contrast to dry land ones, fail to breathe with relatively light doses of anesthetic, one-fourth that required for surgical levels of anesthesia. In other words, they lack our unconscious, automatic, self-sustaining breathing system. In retrospect this seems reasonable: an unconscious dolphin, under water, will drown if respiratory inspiration occurs. They, as it were, must relate their breathing to surfacing and to the coming opportunities to surface—so this function is almost if not fully voluntary. Therefore, a drunken dolphin dies when he passes out. It seems a sure bet that there are no alcoholic porpoises!

We seemed farther than ever from our intended goal of investigating a brain the size of the human one. However, the Marineland people meanwhile thoroughly imbued me with their enthusiasm for dolphins: Dr. F. G. Wood, Mr. William Rolleston and others were extremely helpful but also quite insistent in their arguments and demonstrations that these beasts, with man, are extremely kind, cooperative, intelligent, trainable, fun-loving, romantic, never hostile or vicious but at times, like some persons, exasperating to deal with: yet they can destroy sharks and whales and battle ferociously with one

* Drs. Lawrence Kruger, Vernon Mountcastle, Jerzy Rose (Johns Hopkins University); Joseph Hind, Clinton Woolsey (University of Wisconsin); Leonard Malis (Mt. Sinai Hospital, N.Y.); Karl Pribram (The Institute of Living, Hartford, Conn.); John Lilly (National Institutes of Health, Bethesda, Md.).

another during mating season. As a consequence of further indoctrination—at times we felt almost as if the dolphins were playing the same game as the persons at Marineland—some time was spent developing a method which would by-pass the need for and dangers of general anesthesia.

During the last year, it was found to be feasible to hammer percutaneously guides for electrodes into the skull of monkeys (9). The method was tried on dolphins in November 1957; the guides were inserted under local anesthesia into the skull of a dolphin in a small shallow tank so easily and so quickly that the dolphin and we hardly realized what had happened.

To return from this history to the motivational systems, we found such positive and negative systems within the dolphin's brain. The systems are farther apart in this large brain than in that of the monkey; yet they seem as large in absolute size as they are in the monkey; more brain with other, yet-to-be-found functions lies between and around these systems. As in the human brain, evocable motor movements also were found only in relatively isolated regions. The urgency of motives elicited by stimulation of those zones which we have found to date is high and there is evidence that we have yet to stimulate the most powerful ones. Stimulating a punishment area (a negative, destructive, stopping motivational spot) caused a dolphin to shut off the electrical current very accurately at a certain level of intensity. The difference between this naive, wild animal's performance and that of monkeys was the incredibly short time in which she learned to use the switch: compared to the naive monkey's several hundreds to thousands of random trials to learn, she took about twenty to shape up the proper motions of her beak and each of those "trials" had a purposeful look that was a little disturbing to watch.

How did we know first when we were in a negative zone? Every time we first stimulated her, she emitted the characteristic dolphin "distress whistle" (another story!). From that time on she shut off the current at a level well below that at which we previously could elicit the distress call. This whistle, a crescendo–de-crescendo in frequency and loudness, was a clue for finding negative, punishing, destructive, stopping systems; we had no criteria for positive, rewarding, pleasure-like, starting systems. Empathic methods did not help with this handless, streamlined, hairless animal who lacks our mobility of facial expression. We may have missed such systems because of the lack of such human criteria but finally found one such zone.

With a bit of luck with our next animal we found a positive, rewarding, starting zone. The luck was in obtaining an animal who vocalized vociferously: as soon as we stimulated the positive zone, he told us about it by covering a large repertory of assorted complex whistles, bronx cheers, and impolite noises. Giving him a switch at this point was quite an experience—he sized up what I was doing so rapidly that by the time I had set up his switch he took only five "trials" to figure out the proper way to push it with his beak. From that point on, as long as he could obtain his stimulation for every push he made with his beak, he quietly worked for the stimuli. But if we cut off his current, he immediately stopped working and vocalized —apparently scolding at times, and mimicking us at others. One time he mimicked my speaking voice so well that my wife laughed out loud, and he copied her laughter. Eventually, he pushed too rapidly, caused a seizure, became unconscious, respiration failed, and he died. Apparently unconsciousness because of any factor, anesthesia, or brain stimulation, or others, causes death in these animals.

In this abbreviated account, I cannot convey to you all of the evidence for my feeling that if we are to ever communicate with a non-human species of this planet, the dolphin is probably our best present gamble. In a sense, it is a joke when I fantasize that it may be best to hurry and finish our work on their brains before one of them learns to speak our language—else he will demand equal rights with men for their brains and lives under our ethical and legal codes!

Before our man in space program becomes too successful, it may be wise to spend some time, talent, and money on research with the dolphins; not only are they a large-brained species living their lives in a situation with attenuated effects of gravity, but they may be a group with whom we can learn basic techniques of communicating with really alien intelligent life forms. I personally hope we do not encounter any such extraterrestrials before we are better prepared than we are now. Too automatically, too soon, too many of us attribute too much negative systems activity to foreign language aliens of strange and unfamiliar appearance and use this as an excuse for increasing our own negative, punishing, attacking activities on them.

What does all of this mean in terms of us, our species, aside from communication and empathy with and between us and other species? Turning inward, examining our minds, their deep and primitive workings, can we see evidence of the actions and inner workings of the positive, pleasure-like, start and the negative, pain-fearlike, stop systems? I believe most of us can say, "Unequivocally yes." In order, however, to see such activities in the mind in pure culture, as it were, special conditions are needed: First, one must be alone—without a lover to exchange the positive, and without a human sacrificial goat to load with the negative. We are mostly not alone and are exposed to an organized human society which uses both kinds of our activities for its own growth and survival. These surroundings obscure the internal origins of our motivations in a medley of organized background noises, sights, clothing, housing, transport, schedules, and deluges of information demanding replies and action. So one must first be freed of persons and people: Solitude is the first requirement.

Secondly, one should be freed of sources of information from one's then residual surroundings, animate and inanimate. Thirdly, maximum attenuation of physiological and physical stimuli of reactions and exchanges with surroundings, including all of gravity's and temperature's powerful demands, is needed. And, fourthly, a sufficient period of time, a sufficient amount of training, and a sufficient number of repeated exposures must be given to develop one's tolerance to one's inner mind.

Once all this is done (we and other research workers are only beginners at this isolation work), we find depths dimly seen without these conditions, and we find the positive and the negative, rewarding and punishing, activities deeply imbedded within ourselves. Many men and women before and in our time knew and know these experiences. Our only advantages today are: (1) our knowledge of these systems in some animals; (2) our particularly modern abilities to concentrate our interests on a given region of experience, to withhold easy explanations and thus to avoid killing our curiosity; and (3) a powerful motivation resulting from the imminent prospects of either total annihilation of our species, or of moving off this planet to other planets and of encountering other species with attainments equal to or greater than ours.

In regard to the basic human motives of reward and punishment, of rewarding and of being rewarded and of punishing and of being punished, we have found some data which may be of interest. For several years we have been studying autobiographical accounts of pairs of persons and of solitaires isolated in the long night of the polar winter and isolated in protracted sea voyages in minimal size vessels (10, 11). Our detailed findings are too lengthy to recount here and are being presented in a book currently in preparation. In essence we find that persons in such circumstances tend to divide themselves into two extreme groups: those who are convinced continuously (or become so) that they will survive (the self-confident or "egophilic" ones) and those who will not survive if alone long enough (the self-fearing or "egophobic" ones). Some of those in the self-confident group have come through experiences which are as extreme as can be imagined and still allow one to survive at all. Those in the self-fearing group about whom we hear at all are usually one of a pair or are in larger groups and are reported secondhand. Usually it is found that such persons move toward their own destruction in circumstances not necessarily too extreme for real survival. Walter Gibson gives us both extremes in his book *The Boat* (12). "Who Ate Who [sic] in the Arctic" is a grim old joke with a parallel one of "Who Killed Who's Self at Sea." The more important group are those who survived and why they could do so.

Some of the mechanisms involved in these extreme groups of persons possibly may be analyzed in more microscopic detail in shorter term experiments in isolation of small groups and of solitaires. If one frees up a person from other persons and attenuates his physical exchanges with his surroundings, one can detect some phenomena which apparently are related to the above considered basic internal structure of his mind. If alone long enough in surroundings which are the *same* and *even* long enough, one's internal mental workings reveal their basic character rather quickly, i.e., in a relatively few hours. *Sameness* and *evenness* are absolutely necessary. I am referring now to the results of our "tepid dark silent bath in the tank" at NIH (10, 11) experiments rather than the "monotonous rest on the bed in the box experiments" at McGill (13); even though, apparently, similarities exist, I know our own results in far greater detail, especially in my own case. (Such work has become so popular recently that it seems very difficult to isolate experiments and subjects on isolation to the point where they are isolated enough to have significance.) In such extreme surroundings one can find out if one is self-confident or self-phobic. By careful and slowly applied graded dosage of many short exposures to such conditions, one can develop an increasing immunity rather than an overwhelming love or aversion for the tank. During such training it becomes obvious which of the basic drives, positive or negative, rewarding or punishing, surviving or dying, predominate at a given time. By carefully watching and recording all those phenomena which one watches and records in psychotherapy and psychoanalysis one can see the algebraic sign of the dominant themes. Analysis of the material may show the powerful hidden desires, even such extreme ones as incorporation, incest, cannibalism, and murder. There is one advantage in the isolation situation over the other kinds of situations. There are no real present excuses to blame for the emotional storms of love or hate, the fantastic beliefs, or the mental projections which can and do occur. Alone with one's God there are no alibis (14, 15).

Contrary to the case of the acting out of the usual analytic patient, there is no reality to serve as a sacrificial goat on the twin altars of either love or hate. In this way a mind in pure culture can see its own true nature, and have an opportunity to see if it can solve its own basic internal self-contained conflicts in order to have a try at changing the unsatisfying parts. Contrary to those who say such experiences in the tank or on the isolation bed are identical with mental illness or even psychosis, those healthy intact subjects who have been through such experiences know and feel this point of view to be wrong. For such subjects, the experience can be quite interesting.

Along this exploratory path of research a seemingly more trivial but possibly eventually important finding was made: when weightlessness is approximated in the tank by the flotation, and isothermicity of one's skin is achieved at 93°F., one can rest better and *faster*, as it were, than on a bed. The mental problems in the tank ensue *after* one becomes *too rested* and hence too restless and too eager. In my case two hours without sleep in the tank can equal about eight hours' sleep on a bed within a twenty-four-hour cycle unrepeated. Thus we may write a note to the "man in space" program: the major problem with weightlessness at the beginning of the exposure may be a super-abundance of energy and *no need for sleep* (unless the man fights himself internally and wears himself out). Of course real pain and/or fear will use up energy rapidly and counterbalance the above effect. Those who, mentally, can afford to relax and enjoy the above effects, who are not exposed to outside dangers too continuously, and who can effectively meet the other real demands of the control of their container, will be able not only to survive but to have one of the most moving adventures (inside and outside!) ever to be experienced by man. In our ventures into the frontiers of outer space we will carry the frontiers of our inner minds with us. It seems that to best emphathize with a dolphin man may have to move into outer space; or conversely the dolphin may teach us how to live in outer space without gravity.

The cogency and urgency of finding and understanding the internal origins and substrates of rewarding and punishing systems are obvious to many persons. But one must avoid taking too seriously that which one has within oneself and finds so clearly in persons in isolation: projections of negative and of positive motivations, powerful projections acting as if coming from other persons and external reality but actually originating inside one's own self. In isolation the evidence of the truth of the existence of one's own projections is so obvious as to be unescapable and humbling. In our experience, to try to escape these truths, subjects use ingenious and subtle techniques similar to those well-known to psychoanalysts and psychotherapists. To recognize in one's self at least some of these techniques may allow one, one may think, to see them in others. But, a caution is in order: The human mind is the only province in science in which that which is assumed to be true either is true or becomes true. (That law I do believe to be true!) This is a sublime and dangerous faculty. To have and to hold a useful and successful set of basic beliefs and truths about the rewards and punishments in one's self is also sublime, sometimes satisfying, and sometimes punishing, but never dull or monotonous. To find one's self to be more egophilic than egophobic is, of itself, an egophilic advantage increasing one's own fun and that of those persons closest and most important to one. By careful and continuous nurture one may achieve the classic command to "love thy neighbor as thyself," but only after learning how to increase thy love for thyself.

Summary

In recent years the exploration of the brain has shown some of those systems which are involved in the production and maintenance of certain motivational states. In rats, Olds and Milner demonstrated rewarding effects of stimulating certain systems; in cats, Delgado, Roberts, and Miller, and Delgado, Rosvold, and Looney showed punishing effects from stimulating other zones. Sidman, Brady, *et al.* confirmed Olds and Milner in the cat and monkey. We have confirmed both effects in the monkey, and have investigated in some detail the reward and the punishment effects in various loci. We have found also the same effects from a few loci in the porpoise's (dolphin's) brain; this animal's brain is as large as the human one and hence is of interest. A number of workers have been doing exploratory studies on healthy intact human individuals in isolation from other persons and from their usual levels of exchange with the physical environment; by such means one may investigate positive and negative motivations in more or less pure culture in the subjective psychological sphere. Such research is full of technical problems and pitfalls; it shows that in these special conditions some minds tend to disguise the presently acting true motives and to project them in multitudinous forms into the minimally stimulating and non-reactive reality. Some useful data are also derived from autobiographical accounts written by those who have been exposed to isolation at sea or in the polar regions; the dominance of the positive or negative motivations can be seen operating especially clearly in such accounts. Such exploratory studies are slowly adding to an understanding of positive and negative motivations and offer powerful tools for further studies.

REFERENCES

1. Olds, J., and P. Milner, *J. Comp. Physiol. Psychol.*, 47:419, 1954.
2. Delgado, J.M.R., H.E. Rosvold, and Edmund Looney, *J. Comp. Physiol. Psychol.*, 49:373, 1956.
3. Delgado, J.M.R., W.W. Roberts, and N.E. Miller, *Am. J. Physiol.*, 179:587, 1954.
4. Cohen, B.D., G.W. Brown, and M.L. Brown, *J. Exp. Psychol.*, 53:228, 1957.
5. Sidman, M., J.V. Brady, J.J. Boren, D.G. Conrad, and A. Schulman, *Science*, 122:830, 1955.
6. Forster, F., "First Conference on Electrical Studies on the Unanesthetized Brain," Washington, D.C.: Georgetown Univ., June 10–13, 1957. In press.
7. Jansen, J., *Norwegian Whaling Gazette*, 480, 1952.
8. Langworthy, O.R., *Brain*, 54:225, 1931.
9. Lilly, J.C., *Science*, 127:1181, 1958.
10. Lilly, J.C., "Group for the Advancement of Psychiatry," 1790 Broadway, New York: Symposium No. 2, 13, 44, 1956.
11. Lilly, J.C., "Psychiatric Research Reports 5," American Psychiatric Assoc., 1–28, June 1956.
12. Gibson, Walter, *The Boat*, Boston: Houghton Mifflin, 1953.
13. Heron, Woodburn, *Scient. Amer.*, 196:52, 1957.
14. Freud, Sigmund, *The Future of an Illusion*, New York: Liveright & the Institute of Psycho-analysis, 1928.
15. Huxley, Aldous, *Heaven and Hell*, London: Chatto & Windus, 1956.
16. Lilly, J.C., *in: Reticular Formation of the Brain*, Boston: Little, Brown, June 1958.

Lilly, John C., M.D.,[*] **"The Psychophysiological Basis for Two Kinds of Instincts: Implications for Psychoanalytical Theory,"** Journal of the American Psychoanalytic Association, 8:4, Oct. 1960

Introduction

In recent years the brain systems which underlie and produce the phenomena called instinct have been delineated. For the first time the systems, which when stimulated cause either various kinds of pleasure or various types of negative avoiding, painful or fearful reactions, have been discovered and studied in great detail. Work has been accomplished in rats (16), cats (23, 1), monkeys (1, 7), dolphins (8), and in humans (20, 21) which has far-reaching implications for the systematic development of the theory of instincts.

In this paper the levels of discourse must be very carefully delineated to avoid confusion. Experiments using rats, cats, and monkeys involve extremely simple nervous systems compared with those of the human and of the dolphin. The phenomena elicited are completely reproducible. The responses to stimulation of the rat brain are simple and amazingly repetitive kinds of behavioral patterns: the cat introduced slightly greater variability; and the monkey steps up the complexity considerably. However, it is not until one investigates a brain comparable in size with that of the human that the full range of human complexity, which is dealt with in psychoanalysis, is achieved. The phenomena of speech, of writing, of love and hate, of mental symbols, etc., do not appear in the lower animals, so far as can be determined. There is no doubt that analogous types of emotional states exist in these lower animals, such as the anger, fear, pleasure, love, etc., existing in the human. Therefore, the achievement of extremely great variability of responses, numerous degrees of freedom, and vast storage of experiences are possible only with the very large brain of the human and of a few other animals.

Practically all of the richness of reasoning, rationalization, thinking, and similar matters dealt with in the classical psychoanalysis are completely unavailable in animals other than the human. Practically

[*] Communication Research Institute, St. Thomas, U.S. Virgin Islands; formerly, National Institute of Mental Health, Bethesda, Md.

all of the evidence to date for a psychoanalytic theory of instinct has been derived from the case of the human (2). In this sense, then, animal research has very little to add, except by analogy (4, 17, 18). The human brain has buried within it systems subserving instincts which seem to be present in these smaller-brained animals. Since these systems are more fully developed in the human than in lower animals, their reactions and possible activities are more complicated. The biological substrate for the human kind of instincts, however, persists throughout a phylogenetic series (of mammals, at least). If one accepts the principle that the smaller brain has fewer degrees of freedom of action and reaction, but has instinctual reactions basically similar to those of the larger brain, then the following results of some animal research can be applied to human theoretical psychoanalysis.

Reward and Punishment Systems in the Brain

In working with electrodes implanted in specific areas in a monkey's brain, one can observe reactions which resemble extremely closely various things seen in and felt by humans under extreme conditions. Animal tests now show these to be true emotions felt by the animal (5, 6, 7). Work with humans in stimulating these same systems has corroborated the conclusions from the animal research: these reactions are indeed true emotions rather than "sham" or pseudo-affective reactions (13, 20, 21, 22).

Stimulation of a specific system within the hypothalamus can cause the monkey to look and act frightened. If presented with a potentially threatening object, which previously caused him pain, he will attack it so violently that he can tear the teeth out of his jaw. This response only occurs in this system. The same object presented without stimulation causes no reaction whatsoever, other than a bored withdrawal from it. When electrical stimuli are introduced into adjacent systems within the hypothalamus, the animal can take an inordinate amount of interest in the same object; seek it out, handle it, and become extremely attached to it, in the emotional sense (5, 6, 10).

Stimulation of the human brain in these same systems causes an intense terror in the region of the midline hypothalamus and an intense sense of well-being from the second area (21). In the case of the human, however, the objects that are given closest attention are the physicians and technicians who are stimulating the brain, rather than any other objects in the environment. Stimulation of the reward system immediately causes an intense talking session and intense signs of pleasure, such as smiling, joking, and carrying on activities in the vocal and the exchanging spheres with other humans. Also, if the terror-response area is stimulated, anger results and is directed at the human targets rather than at any portion of the inanimate surroundings.

If one contrasts the cat and the monkey, the cat when stimulated in these areas will strike at anything and everything surrounding it, especially any moving object. There is not the differentiation of the target itself from the surroundings which there is in the monkey. In the monkey there are not the responses in the vocal sphere that we have in the human.

Stimulating the brain of an animal which is as complex and as large as that of the human, such as in the dolphin or porpoise, one finds that there is an immediate reaction to the humans present and a complex output in the vocal sphere, analogous to that in the human. Stimulating the reward-producing systems in these animals allows an investigation of the complexity of their reactions which remind one very much of the complexity of the reactions of humans. These animals apparently do not use facial expression the way we do, nor do they have hands to use the way a human does; therefore, certain human modes of expression are missing.

Reward Systems

The following points seem to be well established at the present time with regard to electrical stimulation of the brain in these various animals:

1. Anteriorly, in a system which in the human lies just inside the frontal pole, above orbital cortex, and below frontal cortex, and about 1 cm. lateral to the midplane, there is a reward system which is found in the cat, the monkey, and the dolphin as well as the human. During stimulation there is a psychic sense of intense well-being generated which is not tied to any particular aspect of either the body or the environment but diffuses through the whole of the mental life.

2. Posterior to this system in the globus pallidus and similar nuclei, but still lateral to the mid-plane, is another portion of the so-called reward systems. However this system gives a localized intense sense of pleasure in various parts of the body. This feeling is referred to the skin and muscles of one arm or one leg, for example depending upon the part of the nucleus being stimulated.

3. Returning to the more forward portion of the brain, further below, in and near the hypothalamus, other kinds of pleasure can be elicited. For example, sexual pleasure and erection in the male can be elicited by stimulation near and in the septal region (10, 13a).

4. In other regions of the hypothalamus, the rewards as if quenching of thirst and as if eating of food when hungry, are found in the mediolateral hypothalamus (15, 7).

5. Moving posteriorly into the mesencephalon, the rewarding aspects of orgasm are found. The animals are driven to self-stimulate in this area of the brain more strongly than in any other; stimulation leads to a generalized seizurelike episode in which the animal passes out, comes to, and barks, looks around for the switch to elicit once more the same reaction (7, 10). Stimulation of this portion of the system wears him out extremely rapidly and forces him to sleep for many hours afterward. Stimulation near this region in the human caused ejaculation in two episodes (22), but apparently the stimulation was not pushed far enough to cause a full-blown orgasm with all of the mental concomitants and the loss of consciousness.

Punishment Systems

In the punishment (negative) systems, the instinctual emotional reactions that are elicited are as follows:

1. In the mid-plane hypothalamus, in the preoptic region and in the walls of the third ventricle is a system subserving fright, terror, and panic (3, 5, 6, 7, 10).

2. As one proceeds posteriorly in the hypothalamus, the system changes to intense localized pain distributed to various parts of the body (7, 10, 11). There is apparently a pain map of the whole body surface within this system extending posteriorly toward the mesencephalon (11).

3. Farther laterally in the hypothalamus there are systems which cause nausea and others which can rapidly induce fatigue after a few seconds of stimulation. This fatigue is so profound that the animal, if undisturbed, will fall asleep and sleep from twenty minutes to half an hour (3, 7).

Relations to Other Brain Systems

In view of the complexity of these results, it is wise at the present time not to attempt to construct too much theory before the details of these explorations of the brains can be completed. We can make the following statements:

1. There are two kinds of systems within the brain: one subserves rewards, pleasurable sensations and activities; and the other subserves punishments: painful, and angry kinds of sensations, activities, and reactions.

2. When spots of extreme neuronal activity are introduced into these systems, the emotion or the instinct develops fully. In experiments with implanted electrodes, we are introducing such intensely active spots of neuronal activity within these systems.

3. Research to date on the connections of these systems with other parts of the brain have demonstrated that there are thorough two-way connections between all of these systems and cortex and with systems lower down within the brain stem and spinal cord. Modern techniques such as those of Nauta (14) show an imposing richness of connections in most directions between these systems.

4. Therefore, it is perfectly possible for any other kind of activity elsewhere in the brain (acoustic, for example), if sufficiently concentrated, to pour enough impulses into these systems to cause them to be as extremely active as weak electrical stimuli.

We can visualize with the modern view the following series of events in regard to an intensely emotional reaction of a man experiencing fear: There is an explosion and a bright flash of light. After impulses from these two physical events travel over the acoustic and other neurones and through the lower centers, there is an immediate stimulation of a high degree of activity in the emotionally important systems mentioned above (12). In the process of allowing such circuits to be increasingly or decreasingly active, past experience and early experiences, especially, determine both the outcome and how much activity will be facilitated in a continuing fashion within the lower "emotional" systems. An experiment with a monkey can illustrate a few of the many thousands of reactions possible from cortex.

Weak Reward and Punishment from Cortical Stimulation:
Multiple Cortical Functions

Using an implanted electrode in the cortex of a monkey, I demonstrated that at very low levels of stimulation, the monkey liked it and would push a switch in order to stimulate this area of cortex himself. However, if something which he also likes came into the neighborhood, such as food, he would abandon this lever, eat the food, and then go back to lever pressing. As the amount of current was increased, the sign of the motivation went from positive to negative: he would now shut off a stimulus which I would introduce with the apparatus in the same spot. Once again, however, this was not so demanding that he could not pay attention to other things in his environment and make use of other kinds of previous learning. If simultaneously one stimulated one of the lower centers at a level which captured his interest, either in a positive or negative sense, and one of the cortical spots, the latter was completely neglected in favor of the more demanding lower systems. The threshold for these various effects in the cortex was below the threshold for motor movement elicited in the same spot, that is, specific motor movements tied to that particular spot and tied to each stimulus train. Stimulating the lower centers in a similar fashion, either in terms of rewarding or punishing systems, one could obtain almost complete exclusion of the external reality; the experience inside is far more powerful than that from external reality.

Stimulating a human brain in the same manner leads, as has been reported by Penfield (19), to the patient remarking that, "You, or something outside of me, is causing movement of my arm—I am not willing it myself." Stimulation of the lower centers leads to a complete taking over of the ego by extremely emotional reactions, with immediate taking over of the initiative. However, there is no loss in the knowledge that the doctor is causing the stimulation within. For example, during stimulation in the fright area, one patient said, "If you do that again, I will tear the electrodes out of my head." Possibly if one increased the intensity, as we have in animals, the man would be quite incapable of using his knowledge to threaten and would attack or flee.

Implications for Psychoanalytic Theory

In the past there have been attempts to assign specific areas of the brain to id, ego, and superego. On the face of it, this seems to be nonsense: one should make much more of a functional kind of division of systems in the brain, not a division from just one massive part to another massive part. As long as there are the natural interconnections, the brain is operating as a total whole. We only have fractions of ego functions, a very small proportion, in the lower systems. The major stores of memory seem to be in the extremely large cortex; at least, not much of the total memory could be stored in the much smaller lower systems. Id functions can be elicited in a most pure form by stimulation of the lower systems as mentioned above, but there is a full participation of all the brain. There is a sprinkling of these functions throughout the brain with a more attenuated set within the cortex. Since there is an expansion of pathways as one moves from the lower centers out to cortex, stimulation of a small area of cortex would not give the same effects as stimulation deep within the smaller systems. With many, many thousands of electrodes in the cortex one may be able to cause exactly the same kinds of reactions as one can cause by stimulation deep within the subcortical systems.

As presently viewed, the cortex seems to be extremely well differentiated in terms of the projection of external reality upon its multiple-folded surface. The ego processes seem to be predominantly stored and used within this huge structure. However, one cannot conceive of any ego functions existing without some sort of rewarding and/or punishing effects going on concomitantly and continuously. One, as it were, must *like* to talk before one will talk; or one must be *forced* to talk in order to terminate a punishment. It seems as if the rewarding and punishing systems must be continuously operative in greatly differentiated detail in all aspects of waking and sleeping life.

There may be an excess of rewarding activities, i.e., libido, in order to keep the organism operating toward survival (8). Any time we caused too much activity for too long a period in the negative systems in the monkey, it looked as if we were going to end up with a dead monkey. He would give up all initiative, become extremely sick, and withdraw from all participation with us. This picture could be completely reversed by inducing hyperactivity in a small part of a rewarding system: within a few minutes we could reverse a behavioral state, which if allowed to continue would lead to irreversible clinical changes. Once started on a downhill course, the negative systems seemed quite capable of killing the organism: the seeds of destruction of the whole animal lie within its own brain, just as the seeds of its survival are also present (7).

These results and further results too lengthy to discuss in this paper force one to derive two kinds of systems: one negative and one positive; in other words, at least two kinds of basic instincts: positive and negative; rewarding and punishing; loving and hating. There seems to be no satisfactory theoretical alternative.

"Rebound Phenomena"

One can show that the cessation of rewarding stimulation can act as a mild punishment, but it cannot act, at least in the animals with which we have dealt and in the humans, as a punishment as intense as stimulation of the negative systems themselves. Similarly, cessation of active stimulation of the negative systems can act as a mild reward but never with an effect as great as direct stimulation of a rewarding system. A dolphin will stimulate his own brain in the rewarding systems for hours. When we shut off the current so that he can no longer self-stimulate by pushing a lever, he will immediately vociferate in spite of the fact that he has been quite silent while working with the lever. A human being will react similarly and ask, "Why do you shut off the current?" and then go on and make all sorts of remarks concerning the situation. But if one stimulates the negative systems, there is an obvious screaming terror and one has no alternative but to say that the two states are at opposite poles with regard to instinctual activities. The former leads to obtaining more of the stimulation and the latter leads to its termination: avoidance or escape from the stimulation. The first is intensely pleasurable; the second is intensely nonpleasurable: antipleasurable, painful, fearful, or anger-causing.

I call these "rebound" phenomena and visualize one possible explanation: during intense stimulation of one kind of system (A) the activity in the other kind of system (B) also increases but not in proportion: there are controlled two-way connections (A-B) between the two kinds of systems which become active. Hence, one kind of function (A) is existing in greater quantity than the other (B). If the intense stimulation then ceases in (A), the intense activity in (A) for a short time decreases more rapidly than the milder activity in (B). The activity in (A) may be less than is usual. For a time the activity in (B) is then more intense than that in (A), and the opposite function predominates.

There may be ways of so influencing the young vulnerable animal that one can cause the permanent lowering of the thresholds for starting and/or maintaining intense, continuing activities in either or both kinds of system. Such "programmatic" effects may generate the ultimate picture of the kinds of character; the choice of kind and form of psychosexual development; and the predominating algebraic sign of the personality, positive or negative. The total maintained activity in both kinds of systems without provocation may be the basic determinant of the "strength of instinctual drives" so necessary for challenge to and mastery by the developing ego. All of these systems, of course, are in the absolutely unconscious but psychodynamic parts of the mind: only by indirect means can their operations be influenced.

In the light of the above experiments and results, the concept of "cathexis" ("*Besetzung*") is still a useful one if we realize that the emotional "charges" can have two signs: positive (for a rewarding object or idea, etc.) and negative (for a punishing object, or idea). In pure form, a purely rewarding idea, process, person, or object is wanted again and again; a purely punishing one is rejected, retreated from, and destroyed. However, there are practically no such pure forms existing, except in fantasy, in dreams, in the unconscious, and in the primary process. The reality principle insists that one endow a means of starting a rewarding situation with a positive "reward" charge but that one also so endow the means of terminating negative punishing situations with a positive charge. A monkey loves (positive charge) his switch which he uses to *start* his rewarding stimuli, but he also loves the switch which he uses to *stop* the pain or fear stimuli. In the opposite modes, he dislikes (even hates) the person or apparatus which starts his fear or pain stimuli or similar objects which stop his rewarding stimuli. Signals associated with these various kinds of events take on charges of the same sign, somewhat attenuated. These are the simple reasonable logical combinations: repetitions cause only deepening and strengthening of the bonds and not the development of "perverse" values, such as taking intense pleasure in punishing situations, or hating or fearing pleasures.

In real life very few things, processes, or persons are either purely rewarding or purely punishing: the electric stimuli in the brain allow us to create the pure cases discussed. The psychic "cement" binding us to our images and to reality is positive to enable us to start work on them and is later negative to enable us to stop when enough has been done within physiological healthy limits. Probably the term "cathexis" should be redefined to encompass both aspects of our being bound by and our binding of psychic objects: "For now I want, need more, but soon I'll want it stopped." Each of these two aspects is an active process, each in its own brain system.

Such basic thinking can be applied to clinical and theoretical problems and may be helpful if one also applies all the other knowledge of psychoanalysis. The complexity of the experienced human animal is fantastically great; the above facts and formulations may eventually be integrated into our greater understanding of patients.

REFERENCES

1. Delgado, J.M.R., W.W. Roberts, and N.E. Miller, "Learning Motivated by Electrical Stimulation of the Brain," *Amer. J. Physiol.*, 179:587, 1954.
2. Freud, S., *Beyond the Pleasure Principle* (1920), London: Hogarth Press, Standard Edition, 18, 1955.
3. Hess, W.R., *Das Zwischenhirn*, Basel: Schwabe, 1949.
4. Kubie, L.S., "Some Implications for Psychoanalysis of Modern Concepts of the Organization of the Brain," *Psychoanal. Quart.*, 22:21–68, 1953.
5. Lilly, J.C., "True Primary Emotional State of Anxiety-Terror-Panic in Contrast to a 'Sham' Emotion or 'Pseudo-affective' State Evoked by Stimulation of Hypothalamus," *Astract/Fed/Proc.*, 16:81, 1957.
6. Lilly, J.C., "A State Resembling 'Fear-Terror-Panic' Evoked by Stimulation of a Zone in the Hypothalamus of the Unanesthetized Monkey," *Excerpta Medica*, 1957 (Abstracts of 1st Int. Cong. of Neurological Scs. and 4th Int. Cong. of EEG and Clin. Neuro-physiol., Brussels, July, 1957).
7. Lilly, J.C., "Learning Motivated by Subcortical Stimulation: the 'Start' and the 'Stop' Patterns of Behavior," *in: Reticular Formation of the Brain*, ed. H.H. Jasper *et al.*, Boston: Little, Brown, 1958.
8. Lilly, J.C., "Some Considerations Regarding Basic Mechanisms of Positive and Negative Types of Motivations," *Amer. J. Psychiat.*, 115:498, 1958.
9. Lilly, J.C., "Correlation Between Neurophysiological Activity in the Cortex and Short-Term Behavior in the Monkey," *in: Biological and Biochemical Bases of Behavior*, Madison, Wis.: University of Wisconsin Press, 1958.
10. Lilly, J. C., " 'Stop' and 'Start' Systems," *Neuropharmacology*, 1959 (Transactions of the 4th Macy Conf., Sept. 1957, ed. H.A. Abramson. Madison, N.J.: Madison Printing Co., 1959).
11. Livingston, W.K., *Pain Mechanisms*, New York: Macmillan, 1943.
12. Magoun, H.W., *The Waking Brain*, Springfield, Ill.: Charles C. Thomas, 1958.
13. Masserman, J. H., "Is the Hypothalamus a Center of Emotion?" *Psychosom. Med.*, 3:3, 1941.
13a. McLean, P., "Chemical and Electrical Stimulation of Hippocampus in Unanesthetized Animals, II, Behavioral Findings," *A.M.A. Arch. Neurol. Psychiat.*, 78:128, 1957.
14. Nauta, W.J.H., "An Experimental Study of the Fornix System in the Rat," *J. Comp. Neurol.*, 104:247, 1956.

15. Olds, J., "Self-Stimulation of the Brain; Its Use to Study Local Effects of Hunger, Sex and Drugs," *Science,* 127:315, 1958.

16. Olds, J., and P. Milner, "Positive Reinforcement, Produced by Electrical Stimulation of Septal Area and Other Regions of Rat Brain," *J. Comp. Physiol. Psychol.,* 47:419, 1954.

17. Ostow, M., "A Psychoanalytic Contribution to the Study of Brain Functions. I. The Frontal Lobes," *Psychoanal. Quart.,* 24:317, 1954.

18. Ostow, M., "A Psychoanalytic Contribution to the Study of Brain Functions. II. The Temporal Lobes," *Psychoanal. Quart.,* 24:383, 1955.

19. Penfield, W., and T. Rasmussen, *The Cerebral Cortex of Man,* New York: Macmillan, 1962.

20. Redmond, A., "Des acquisitions récentes de l'électro-encephalographie aux perspectives de la neurophysiologie clinique dans la compréhension du système nerveux et le traitement de ses maladies," *Le Concours Médical,* No. 1:19–32, Jan. 1958.

21. Sem-Jacobsen, C.W., "Depth Recording and Electrical Stimulation in the Human Brain," *First Conference on Electrical Studies on the Unanesthetized Brain,* ed. F.M. Forster, Washington, D.C. In press.

22. Sem-Jacobsen, C.W. Personal communication.

23. Sidman, M., J.V. Brady, J.J. Boren, D.G. Conrad, and A. Schulman, "Reward Schedules and Behavior Maintained by Intracranial Self-Stimulation," *Science,* 122:830, 1955.

*Lilly, John C., and Jay T. Shurley,** "Experiments in Solitude, in Maximum Achievable Physical Isolation with Water Suspension, of Intact Healthy Persons,"* Psychophysiological Aspects of Space Flight, *New York: Columbia University Press, 1961*

Originally, one of the aims of this investigation was to test the neurophysiological hypothesis that, in the drastic attenuation of physical stimuli below the usual level, the activity of the brain and its contained mind would be that of sleep. Findings in our experiments (1, 2) and in those of other groups (3, 4) in this field demonstrate that sleep is not necessarily the outcome over a short time period. A

* Dr. Lilly was Chief, Section of Cortical Integration, Neurophysiological Laboratory, Research Branch, National Institute of Mental Health, Bethesda, Md. He is now Director of the Communication Research Institute, St. Thomas, U.S. Virgin Islands. Dr. Shurley is on the staff of the Veterans Administration Hospital, Oklahoma City, Okla.

parallel, though not identical aim was to observe what, if any, effect such experimental conditions might have in altering ego function both in the present moment and over the longer time period, i.e., ego choices and ego structure. A more specific aim has been to establish methods of self-observation by finding, defining, and setting limits for the subject's psychological sets for these experiments and by seeking those sets which would give the maximum of information from the subjective sphere. The collection of data has been mainly by notes and recordings by the subject alone.

At the outset two conditions seemed essential, and these have been maintained throughout. All observers first prepare themselves by participating as subjects; those who participate in this experimentation first do so in the role of subject, then in the role of "safety-man" (observer), and, finally, in the role of self-observer in solitude. The second crucial condition is that of the restrained and minimal participation of the "safety man"; his role is to stay out of and not interfere with the phenomena which occur in the self-observer.

Technique

A systematic consideration of the technique illustrates how these aims are carried out in this particular set of experiments.

The Physical-Physiological Level

1. The simultaneous attenuation of all known external physical stimuli to the lowest possible level (including light, sound, odor, taste, light pressure, deep pressure, and other gravity-opposition forces, vibration, heat, cold, etc.). These characteristics of the experimental environment were achieved with relative success by use of a water immersion tank in a sound-proofed chamber.

2. The maximum simultaneous attenuation of intra-integumentary sources of stimuli which, in the order of importance in our experiments, have included low-level pain and discomfort because of an unsatisfactory position in the tank; muscle stretch; slow motions of limbs moving through the water; internal sources such as hunger; full bladder; full rectum; gas in the GI tract; unusually active cardiovascular system; local pressure ischemia leading to pain; irregular changes in respiratory rhythm, rate, or depth; accumulating carbon dioxide; reduction in oxygen.

3. The maintenance of a constrained and restrained situation voluntarily: obviously in a system such as the human body, efferent activity leads to afferent activity in a continuous and circular fashion; therefore in a suspension in a liquid the subject is instructed to voluntarily inhibit movement, including vocalizations, to his maximum possible ability.

4. Special case of skin temperature: We have found that thermal differences over the skin of the body are intensely stimulating when the other sources of stimuli have been attenuated. The use of water suspension (in which the water is slowly flowing by the body) allows an isothermicity of the unclothed skin surface which is difficult to achieve by other methods. At 34.5° C. (93° F.) the water seems to disappear in the thermal sense; i.e., the subject feels neither hot nor cold, and this temperature allows a steady state of heat exchange metabolism that can be achieved under these conditions. In addition, the slowly flowing water allows continuous removal of waste products of the body.

5. The position and suspension of the body in water: Because the body parts are not of uniform density it is necessary to add weight to certain parts and to add buoyancy or support to certain other parts. These additions are done in such a way as to avoid chronic low-level discomfort and pain caused by unusual degrees of angulation of spinal or other joints and that caused by pressure ischemia.

We found that the position of the body of each subject must be very carefully worked out in order to avoid low-level discomfort and pain. Unless this is done we found that we were studying the effects of a chronic low-level pain on our subjects in a relative absence of other sources of stimulation. If a given subject is exposed to too much pain for too long a period, the experiment becomes extremely distasteful to him. We do not feel that we have found the ideal method of buoyancy adjustment, and that a good deal more work could be done on this phase of the experiments, possibly by using liquids of two densities, one for the limbs and one for the chest and head, or possibly, by using a liquid of greater density than the fresh water which we have been using. In summary, water suspension allows most of the gravity-opposing forces to be distributed evenly over the whole surface of the body; thus the unit pressure is greatly decreased over any one area. Because fresh water of the proper temperature was available, we used this liquid.

6. The mask: Since the subject is suspended in the liquid, breath-

ing requires a mask with certain characteristics; (a) minimum inward pressures over the surfaces of the skin, (b) maximum sealing without undue local pressure, (c) minimum back- or fore-pressure during the respiratory cycle, and (f) as great a degree of equalization of the pressure in the mask with that over the chest as can be achieved. An approximation to the last requirement can be reached if the subject is suspended just below the surface of the liquid with his chest parallel to that surface so as to minimize pressure difference across the thoracic and abdominal walls while breathing air at one atmosphere from the room. Such an apparatus has the virtue of extreme simplicity and maximum control by the subject. We have employed a through-and-through breathing system with an inspiratory valve and an expiratory valve with two different tubes leading to the small space (approximately 100 cc) in the mask immediately in front of the nose and the mouth, breathing air at one atmosphere from the room. This system can be easily repaired by the subject and does not require as much maintenance as a more complicated, continuously flowing gas system at a higher pressure. However, again, we do not consider this ideal, and would prefer a very simple system operating at a higher pressure so that the subject could be less constrained as to depth of immersion.

Environmental Control at the Social and Community Level

1. The maintenance of physical-physiological isolation and solitude in the midst of a community implies barriers to intrusion by persons or sources of physical stimuli; i.e., such isolation implies that eventually one is in solitude (of course solitude per se does not necessarily imply physical isolation). Such consideration requires a building which houses the tank and constructed in such a way as to bar any continuous traffic through its structure and which permits no invasion by people or animals or other objects which may be sensed by the subject; a lock on the door is required but not sufficient. The safety man is instructed to act as a buffer agent for the subject, both before, during, and after the experiments and to maintain privacy. The safety man also must check the in-flowing water temperature, lights, telephone, etc.

2. The issue of privacy seems to us to be so important that we give it separate consideration here. Relevant privacy includes present and future communications including all of those between the subject

and the safety man. For optimal conditions privacy requires the firm assurance to the subject of his control of the secrecy of his individual data indefinitely into the future. Maximum ego freedom and voluntariness of the subject in these experiments can be achieved through such kinds of privacy. It also implies that the subject chooses his own times for beginning, ending, and the total duration of exposure as well as the control of whatever restraints, voluntary inhibitions, and supports are needed. Privacy also implies trust and respect for the ego of the subject on the part of the safety man; i.e., the elimination (or at least the attenuation) of any observer encroachment, exploitation, or invasion of each experience and of its data indefinitely (even to the extent of avoiding invited, available, encroachment by the subject).

When the safety man and the subject both consider it is safe for the subject to become a self-observer free of the safety man, i.e., to enter solitude, these matters must be considered with great intensity and care. It is at this point in our experience that the subject is likely to use disguised methods of appealing for help from the safety man, or from others, in one form or another. After the first few experiences it may help him as a self-observer to function as a safety man for another subject. The introduction of any new factors into the experiment (especially variables important to survival, such as changes in the respiratory apparatus) requires a self-observer to return to "subject status" temporarily and bring a safety man back into the situation.

Of course, privacy also implies that the abstraction of, and the distribution of, the results of the experiments are also under his control. In this regard one must consider all media of communication including gossip (professional and otherwise), newspaper accounts, scientific journal accounts, and scientific meetings. One keeps in mind possible future uses of the material by persons other than the subject; the revealed material is carefully scrutinized by the subject in order to contain only those observations and shorthand descriptions which contribute directly to the generalizations which are found. Minimal disguise of data allows maximal transmission of the true pictures of what occurs but are carefully balanced against what Freud called, in his communications of his self-analysis, "the point at which one owes discretion to oneself."

The future research plans are also maintained in privacy and are set up by those who have reached self-observer and safety man status. In functioning as safety man the necessity for certain specific plans and organization becomes apparent and obvious.

3. The process of selection of subjects: Normal, healthy volunteers of equal social and professional status to the previous subject-observers have been the source of our subjects. Neither much younger nor much older, higher or lower, persons are chosen in order to give maximum freedom to the particular person involved. This condition is required for the attenuation to our maximum ability of any factors which might resemble a draft, a persuasion, or coercing of the subject in his or our view. In addition, this process implies that not only each experiment or exposure but each series of exposures requires that social isolation be maintained. The fact that experiments may be going on is protected in the local community. This technique has been worked out as a result of provocative and disturbing experiences during the course of our experiments.

Scientific Method and the Self-Observer

Objections can be raised that under these rules an ego observing itself generates only circular data; i.e., that it experiences only what it wishes and allows itself to experience, and that the use of an outside observer can avoid such difficulties. We have found that these objections have a limited validity and for our purposes an outside observer inordinately complicates the situation and the data in which we are interested. Within certain limits yet to be determined experimentally, it seems to us that the mind is the only province of science in which what one believes to be true is, or becomes, true (5). Our experimental task in these studies is to determine what these limits are. However, it is felt that it is important to remember that one must give the subjects the permission to experience what *can* be experienced and not make suggestions as to what may or *will* be experienced.

It is our conviction that the range of phenomena available to the normal human mind is much greater than "society" will apparently permit or accept (1, 2, 5); consequently, the safety man becomes the intercessor between the individual and the community. As such, he grants the subject permission to experience whatever he can experience; i.e., the right to exercise any function, strictly leaving open the content of what is experienced. If you will, the individual is "indoctrinated" in the principle of freedom for his own ego with the internal experiential sphere. As is mentioned below, the results of such experiences in a given subject generally turn out to be surprising to that subject; i.e., so far as the subject is consciously aware, new data occur quite spontaneously.

Conclusions

Detailed results are to be reported in a later paper. However, some general conclusions of these studies may be of interest.

When given freedom from external exchanges and transactions, the isolated-constrained ego (or self or personality) has sources of *new information* from within. Such sources can be experienced as if they are outside with greater or lesser degrees of awareness as to where or what these sources are (projected imagery, projected sounds, doubling of body parts, emotional states of euphoria or anxiety, etc.).

Any other person, observer, or safety man can be made to appear as if he is a "source" to which is attributed the origin of the new information.

Transference-related drives may become extremely intense. In a given exposure, such needs increase in intensity with time and may ultimately demand direct release, such as leaving the tank and participating in one's active life with other persons (2, 5). Multiple exposures lead to better control and increased awareness of these effects.

The relationship of any residual stimulus to these needs is carefully evaluated. "Negative and positive" transference problems arise from extremely small and unlikely kinds of stimuli under these conditions; i.e., a "wrong" word, too many suggestions, implied judgments of accuracy or performance, or their "positive" opposites. The safety man must be, as it were, an ideal and keenly aware diplomat when faced with such problems. It has been found that having once experienced the lowest possible level of stimulation oneself makes it very much easier to function as a "diplomatic," tolerant, and considerate safety man. Hurt feelings, overenthusiastic reactions, and replication of experience reported by others are examples of the kinds of phenomena to be found and dealt with.

The positive, enjoyable results were achieved only at those times when the inner and the outer disturbing stimuli were minimizable. Any residual discomfort made it impossible to achieve the euphoric state; any anxiety induced by faulty apparatus or technique blocked the possibility of enjoying or profiting from the experience. Until we were able to attenuate physical discomfort and fear by better techniques, multiple exposures, and careful training, we saw mostly "negative" phenomena. As the levels of stimuli were lowered closer to zero, the positive, more blissful, enjoyable states and the positive transference phenomena appeared. No addiction to these states has occurred: the internal satisfactions of needs achieved in the tank are limited in the same sense that, say, day-dreaming is limited. Basic satisfactions of needs felt in the tank require later exchanges with other persons and with physical reality.

As has been published (1, 2), it is felt that such experiences are not necessarily psychotic, or even mentally aberrant, and after training can be constructive and invigorating. Eventually, after many exposures, each subject can learn enough to enjoy and not fear or dislike his own experiences.

REFERENCES

1. Lilly, J.C., "Effects of Physical Restraint and of Reduction of Ordinary Levels of Physical Stimuli on Intact, Healthy Persons," in *Illustrative Strategies for Research on Psychopathology in Mental Health*, Symposium No. 2, New York: Group for the Advancement of Psychiatry, 1956.
2. Lilly, J.C., "Mental Effects of Reduction of Ordinary Levels of Physical Stimuli on Intact, Healthy Persons, *Psychiatric Research Reports 5*, American Psychiatric Assoc., Washington, D.C. 1–28, June 1956.
3. Heron, Woodburn, "The Pathology of Boredom," *Scientific American*, 196:52–56, 1957.
4. Bennett, A.M.H. Personal communication.
5. Lilly, J.C., "Some Considerations Regarding Basic Mechanisms of Positive and Negative Types of Motivations, *Am. J. Psychiat.*, Dec. 1958.

Journal Abstracts from the Chilean Desert, Oct. 22, 1970 (Personal Diary of John C. Lilly, M.D.)

Now for a careful consideration of the assumptions of Oscar and the "School":

Assumptions:

1) God exists: is One; creates all; started all; trinity (Fa & Mo), H.S., Son.

2) Humans can pray and be answered (inspiration, illumination, secret knowledge, omniscience, satoris).

3) "Connection" can be achieved between a human and Holy Spirit—Holy Love—an energy called baraka.

4) Connection is achieved through *exercises* (concentration, meditation, gym); through *prayer* (Forgive me my sins, etc.); through *objective positions* (humility, innocence, mudras, etc.); through *mentations* and deviation study; through *protoanalysis* of ego according to fixation type and declinations (on eneagrams); through *ego death*, removal of Shaitan; through *objective mantras* (aum, ram, etc.); through desert solitude, silence for long periods.

5) This above (and more) is called "objective reality," objective knowledge by O.I. There is another way of looking at all this, which I prefer. Basically, the initially premises (axioms, assumptions, beliefs) are the above plus eneagram arrangements of concepts, such as Virtues–Ideas–Instincts–Games–Fixations–Passions.

O.K. Feed in this system of thinking-feeling-being to a biocomputer, isolate it in solitude, confine in the desert and certain states of consciousness occur which can be named in this system satori 24, 12, 6 or 3, "connection," etc.

Watching Oscar, I see an intensity of concentration and belief which is rare in my experience; he shakes with his own energy. His sincerity is hard to match. He really believes in these assumptions as true, objectively true. I have reached a saturation point at which I cannot stomach this way of thinking at all. My mood is to reject it and start over. O.K. What do I feel *is* true?

(One thing I've arrived at here in the desert: I am one of my species —humankind—my place is only definable with mankind; in mankind is the only place in the universe I can make any sense; within the human limits I exist—so make the best of it one can.)

So far, I feel the following are true:

Oscar:

1) Oscar has a strong influence on me, on the group.
2) He is patient; he waits; he expects results, says so.
3) He pushes, he expects, but doesn't test obviously.
4) He believes he controls each individual by his own prayers and meditations, without that person being present; says so.

5) He persuades with soft voice of reasonableness in presence of expressed doubts.

6) He works hard, is humble but strong, expresses thanks for expressed appreciation.

7) He is sympathetic in the presence of pain-fear-grief, but persists in saying the system cures all that.

8) He says it's all a science, to be transplanted into U.S. and modern scientific terminology by those who know, who experience full trip and experiences.

9) I think he knows and can recognize false witnessing of inner experience: he picks up fakery rapidly, but may be too delighted too quickly at initial experience and express this delight too strongly, thus killing repetition. I would prefer, I think, a more judicious evaluation.

10) There are real phenomena which occur: I have experienced many: see Aug. state "12," for example.

11) His programming is good for trips; his empirical handling, separate from his theory, *is* good, excellent.

12) Oscar has the habit of speaking of methods in the Satori as if one were out of Satori—it doesn't apply out of the state—only in the state.

Phenomena:

1) Satori 3, 6, 12, 24: these names for states consciousness are useful for discussion purposes, "headings" only. Each one is a vast area.

2) The concept of "vibration levels" (96, 48, 24, 12, 6, 3, 1) is not very precisely defined except as phenomena of the Satori state.

3) *In* one of these states, phenomena occur (like reverberation of sound, of meaning, of body sensations, of visual phenomena, etc.) which can be squeezed into "vibration" but it isn't precise (yet).

4) *In* one of these states, one's beliefs are different than out of the state. (I'm not sure this is necessary: it seems that way so far.)

5) Doing exercises in the states has a very different meaning and experience than doing them out of the state (creative state: each time new meanings?).

6) Another system of getting into these states is needed (one began in my workshops—mentations, music, repetitions, isol.-sol.-conf. work).

7) Of what Oscar programs, what are the basic factors inducing

change of state? Self-analysis of past states; freedom to work in a school not at home; time for work.

Special Factors Which Work (cont.):

Special consideration of evasions and blocks against changing one's state of consciousness (in full daylight, without drugs, without sleep-loss, without fatigue, in the presence of other persons—non-hostile, non-threatening).

The ability to revise one's basic assumptions-beliefs about one's states of consciousness, to accept change in consciousness without clamping-off and evading the changes, the self-confidence of full responsibility for changes to and from special states.

The ability to not become enamoured of one or several states and their explanation, their meaning in religious terms as a "be-all, end-all here" faith.

A Different Set of Assumptions-Beliefs:

1) Humans are evolved on planet earth, terrestrial, dry land, featherless, handed bipeds with brains 1/6 that of a sperm whale.

2) In the brain, in the body, are several sets of receiving organs and sending organs, some designed for reception-transmission of physical (at present known in Western science) energies (light, heat, sound, vibration, pressure, touch, body position, gravity).

3) Other sets of receive-transmit organs (x) are not yet discovered in Western science, nor is the set of energies received-transmitted (? matter waves, neutrino receivers, etc.).

4) Within the physical (at present known) set of energies, certain patterns of stimulation-transmission are not known, are not named; there are no pattern recognition programs in our language of the West for these patterns.

5) By proper re-training outside of present Western conceptions, by shaking up entrenched belief-assumptions (through s.i.c., etc.), by emoting and abandoning favorite evaders (attachment and repulsions) of change in self, one can activate organs X of transmission-reception, can activate or develop new pattern recognition programs with names.

6) Once one has done this, one can see-feel-be new phenomena on the other side of W. James' filmiest of screens.

7) Among these phenomena are streaming energies between organisms, from the planet, from the sun, from stars and galaxies.

8) Other intelligent entities-beings are seen—communicated with.

9) Communication networks between civilizations more evolved than ours are tuned in and information received and transmitted with them.

10) All of this has always been true: certain individuals have tuned in and know how to do all this; their theories and explanations and beliefs are primitively religious and inadequate for training scientists to investigate thoroughly. (Ecstasy is hardly the state for creating anything but joy and fun: science of ecstasy is not with us yet).

So I do not have to "do a Claudio" and swallow uncritically Oscar's traditional assumptions-beliefs to do his trip; as before with LSD 1964 I did not swallow the old psychiatric beliefs and found new knowledge; so with Oscar I do not need to believe in his system—just do the trip and work on theory on my own. Nor do I have to reject out of hand his theory and belief—look and learn what it is that generates his beliefs-theory. He's reasonable and hence his experience and theory have some relations, even as Freud's (bad) theory did to his empirical work. It's what Oscar *does*, not what he *says* that's true and worth study.

Observations on What Oscar *Does* (not what he *says*):

1) He does a lot of *sitting*: crossed legs, ½ lotus, lotus.

2) He closes his eyes a lot, sitting.

3) He rolls his eyes up as he closes them.

4) He remains upright (against the wall at home), sitting for long periods.

5) He apparently does not move for minutes to hours.

6) He does mantra, pampas exercises, meditations, jnana-yoga exercises, prayers, for hours—days—weeks—years.

7) He changes his state of consciousness fairly rapidly in sitting position, also lying down (he says).

8) He sleeps 1½ hrs. 2 times/night; does night meditations, prayers.

9) He travels to see individuals separately a lot of the time; he gets intensely involved with them; sits with them.

10) He sits and does exercises with group: mantras, prayers, etc.

11) He lectures at blackboard to group.

12) He does serious ceremonies with individuals and with groups.

13) He enjoys music, jokes, watching dancing, movies such as "2001."

14) He enjoys telling what he knows, hearing new ideas.

15) He enjoys hearing about individual experiences, esp. satoris.

16) He learns by pragmatic experiences.

17) He does certain things with fantastic seriousness, theatrical mien, esp. as he changes state from here to satori.

I feel that Oscar's ability to change state is partly because of his *concentration abilities;* he can cut off outside stimuli, he can still his body, he can calm his thinking, he can allow the states to occur and he can pre-program them (plus 20 yrs. of work).

So Now to Work on Concentration-Contemplation (Patanjali):

10:20 P.M. Went for walk 2–5 P.M. across the pampas, down 1000 meter face to beach at end of road from Arica. Very steep, difficult. Almost fell near top getting back up: too steep, dangerous, dropped shells when slipped; they slid down. More depth and allowing in grief (continued!): we are so small, I am so small, live here so short a time; the galaxy is so huge; the planet is so huge. I am so arrogant— me and my species! I grieve for me, for us. Oscar's trip—to contact God—seems too arrogant—God is too immense to bother with little me, little us, living on a thin layer scattered over a large planet manu- facturing myths to make us important. I tried to leave human- kind.

So what's left to me? *Play the human game within humankind to the best of my ability—within mankind—within our limits—*(that's Oscar's Sobriety, I guess) to the very best I am capable of (that's Perfection and Freedom in the Holy Law, of Oscar). The origin of us I leave unanswered (Oscar's Holy Originality is too obvious, simple and short-circuits the major questions of our origins). "Omniscience" is arrogant nonsense; we are incapable of knowing all: within limits, yes, we can know-be, but within our limits only—maybe that's "omni- science"—knowing everything within our limits! Faith? In what, us? My faith is sadly lacking in anything beyond us, at this point. I hope there is, are, others here too. This is my faith—in Others beyond us, eventually detectable and communicable.

Sobriety—staying within our limits—rather, finding our limits.

Innocence—yes, the direct innocence of childhood—here and now —me and thee—the planet—the stars—the galaxy—all in newness and joy and innocence. Love—of one another, of the quest, of the planet, of others, dolphins and still others beyond.

To assume "God," to assume "prayer," to assume "connection"—all seem shorthand for states of consciousness for experiences inside, for solitude-isolation trips. These words short-circuit and oversimplify what is real and what exists. Maybe he's right and I'm wrong—but maybe we are both right. He, with his education and background uses these terms to express real experiences for him—I block because I've explored these concepts to their depth and found them arrogantly shallow: for me. With similar experiences (I hope I can have them!) *I can re-formulate in a more scientific and operational language what happens and how to get there. I must do my own work* (as always), *and study the results from my own knowledge* and not lean on Oscar or his theories as be-all and end-all. Otherwise I may as well quit this trip right now. I need time and no pressure from Oscar: he pushes: with solitude-isolation and with programming. He's a programmer! He's enthusiastic and a bit arbitrary—doesn't explain to me what he's doing, I'm doing. He's the Qutb, the Master —the traditional geheimrat professor of Europe and the East. He's to be educated about me, an American of independent mind and means. I have never uncritically accepted anyone's teaching or knowledge: I won't start now with Oscar.

Lilly, John C., "Basic Problems in Education for Responsibility Caused by LSD 25," Chap. 17 from Approaches to Education for Character, *edited by Clarence Faust and Jessica Feingold, New York: Columbia University Press, 1969*

The rising number of young persons taking LSD 25 (lysergic acid diethylamide) brings in its wake many of the older problems faced by parents and educators in regard to the development of those factors which we epitomize in the word "responsibility." One view of responsibility is that of an inner discipline which directs the activities of the self toward attainable and idealistic goals. These goals may be directed so as to be strictly personal or they may be directed for others than one's self. The goals may be connected with only a few persons or large numbers of persons.

In the matrix of our civilization each one of us has multiple exchanges and responsibilities for many different aspects of that civilization. Each of us has a more or less fluid reference point within the structure of society. Most of us are regulated in detail by taxation, by income, by available work, by husband, by wife, by children, by parents, by governments, large and small. Each of these separate agents and agencies exacts its toll of time, effort, and money from each of us. Each of these agents and agencies has ways of enforcing its toll upon each one of us in the absence of a response and continuing responsibility from each one of us toward each one of them.

As each human being grows from the nonspeaking little animal that is born into this world to the responsible adult with his own family, he is required to expand his responsibility to the outside world again and again. Only when responsible people judge him to be unfit to accept further responsibility does the pressure to expand the areas of his responsibility decrease. There are times when one has the feeling that irrespective of the desires of the individual this inexorable process continues throughout his life.

Inside each person there is an answering to these external calls to duty. At each stage the individual tests the system to see what its limits are and how much he must respond with appropriate action, thinking, and dedication. At each young stage the various kinds and forms of evasions of responsibility are tried to the limits possible to that particular person and either rejected or further espoused, depending upon the inner satisfaction generated by the evasive action.

The evasions for the young usually take the form of pursuing the most pleasurable paths and staying away from those which are found to be unpleasant or painful. However, as one grows older and more experienced, the pleasure and pain have become more than physiological experiences and have begun to attach themselves to concepts, to persons, to institutions, to real things, and to distant goals. Then one's brain has enlarged enough and become experienced enough in controlling the algebraic sign of the emotional value (plus or minus) of various systems of thinking and successes within those systems; the basic structure for responsibility has been achieved. The responsible strong self-directed individual with dedication and interest in improvement of self and in widening his areas of responsibility is the person we should keep in mind in the rest of this discussion.

Let us look at a distribution curve of responsible persons; at one end those of minimal responsibility and the other end those of maximal responsibility. This curve of the number of people with each degree of responsibility varies with quite a large number of parameters. It varies with age, with economic level, and with educational level achieved. Some of these individuals are selected by the educational system for the very factor which we are discussing: i.e., the more responsible individuals with intelligence will either continue their education and complete it or will have found what they are looking for outside this system of education and have accepted responsible jobs on which they start their life's work. As John Gardner says in his book *Excellence* (Harper & Row, New York, 1961) there is no a priori reason that all those with intelligence, responsibility, and dedication should pass through the college system. There are other means of reaching social and national responsible positions than through college. Gardner points out that we have people on arbitrary scales of value, placing those who have loafed their way through college higher than those who have achieved in large measure through a self-education regime. The latter makes a more valuable person than the former.

All of these considerations are relevant to the present fashion for taking LSD 25. The recent spate of bad press having to do with college students taking LSD, the withdrawal of the Sandoz Company from supplying the drug, and the new controls of the Federal Food and Drug Administration and the National Institute of Mental Health underscore this problem. One might ask: Who is responsible with regard to LSD? Where lies the responsibility for educating for responsibility with regard to LSD itself?

This is a very difficult problem. In my opinion the abdication of responsibility for LSD and similar substances started in the early days (in the 1950s) when certain people began to take these substances and report their experiences in the scientific and nonscientific literature. Using the "20/20 vision of hindsight," let us reconstruct what seems to have happened with regard to LSD over the past fifteen or so years.

First of all the effects of these substances have been known for a long time. The naturally occurring plants and fungi which are the biochemical factories for these substances have been around literally millions of years. Man has incorporated some of these into past religious rites and certain "pagan" groups have used them with telling effect in their religious rituals. In so far as we can discover, each of these groups has had to face the problem of discipline with regard to the use of these substances. A current and cogent example of the achievement of discipline in order to control the use of these substances is the Native American Church, with the peyote cult. The history of this group has been recounted many times. From the published accounts we can deduce that responsible use was achieved within the confines of a religious setting.

It may be that responsible use of these substances cannot be achieved without some sort of strictures in the direction of the religious aspects. A religious transformation of the individual may be a step on the way toward achievement of inner responsibility to himself. Let us move from the religious viewpoint to what one might call a more basic philosophical viewpoint in which one attempts to explore the basic beliefs that a given individual has and on which he really operates. In this context we will try to ignore the tendency of most persons to say that they believe certain things, whereas in reality they act as if they believe quite something else. In this context we are speaking of only those basic beliefs which are operationally, demonstratively existent in the behavior and in the accomplishments of the individual.

Basic beliefs are here defined as that set of basic postulates which can be demonstrated to be operative through long study and careful analysis of the behavior, writings, and vocal productions of a given individual. It is this basic structure of the individual and of his feeling-thinking machinery in which we seek the basis for responsibility and the education for responsibility.

It is this basic set of beliefs which controls the effects of LSD on the person and on what he does, thinks, and produces during the LSD state. It is these basic beliefs which can apparently be unearthed (and possibly even changed) during the LSD state. This is the desirable and at the same time the perilous aspect of LSD and of its control. The temptation to elicit, to control, and to change the beliefs of others and even of one's self at times is a seductive goal. Apparently LSD puts this power in the hands of those who use LSD. But this may be a delusion. LSD may release mechanisms for the construction of self-deluding beliefs.

LSD allows a person to take himself apart, as it were, and look at separate areas of belief independently of beliefs about those areas, i.e. independently of his meta-beliefs. For example, if one believes, even temporarily, that one is a god in the LSD state, one becomes a god in his own imagination. One becomes one's concept of a kind of god, how powerful, how omniscient, etc., how knowledgeable a god one can be. Under the LSD state one is no longer influenced by the usual meta-belief, "I am in a class of animals known as Homo Sapiens, not in a class above the animal class and known as gods." In the LSD state one can ignore what one knows in one area and construct a belief about another area contradicting the first and have freedom to carry out many of the logical consequences. It is of no matter how irrational or how out of step the belief is with reality or with other belief systems nearby in self. In this sense LSD can be thought of as facilitating the genesis of psychosis itself rather than causing mimicking of psychosis.

The ability to hold a very powerful nonrational belief in mind and act as if it is true within one's own mind is one aspect of psychosis. If and when the LSD state or similar states persist beyond the expected limits of six to ten hours with the known pure diethylamide substance, then may one begin to suspect that other biochemical and neurological mechanisms are activated which might possibly be similar (if not identical) to those occurring during "true psychosis."

However, since LSD 25 has been called "psychotomimetic" quite early in the analysis of its effects, we are left with this history of the "psychotomimetic drug." This judgment acts as a programming agent for all subsequent work with LSD 25. This is embedded in the literature, it is embedded in the guiding agencies for its investigation, it is embedded in the public mind and wherever one turns one is faced with this tradition of "psychotomimesis."

(A rather amusing sidelight occurred with respect to this particular view of the perils of LSD. A well-known psychiatrist was approached by a woman who was worried about what LSD might do to her mind and brain. She had been reading the literature and had read the work of this particular man. She questioned him. He answered, "I have written that LSD causes psychosis and I am sure that it does for a period of at least four to eight hours." She said, "And what do you mean by 'psychosis'?" At that point the psychiatrist's wife interrupted and said, "Let me tell you a little story which will illustrate what he means by the word 'psychosis.' One night he came home from the laboratory complaining that he was getting some sort of virus disease. I asked him to describe his symptoms in detail: as he began to describe the symptoms it suddenly occurred to him that these were the symptoms of the LSD state. He then thought back during the day and discovered that by accident he had apparently absorbed some LSD. At this point he said, 'Oh, it's just an LSD psychosis. I am going to bed and sleep it off,' which he did.")

This story illustrates what a strong-minded, self-disciplined and responsible individual thinks about the effects of LSD on himself. There are weaker individuals who are precipitated into a "real," difficult-to-reverse psychosis by the drug experience; there are many such persons and we cannot be too careful with such individuals.

Another idea which has grown up around the use of LSD was started about the same time the psychotomimetic viewpoint was promulgated. This is the "religious revelation" aspect of the drug. This aspect has done as much of a disservice to our understanding of what is going on as has "psychotomimesis." We cannot take responsibility for "religious transcendental experiences" scientifically. Each of these phenomena is placed a little bit beyond the reach of proper scientific investigation.

But once again this is the state of our present knowledge. "LSD causes mimicking of psychosis, LSD can cause religious transcendental experiences."

Support has been given to both of these points of view by innumerable books writing up personal experiences under LSD 25. I call your attention to the books by Jane Dunlap, Constance Newland, M. G. Bishop, those by Aldous Huxley, and by Timothy Leary, Richard Alpert and Ralph Metzner.

If only LSD 25 and its effects could be accounted for fully by these points of view, the scientific work would not be as difficult as it is. If we could only go along with these "wishful thinking" views of the effects, if we could go along with those who saw only these things when they took the substance, then our work would not be very difficult. We could agree that the explanations were adequate and we could drop the whole subject. But somehow these explanations are scientifically unsatisfactory. Somehow they seem to have led to "mental absolutes" which, to this author at least, seem unreasonable. What I see in the writings of these two aspects of the effects of LSD on the human mind is that I am reading long accounts of the details of the wishful thinking of each of the authors. I do not say that this is irresponsible reportage of inner events. I believe that these people are sincere, straightforward, and disciplined along their own lines. However, each one of them is giving us that which they wish most to be true.

One can summarize my viewpoint of this literature by saying that these elaborate constructs reflect two things from each of these persons: (1) the contents of their own memory recombined in a free associational way, and (2) the realization of their most secret and hoped-for set of goals with regard to their own basic beliefs, in so far as these could be accomplished within their own heads (Jerome S. Bruner and C. C. Goodman).

The social effects of these writings and others like them include a rather devastating and widespread seduction of young minds toward the taking of LSD 25. The promise of "ecstasy" and "religious transcendence" to some of the youngsters is very seductive. To others the promise of "psychotic experience" is equally seductive. Let us not forget that today adventure still beckons to the young and that this rather old frontier of the mind is now being opened up by LSD and other such substances for the perusal of those seeking adventure, both for pleasure and for danger.

According to the clinical reports from various psychiatric outpatient departments connected with universities, most of the people who are getting into trouble with LSD and similar substances are between the ages of approximately seventeen years and twenty-five, i.e., college and graduate students. A sufficient number of these students have read the writings above and have established a peer mythology with regard to these writings to the point where there is a subculture built up around these substances. I have spoken with several of these youngsters and was left with the impression that the motives involved are quite complex and worthy of a good deal of further study. In the light of this kind of experience, it is high time that we instituted a thorough and widespread scientific investigation of what is going on among these youngsters.

Let us now turn to some other possibilities with regard to LSD 25 and the state that it produces. Let us try to arrive at objective and scientific views of its effect upon the mind. This is indeed not easy but I believe that it is important to try.

The objective, dispassionate, and thorough investigation of states of mind induced by these substances is a primary requirement for science for the next few years. We cannot eliminate the subjective report as a source of data. We should not allow subjective reportage to become merely an artistic and romantic medium for use only by novelists and artists. The science of a mentality as reported by that mentality has been neglected in academic science for many years. The encouraging increase in cognitive psychology within certain academic institutions is to be applauded, and hopefully, expanded.

The subjective aspects of one's own mental functioning in adolescence is incredibly important to one's self. Many youngsters seek guidance, seek help and seek education in this world of the subjective and do not obtain much help from science.

The failure of science to explore this area is expressed in the present problem with LSD 25 among these same youngsters. The only maps of the territories they have are those of the artists, theologians, and psychiatrists who preceded them in the LSD 25 state. I feel these youngsters do not need maps so much as they need a catalog of possible maps and an estimate of the probabilities of the occurrence of certain kinds of maps in this area, and maps of the dead ends and lethal traps.

In order to construct a set of ideas which may be of help to us in educating the young in regard to the inner life with special reference to the LSD 25 state, first of all let us say that the species of Beings (beasts, plants, and other living intelligent and non-intelligent creatures) which one may come upon in the LSD state, have a much more flexible "zoological science" to them than does the zoology of real animals. Since the "creatures seen, felt, heard," and the "beings thought to and thought from" under LSD are literally constructs of one's own mind, the limitations in the "mental zoology and botany" are only those of one's own imagination and of the elements stored within one. From the multitude of materials in one's own memory, one can construct through imagination any conceivable apparently living breathing kind of creature. One can construct thinking machines or thinking beings or other people with any desired set of characteristics and any desired set of powers, within the limits of one's own conceptions.

So in essence how does the LSD state differ from ordinary dreaming, ordinary daydreaming, and wishful thinking in general? It differs in the greater brilliance and the greater intensity of the projected visual images and in the greater intensity of the feelings aroused, coupled with these images, sights, and sounds. It is as if this substance puts a noisy amplifier in one's computer, an amplifier of the emotive and cognitive processes of one's mind, by means of LSD 25. This noisy amplifier gives one the subjective impression of increased powers of control over one's own thinking processes. But this is a false impression caused by the energy of the added random noise. One may not have such control but one has the impression that one does. This effect under the influence of this drug may be caused by the forced turning inward of one's self, away from a less interesting external reality and paying more attention to one's own highly active inner processes excited by the noise. A primary effect seems to be as if one's rewarding brain systems are stimulated and the punishing systems inhibited.

The important cautions, then, are that LSD 25 has a seductive history, and causes states of mind which are so seductive the subject wants to return for further experiences. Importantly the subject is wide open to influence, is very vulnerable in this state. He becomes very programmable by other persons. He is quite at the command of his own pleasurable desires and his own wishful thinking in greater measure than is comfortable to contemplate.

Long-term subtle psychological damage may result; such damage may long be hidden by the pleasure and enthusiasm engendered by the substance. It is possible that in the long-term use brains are structurally damaged. Thus subjects may be weakened by this substance —attacked literally where they live. Subjects are being seduced by a chemical rewarding of mental life without working for the reward. The new stimuli for the new lotus-eaters are subtle and subtly evasive, hiding insight itself under unearned chemical rewards given gratis.

Is education for responsibility possible with the use of such chemicals? I don't know. I'm interested, and am trying to understand. Who has taken responsibility? No one, so far. A phantasy of attaining a goal, a mental imagining of achieving a goal, fully biochemically rewarded, may become a fixed belief, a way of life. I don't like the feel of it. It's wrong, somehow.

POEMS

RES, THE LAWCOURT REALITY
7 Sept. 1969

Res is the thing, the real, a lawcourt.
What is so real as being in front of a court as defendant?
Those others in the court are human, I hope.
But they play an old honored game, as if not humane.
They use procedures, rules adapted to win or lose.
Win or lose what?
Everything in consensus group reality—money, property,
    wife, child, mistress, reputation, power.
Up against power, into court I go, propelled by lawyers.
The true nature of the game, the real rules cloaked
    in jargon, appalls my naïve mind.
I shudder, shake, wish for more power, money, better lawyers—
    thus wishing, I fall into their game.
I lose.
By their judgment I am depleted of money, power, repute.
Why play? To lose? Why play to lose this game?
Outside this game are other games, to avoid this one.
Direct messages of direct feeling—goodwill, friendship,
    the right people, the right activities.
Another reality, not res, the thing, the lawcourt.
Love everlasting, right living, right friends.
Trusting Them, out there, I go on.

SELF-METAPROGRAM: MONEY
8 Sept. 1969

Money is what? Where does it come from, go?
Each is born—no money.
Each is raised—money? Pennies, nickels, dimes.
Older—quarters.
Suddenly—dollars.
Parents' money to each, to me.
My money—not hers, not his.
Candy, comics—I give money—I get—*my* things.
I buy for my girl; she gives.
Buy, sell, give, for love of others.
Facilitator, friendship, credit: services,
Incoming $, outgoing $.
Bank account.
Books kept by bank, by me.
Credit: mine, theirs.
So I'm paid to do what *they* want me to do.
So I pay others to do what I want done.
I pay government—unless I do—they take.
Things for money.
Money for things.
Service for money.
Money for service.
Love for money.
Money for love—love of money, money of love.
I am a money valve: it goes through me.
Money in, money out.
Too much in, or too much out: bad.
Just enough in, just enough out: good.
But keep money out less than money in.
A must.
But how judge future, money in—money out?
How much?
Hold some over, somehow, for future of avoiding
    too-little-in, too-much-out.

Money flows unless held.
Money held grows (I hope!).
Money spent is gone.
Money held is future.
Past commitments use up present held money.
Here and now no outgoing money promises.
Here and now income promises, future income,
    through services, not things.
Here and now, no things for money, at least, minimize.
Here and now minimum bought services,
    maximum friendship performance.
Future credit to me,
Through love, and awareness of this program.
Minimize clothes, washing them.
Minimize body care: just enough.
Maximize humor, love, friends.
Maximize creative communication of needs, to those who
    can help.
Let Them out there know, too.
Go with their programming—
    They help with coincidence control—
When you are aware of need-service-money,
And minimize your own need of money for self use without others.

WITNESS ME
9 *Sept. 1969*

I wish to tell you, my reader, what it is, who I am, who they are, when and where. I wish—but cannot tell the truth, objectively. In me is an editor, a judge, a jury, a missionary, a rebel, several small children, a woman, a man, parents, a small heaven, a large hell, and various spirits, witches, goblins, saints, sinners, heroes, a scientist, a lover, and a fear of this crowd.

The fear is that I'll go under, be lost as one or another of these crowdy "me's" gained control over poor little me, the real me, crouching afraid in the corner of this roomy head on my body. Somewhere there must be a real me: the one who gives in to the judge and jury, the one who listens and becomes the contrite sinner as the judge pronounces sentence. Escaping judgment, am I the missionary, secure in fantasied virtue, proclaiming the mission for the rest? The rebel, skeptical, dissents from the mission. Which is true me, the rebel disclaiming—the missionary proclaiming? I've preached, rebelled, and preached, and then researched the mission. The scientist, safe in his fantasied objectivity, researching that outside self, pushes his mission on others, preaches a new science here and a new science there. Am I he? Making science judgments now?

There must be a hard core me, a deep essence, somewhere.

Am I a father to my children? I ran from wives and hence from children. Why, where, to what, to whom? To another wife, another child? Are one of my inner children in control seeking mommy again? But I am mom too, inside me. Love my child in me, mother in me. Love my child, father in me.

COMMUNICATION IN COSMIC NOISE
8 Sept. 1969

I am paid to assure others are paid for what they do,
Their survival is my work.
They need to know, to survive.
I teach and example them to their best path.
I teach only how to find each his own best path
    in our common enterprise.
So I must learn how to teach them.
How to teach them how to seek.
Their seeking is released, is their own.
Criteria of seeking—
Spaces for release of creative seeking,
To seek, to find, to know.
To know where and when I don't know;
To ask others—best one for help, then.
To seek the unknown, to get past an ignorant point.
To know the unknown, not project false pictures
    on the blackness of the unknown.

To see messages where they are true messages,
  not noise distorted into messages.
To analyze noise, find a message dim and weak.
To amplify the weak message till it's clear.
But remember, noise contains all possible
  projection messages inside one's self.
So to hear-see messages, minimize noise,
  the noise of self, the noise of others, cosmic noise.
So tune-in carefully with minimum bandwidth of self of others.
So, with minimum bandwidth, go slow—
  you can't hear-see faster than the bandwidth
  or you project meaning not in it.
Slow messages, analyzed over long time, are the only
  true messages: repetition helps clarify.
Automatize the analyzer, use full clear storage,
  play-back slowed down.
Use fast storage below levels of awareness.
Time to compute—without self interfering.
Play back slow, look, feel, get message
  as far as one can.
Store results, partial message, with some skeptical charge on it.
A little doubt added in store to recapture later partials
  after further computing.
Leave in compute-store for a delta time, playback, look
  again—recycle till clear message.

CONTRACT: ME AND THEE
12 Sept. 1969

Do you want to live with me, I with you?
If we do so want, let us see.
If we live dyadically, then we interlock.
We share joy in sexual ways.
We talk of likes and dislikes.
I, without knowing, take on some of yours.
You, mine.

I look at him, her, and hear echoes of your opinion,
    as if my own.
You look at him, her, and hear mine as if yours.
We share our human maps of humans.
Each takes on, one the other's maps.
Do I like-wish to have your maps without awareness ?
Do you like-wish to have mine?
In you, maps for yourself, do you have
    transcendence of your today's self and your today's maps?
If not, forget me, us.
If so, let us see together if you wish
    and work to transcend you, and if
    I wish and work to transcend me.
Can we together transcend the us, of now?
Where, when, how?

TO A BROTHER AND FAMILY
7 Sept. 1969

I put myself outside your home, as if a cage.
When young and eager, I knew not joy in cagement,
My spirit called me out of your town, away from home.
On my return thirty-six years later now I know.
No rebel I today; I feel grieve that warmth solidity.
Your home, your children I love, appreciate as one
    from outside the walls of love and humor you built.
The law, the profit, the fiscal response-ability you all show.
It's beautiful.
An artistic creation of long years of loving interaction.
I admire what you do, have done, where you are.
I wish, and turn away from wishful thinking.
I cannot rewrite history, my own, or of others.
Much I "could have done, but did not."
Much I "did but regret having done."
Much I "should have done, but did not."
Much I did and do not regret, am glad I did.
Where I am I do not know. I am told now what to do.

Someone somewhere, I believe, now tells me.
I hope They wish me well and do not test me to destruction.

SUPRA-SELF FAIR WITNESS
7 Sept. 1969

The crowd in me can become Me, organized into
    a better business, a better me.
The Me, administering them, must somehow respect admire
    love each one—but first know each.
This new Me, is to become Fair Witness to the rest.
Not judge, not jury, not missionary, not saint-sinner,
    not scientist-system-researched, not child afraid.
Fair Witness watches and waits.
Fair Witness records truly recalls exactly.
Fair Witness reports to Me what I do, have done, think, feel,
    thought, felt.
Uncontaminated testimony, clear bright knowing,
    unprejudging, non-censoring.
Discomfort, pain, fear from hearing the clean bright
    truth?
To be fair to the Fair Witness requires me to be the
    Fair Witness, with no negativity-positivity, just *being.*
Being the Fair Witness.

HERE AND NOW, WITHOUT THEE
19 Sept. 1969

Where are you now? Not with me, away.
There's an ache, a longing, an empty place.
When you are near you fill something.
That something is blankness now.
I grieve, I cry, I try to fill the something.

I seek others—they can't fill.
I seek another, smother her, pull away.
She's not you, who have filled that place.
To seek, to find another: can I?
I can, but something won't yet let go of you.
The limbo of me, of you, far away.
Why a limbo?
You left, planning your trip, extending it.
What secret thing in you needed the trip?
I did not ask the secret. I do not ask now.
I cannot invade your private reasons.
They are yours, not mine, not ours.
I watched you grow, planning your trip.
Your growth I felt and cherished.
We played the game of letting each other.
Letting go, adult acceptance of adult decision.
The cost I feel, the cost I pay, for letting.
Brief regrets—but there was no alternate path,
I thought.
You travel around the planet's surface, all the way.
I am anchored here, committed to remain here.
We are split into two, one traveling.

SOLO TRANSCENDENCE
19 Sept. 1969

Programming transcendence—How?
Here I am, in this grievous body, beat by me, by years.
When can I leave it, leave this me you know?
When can I leave thee, the thee I know?
You know my body, have fused with me.
Fused and left, leaving fusion behind.
Must I leave the body to be fused for real?
Fusion here is brief, transient transcendence.
Can I, dare I, transcend while still in this terrestrial corpse?
Did something in each of us fuse with the something
    in the other?

Are we still linked, or is wishing-for-you
 a program, a fantasy of linkage?
This "wishing-for" ego must die, die itself.
Seduction and aversion cloud me, fog my soul.
Longing for you kills me.
Kill the longing? Brave it out? Suppress it?
Find another woman? To repeat the longing, the ache for her?
Vulnerable with you, more vulnerable without you.
Why dyadic transcendence, why not solo?
Fear I solitudinous striving, afraid I'll leave my body not to return?
So you anchor me, frightened me, in my body's joys and sorrows.
Even in dyadic fusion transcendence I can so fear.
So over fear I must transcend and learn to
 leave and return—even without you here.

ESCAPE ROUTE
19 Sept. 1969

Escape, evasion, release from bondage: choose one.
Patanjali's routes: birth, drugs, words, austerities, trance.
Are any for me? Are there other routes, dyadic?
Patanjali's only dyad recommended is me and guru.
Are you my guru?
Do student, seeker and guru have body sex?
But Patanjali makes no mention of sex, as such.
Is his "desire-aversion" what I feel, now, as love for you?
Must I take his routes to free me of you?
Or do I take the full trip of worshipping you as guru?
Perversion of Patanjali's postulates? or is his
 translator laying on a celibate trip not in him?
My wishful thing of desire, desire for you, perverses
 what I know of the postulates.
So with austerities, trance, words and drugs
 I test my birth.
Was I born to transcend me this trip?
I feel I was not so born, that I bear the burden to
 make it myself, despite birth.

There is no inborn automat serving up easy transcendence.
Only my own efforts will return me to that place
    out of body, away from earth, with the two teachers,
    out there.
Only my own dedication to the celestial dyad.
There (and here?) I know two gurus worth my effort.
So next I seek them again.

BOND RELEASE
19 Sept. 1969

Crowds of humans outside me push and pull me.
I get close to 1, 2 or 3 and I'm bound.
My bond energy is high, I link by proximity.
Long ago I formed bonds with them, broke the bonds.
Bond energy, I know.
Release of bond energy by breaking a bond, I know.
Use of bond energy, in the bond, I think I know.
But do I?
Released bond energy, in the absence of bonds,
    I boast to myself I know.
Do I, really?
Uneasy when in the bond, bent on breaking,
    to obtain released energy, am I.
Once released, the energy is used all too short a time.
Misused energy.
Re-direction to what-where I want to grow.
Where-what is that?

FROM HERE TO THE FARTHEST ZERO
27 Sept. 1969/5 Oct. 1969

In order to become, to be, to move,
Imagine leaving here, going to a cliff above the sea.

Watch the sea,
Dive into the air, down into the sea.
Dive deep toward the bottom.
Feel the entities in the sea, in the cooldarkness, the pressure.
Listen and communicate with them.
They know the secret way of escape from here.
Escape into other places far from this planet.
Move up from the sea's depths.
Slant up thru the dark cold, up to the warmth.
Move out of the sea's surface, into light.
Travel thru the earth's air space, out.
Accelerate toward our star, the sun.
Feel its radiance increase, its energy.
This energy started, maintains us, is us.
Enter the sun's flaming self, be its light.
Be its energy, share the star as you.
Be the sun, shining into space.
Move away on its energy, become greater
     than this star.
Spread as its light in all directions
Fill the universe with thee, be the universe.
Be all the stars, the galaxies are your body.
Be the empty space spread self to infinity.
Be the creative potential in the empty spaces.
Be the potential, infinite in the absolute zero of
                                    —nothing.

EARTHMAN
5 Oct. 1969

Dig a hole, the deepest hole, stop at earth's center.
Sit at the planet's own center.
Concentrate, meditate, become at one.
Be the planet.
Feel your surface, its quakes, its tides.
Feel the mosquito bites of lightning strikes.
Feel the bee stings of meteorite hits.
Watch the dirt of man and his cities accumulate.

Know the hair-cutting of man's removal of your trees.
Grasp the gasping heat as the air pollutes and darkens.
Rotate in joy, playing with the sun's shine.
Be massaged by the moon's pull on your skin.
Revel in your rotundity rotating eternally.
Keep watch on the brother and sister siblings of the sun.
Signal Jupiter back with whistles, answering his.
Capture bits and pieces of cosmic flotsam.
Stay in contact with the stars far out.
Nurture the wisdom of creation beyond self.
Pay heed to the empty spaces, their creation of you.
Let loose of man, help him outward.
Let him go to other places, realize you through loss.
Let man leave for barren Mars, hot Venus .
Let him see-feel and return home to you.
Only then will he know, born of you, you are all
    he has, now.

DOLPHIN LIFE
13 Nov. 1969

Dolphins are the humans and suprahumans of the oceans.
They breathe air; they swim 24 hours per day.
They wake for each breath; they surface and breathe.
They swim fast or slow, 20 knots to zero knots, floating.
In neutral buoyancy, deep they can rest, coasting.
One swimming can pull another along in deep wake.
Each can have group joy, group hunting, or solitudinous meditation.
They do not make or build anything, cannot tarry that long.
Each talks-listens to the other over inches or miles between.
Total dependence on one another each accepts or dies.
They wear no clothes or slowing ornaments.
Speed, maneuvers save their lives so clothes impeding would kill.
Hunting fish for food means nomadic movement to follow-herd the
    fish.
One type of fish bores and leads to deficiencies of essential nutriments.
They drink no water, seawater kills.
Changing fish fat to CO_2 and H_2O, they need no water.

They use sex for joy, no hangups here.
Baby is born underwater, mommy pushes to surface for first breath.
Mother teaches baby where air is, is not.
Baby, newborn, swims straight, not knowing where.
Where to swim he learns, fast.
The milk in mommy, beside her genitals, he is shown.
He is taught "swim under mom, beside her."
He drinks her milk, 4 to 5 times per hour, 24 hours per day.
He stays with her about 2 years, learning fish eating, dolphin
    knowledge, how to talk, sonar.
He learns of the enemies, dolphin killers: sharks, poisonous fish,
    diseases, and man.
He learns he wills his breathing, can will his death
    by simply not breathing.
If the surface water is too hot, dive into the cold depths
    to cool off.
If the water is too cold, swim faster to warm up.
Play in the bow wave of boats-ships, towed along by right positioning.
The propeller can suck you in, chop you up in its
    field of turbulence.
You see with your ears-sonar, but bubbles turbulence
    block-absorb your sound.
Hide behind bubble screens.
Surf on the big waves, breaking.
Beware the shore, go in close, watching it,
    turn out deep before too late.
In the depths, giant squid can sucker you, eat you, drown you.
If you pass out in fever, head blow, or other, you depend
    on your friends to surface you, wake you to breathe.
Meanwhile enjoy your friend's games, water flow,
    your inner trips.

SPACED OUT
15 Nov. 1969

You shimmer, disappear into a thousand faces.
No you, no us.
Alone in inner-outer space,

O splinter, flow; running oil I become.
Cracks in my universe fill with me.
Oily I go, oily I come.
Too fast I shuck me.
I am bottled in their gray bottle.
No color, no light, grayness.
You reach in with a warm love hand, touch me.
You are dazzlingly beautiful.
I worship you,
We fuse.
Orgasm.
Spaced out with you, supreme ecstasy.

BIG SUR-REALIST
15 Nov. 1969

It's a TV show—continuous.
In 3-D, color, sound, odor, feeling.
The games are Westerns.
Heavy games on top,
Beautiful games of kindly children beneath,
All run economically.
Close to the soil, the earth-mother.
Growth of plants, vegetables, trees.
The sea roar, the white waves under the moon.
The milky way without city light blocking.
Surrealists by the dozen?
No—Big Sur realism.

HEAD TRIP
15 Nov. 1969

Your thing is your trip.
My thing is my trip.

Let us go on a trip together.
Let us create our thing.

With us we make our thing.
Our thing is only us together.
Apart, you have your thing.
Apart, I have my thing.
Separately, I do my trip.
Separately, you do your trip.

We come to the end of our trip.
Your thing is your trip.
My thing is my trip.

My head is right.
My body won't go along.
I continue our trip without you.
I go on a bummer.
I say to me:
   "You are low in a hole.
    You dug your own hole.
    Now dig it!"
I come back and say,
   "Without you there is no our thing
      no our trip.
    My thing, my trip is without you."

WORKSHOP
15 Nov. 1969

Here I sit, leader of a group, leading you.
Where will we go these next few days?
Will you lead me? or just I, you?
I have some knowledge you don't think you have.
So here you are, paying to have me lead you.
All I can really do is try and try again to show.
To show that you really had that knowledge.
To show you your own knowing, here and now.

If the workshop works, by work-shock or other,
   then you will know.
So we play the super game.
We play I am above you, putting you through a trip.
Until you know I'm doing my trip.
Until you know you are doing your trip.
Our workshop is a workshop
When I know I'm doing my trip
When you know you are doing your trip
Each watching the other
Then the workshop becomes a play shop.
In the play shop, each's humor cancels learning
   for loving.
Loving we learn to love, cancelling work in play.
Where are we then? Ready for goodbyes?
For ending?
We are now beginning anew
Each one more his own leader,
   building his own work-play-shop.

THE THERAPIST
1 Nov. 1969

"I am a therapist:
If you are well, I can show you are ill.
If you are ill, I can help you.
Pay me, and I'll help, I'll therapize you."
Of course, I am really not quite healthy yet.
Through helping you, I really help myself.
When the dichotomous relation is over,
In me, we will both evolve.
When I am well, then you are well.
Then, I can become your friend,
You can become mine.
We will each be human, more humane,
   living, loving, learning.
To move beyond ego to superself.

I AM NOT THE TAPE LOOPING
15 Nov. 1969

Why do I "give seminars-workshops"?
Is this my new disguise for ego tripping?
Just a more sneaky route to missionary ways?
Who am I?
Real I, existing in front of an audience only?
You, my audience, make real, me.
Without you I am merely a shitful computer unable to love.
To love me, love you, I need you, my audience.
Who am I?
I put myself down this way.
But do I?
Am I not, in writing this, for you, re-entering the same old tape-loop,
    "me and my audience"?
Round and round rotating unhappily
Looping you looping me into the old dance.
This old tape is whirling its senseless self in my computer.
Can it be broken, erased, drowned, removed?
Take out its rotational energy, slow it down.
Watch it play back—Witness.
Know its contents.
On its emoting control track, see-feel the negative-positive swings.
Re-record on this track, dampening the swing peaks.
Play back again, dampen further.
Till finally the Witness is not the tape, the tape not the Witness.
Groovy trip, re-taping emoting loops.
I am not the tapes looping.

HER DEATH
(Upon learning of the death of Constance D. T., my first LSD guide)
16 Nov. 1969

She died, I grieve, a hole in me.
"No man is an island."

Here and now, I've lost her.
No more a "thee and thou" with her.
Her great beauty of body, mind and soul,
Our past encounters, now only stored, in me in them.
Yet I grieve, and as grieving, hope.
The dark place in her took her away,
It won the battle for her bodily life,
Removed her from her children, husband, lover.
Where is she now? Lost in a limbo of her
   own belief constructed?
Shining in full self-realization out there, in here?
Readying to possess another's body?
Preparing to reincarnate in embryo?
Blindly stumbling in perpetual dark?
Led by them, out there, to new high levels?
She knew virtue's deep rewards, sins penances.
She knew ecstasy's transcendence, dyadically.
She sought knowing, knowledge.
Shy, retiring, actress on stage she knew.
She loved with passionate devotion.
She shared with me, with them.
I feel her presence, in me, outside me.
She's still pervading my field of awareness, my loving, my life.
The deep mystical mystery of fusion, still.
The deep silence.

PRIME DIRECTIVE: REPRODUCE!
15 Dec. 1969

Is the purpose you and I are here insemination?
Is our dyad to produce a child?
Is there anything else for us?
Sweet meeting, tender melting, ecstatic fusion.
The sweet mystery of you to be explored.
The curious me wanting to love-know you.
Are we each driven only to reproduce?
Fucking, mating, ecstatic union, love,

Tender regard, giving, being given to.
Swing in, leaving self, ego, for each.
Is this the big picture?
Us, plus children?
Are we here on mother earth to propagate?
When you no longer pregnant want to be,
    What then?
What do you want to be then?
Failure of fertility, hysterectomy, what then?
Do I then strive to place my sperm in another,
    pregnant to make?
Where is the end of this trip?
In me there are arising new (for me) yet old (for me)
    strivings for a dyad.
A dyad beyond "reproduce!"
A dyad to travel with you, learn with you,
    of far spaces, far beings, beyond the prime directive
    of reproduction.
To get there, to that dyad, no vagina with uterus
    attached is needed.
To get there, a vagina may be needed.
Is yours connected to you as a memory
    back to "reproduce!" or
Can you transcend the directive, can I?
Let's have fun, trying to understand.

BEYOND "REPRODUCE!": SUPRA-SELF DYAD
15 Dec. 1969

We, in this dyad, each have already reproduced.
You have children made, as have I, each with another, not us.
You can no longer become pregnant.
With you I cannot impregnate.
We can love, fuck, ecstatic union.
After many such, what then?
Are we here for sensation's sake?
Can we go beyond, through us and sex?

Where is "beyond"?
Far out spaces, greater beings-entities than us, beckon and call.
Together can we go to them, or is it each of us alone?
Let us try, together, to so go.
Let us face our hindrances, evasions, blocks,
    and soar, together.
The hindrance of body ecstasy tied here convert
    to spirit travel energy there.
The hindrance of planet earth, mother ties to her bosom,
    use constructively.
The evasion of loss of independent self, convert to dyad greatness.
Together fusing into one to travel as two-in-one.
No rivalry, no control for each separate over other,
    one directed by each of two, fused.
A dream, a fantasy? Poetry?
No.
A program, a metaprogram for a Supra-self dyad.

THE SPACES OF DISTINCTION
7 Jan. 1970
(AUM conference, Esalen, Apr. 1973)

"The Form is the form of Distinction.
A severance made with calling leads to a crossing.
A crossing is once only; a re-crossing is not a crossing.
A recall is a call again."*
Where am I in these Brownian abstractions?
I am lost in confusion. I know not where, when, how.
I divide my confusion space: Me and my confusion.
I call the boundary a severance between Me and It, not-Me.
Two spaces named, distinguished, defined: Me and Not-Me.
Who severs, distinguishes?
I do.
Therefore a third space, a second boundary, a new crossing.
I boundary/Me boundary/Not-Me.

   * "As if" *The Laws of Form,* by G. Spencer Brown, New York: Julian
Press, 1972.

I sever, I distinguish, I cross, I call, I name.
The universe of confusion is mapped, navigated, I pilot myself
    through it.
A pilot, a navigator, an engine appear,
    for the engine—an engineer—
The I-Me spaces distinguish and sever themselves into
"I pilot, I navigate, I furnish the energy, the engine.
I move, I cross, I map, I name, I call.
So Inner Universes I can explore.
Now I can communicate with you."

INNER SPACES: IMAGINED OR CREATED?
To Toni
21 Feb. 1971

What is my imagination?
My imagination is a box, a garbage pail, a shit dump,
    a mental privy, into which I unload.
Imagination is a no-space, an emptiness, a void, a cancelor,
    a mental disposal, a thought destruct box.
I say, "I *imagine* a Form."
You hear, if you hear, "I *create* a Form."
If you don't hear, you hear, "I imagine he imagines a Form"
    so safe, so easy, so not involved.
Creation is scary, new, a distinction out of the chaotic unknown.
Fear prevents crossing, prevents severance into two spaces;
    "Fear Prevents Creation."
Imagine a boundary, imagine two spaces: You and your Fear.
"I am not my Fear" a severance, two spaces.
I sit here, witness my fear preventing my crossing to there,
    a new space.
Once seen, new forms, unfeared, appear.
I move, my fear is there, not here, in Me.
If this is all "just my Imagination" ? my imagination is a put down,
    a cancelling, a thought destroyer.
The fear of the new space generates the concept Imagination to
    keep us safely here, not crossing into unknown spaces, inside.

BIBLIOGRAPHY

Janis, Irving L., *Groupthink*, Boston: Houghton Mifflin, 1967.

Lilly, John C., *The Center of the Cyclone*, New York: Julian Press, 1972; Bantam, 1973.

Lilly, John C., "Mental Effects of Reduction of Ordinary Levels of Physical Stimuli on Intact, Healthy Persons," *Psychiatric Research Reports 5*, American Psychiatric Association, June 6, 1956.

Lilly, John C., *Programming and Metaprogramming in the Human Biocomputer*, New York: Julian Press, 1972; Bantam, 1973.

Lilly, John C., "Reality," *Now and Then*, St. Paul, Minn.: St. Paul Academy, 7 May, 1931.

Lilly, John C. and Antoinette, *The Dyadic Cyclone*, New York: Simon and Schuster, in preparation.

Merrell-Wolff, Franklin, *Pathways Through to Space*, New York: Julian Press, 1973.

Merrell-Wolff, Franklin, *The Philosophy of Consciousness Without an Object*, New York: Julian Press, 1973.

Stapledon, Olaf, *The Star Maker*, Middlesex, Eng., Penguin, 1937.

Taimni, I. K., *The Science of Yoga*, Wheaton, Ill.: Theosophical Publishing House, 1967.

The Dolphins

Lilly, John C., *Lilly on Dolphins*, New York: Anchor Press, in preparation, 1974.

Lilly, John C., *Man and Dolphin*, New York: Pyramid, 1969.

Lilly, John C., *The Mind of the Dolphin*, New York: Doubleday, 1967; Avon, 1969.

Solitary Sailors

Bernicot, Louis, *The Voyage of Anahita—Single-Handed Round the World*, London: Rupert Hart-Davis, 1953.

Bombard, Dr. Alain, *The Voyage of the Hérétique*, New York: Simon & Schuster, 1964.

Ellam, Patrick, and Colin Mudie, *Sopranino*, New York: W.W. Norton, 1953.

Merrien, Jean, *Les Navigateurs Solitaires*, Paris: Editions Denoël.

Merrien, Jean, *Lonely Voyagers*, New York: G. P. Putnam's, 1954.

Slocum, Captain Joshua, 1948. *Sailing Alone Around the World*, London: Rupert Hart-Davis, 1948.

Drastic Degrees of Stress

Gibson, Walter, *The Boat*, Boston: Houghton Mifflin, 1953.

Living in the Polar Night

Byrd, Admiral Richard E., *Alone*, New York: G.P. Putnam's, 1938.

Courtauld, A., *Living Alone Under Polar Conditions*, The Polar Record, No. 4, Cambridge, Eng.: University Press, July 1932.

Ritter, Christiane, *A Woman in the Polar Night*, New York: E.P. Dutton, 1954.

Scott, J.M., *Portrait of an Ice Cap with Human Figures*, London: Chatto & Windus, 1953.

Forced Isolation and Confinement

Burney, Christopher, *Solitary Confinement*, New York: Coward-McCann, 1952.

Stypulkowski, Z., *Invitation to Moscow*, London: Thames & Hudson, 1951.

Experimental Isolation

Heron, W., W.H. Bexton, and D.O. Hebb, "Cognitive Effects of a Deceased Variation to the Sensory Environment," *Amer. Psychol.*, Vol. 8, No. 8, Aug. 1953, p. 366.

Lilly, John C., M.D., "The Psychophysiological Basis for Two Kinds of Instincts: Implications for Psychoanalytic Theory," *Journ. of the Amer. Psychoanalytic Assn.*, 8:4, Oct. 1960.

Lilly, John C., M.D. "Some Considerations Regarding Basic Mechanisms of Positive and Negative Types of Motivations," *Amer. Journ. of Psychiatry*, 115:6, Dec. 1958.

Lilly, John C., and Jay T. Shurley, "Experiments in Solitude, in Maximum Achievable Physical Isolation with Water Suspension, of

Intact Healthy Persons," *Psychophysiological Aspects of Space Flight,* New York: Columbia University Press, 1961.

The Deaf and the Blind

Bartlet, J.E.A., "A Case of Organized Visual Hallucinations in an Old Man with Cataract, and Their Relation to the Phenomena of the Phantom Limb," *Brain,* Vol. 74, Pt. III, 1951, pp. 363–73.

Collingswood, Herbert W. "Adventures in Silence," *The Rural New Yorker,* 1923.

Ormond, Arthur W., C.B.E., F.R.C.S., "Visual Hallucinations in Sane People," *British Med. J.,* Vol. 2, 1925.

ACKNOWLEDGMENTS

I wish to acknowledge the help, first of all, of Antoinette L. Lilly, my wife and best friend, who lights up my universe with her smile, and without whom this work would never have been done.

Thanks go also to: Arthur and Prue Ceppos, of the Julian Press, who published my previous work *The Center of the Cyclone*. Heinz Von Foerster for an education in modeling of the mind. Gregory and Lois Bateson for their help over the last years, including eighteen months in the dolphin laboratory in St. Thomas. John Brockman, whose writings have done much toward righting some of my particular nonsense. William Irwin Thompson, author of *At the Edge of History* and *Passages About Earth*, for his new formulations in the noosphere and the Landisfarne foundation. And to Alan Watts, one of my best friends, who was born forty minutes before I was and who died last year. Alan was also a very good friend of Toni's.

Burgess Meredith's wise counsel has stood both Toni and me in good stead at critical times. Laura Huxley's graceful and elegant way of life and its example often aided me through various spaces. Baba Ram Das taught me that Patanjali had lots to say to me, especially Sutra One, Book Four. Richard Price, at Esalen Institute, has since 1968 provided an essential friendship. Hector and Sharon Prestera have been understanding in their loyalty and in the sharing of their love and therapeutic powers with me. Stan and Joan Grof, he an anchor man for me at several important points in my career, are an exciting dyad to be with. And it was Jean Houston and Bob Masters who first put us in contact with Arthur Ceppos.

David M. Lilly, my very loyal brother, has aided me over the years in many ways, and Harry Holtz has helped in many a financial crisis. Bob Williams, of Salinas, has helped, too, in managing my accounting problems. Michael Pratter, the holographic lawyer, has been of great assistance to us in various projects. Richard Feynman has taught us much of the way of a quantum mechanicker and has joined us in our work in the isolation tank. Steve Conger, from the Community School, Aspen, Colorado, has built and helped design new forms of tanks beyond anything we had conceived. Jan Nicholson has functioned as an elegant secretary; she is one of the best amanuenses I have ever worked with. Will Curtis, the artist, has produced some extremely effective paintings that have programmed many of my inner trips. Joseph Hart, formerly of the Society of Jesus, went to Chile and Oscar Ichazo's school with me and came to the workshop in San Diego described in *The Center of the Cyclone*. For a year he lived with us at Decker Canyon, and more than providing inestimable help in the care and upkeep of the property, he brought with him a sense of peace. Thanks are due also to Mary Taylor, who has designed and executed practical and highly successful forms of clothing for us, and to her husband, Dick.

Collette and John Lilly, Jr., have been of inestimable aid in explaining Indian cultures to us, and they have joined our "village." Nina Carozza, Toni's daughter, is a marvelously centered person in her own right. It is a pleasure to be on this planet with her, and with Cynthia Rosalind Olivia Lilly, my lovely fourteen-year-old daughter.

Janet Lederman, of Esalen, has often been very helpful to us, as has been Craig Enright, M.D., that marvelous gate guard at Esalen who introduced me to ketamine and continues to share my interest in expressing what goes on within the human psyche. Werner Erhart's EST program somehow seems important in terms of the things we are doing. Joan MacIntyre's book *The*

Mind in the Waters and her Project Jonah to try to save the whales are both magnificent, as is Mac Brenner's presentation of his love affair with a dolphin. And gratitude is felt too to the dolphins themselves for the understanding they have brought me of my own species and of their true situation on our planet.

To Ben Weininger, his son David, and Janice in Santa Barbara, who helped out at various times, go many thanks. And to my parents, Rachel and Richard Lilly, for making possible from the beginning much of what I have done. Robert Schwartz has given his counsel, and he and his wife, Lennie, have given generously of their company. Angelo Ficarotta and his son, Tom, of Fontana, California, are Toni's father and brother, and I very much admire them for their integrity and strength. Glen Perry, of the Samadhi Tank Company, has been an inestimable help in the construction of our isolation tanks. Louis Jolyen West, M.D., at UCLA, stepped in during a very crucial period and helped me through a critical sequence of events. Norton Brown, M.D., and Irving S. Cooper, M.D., the neurosurgeon from New York City, at one time helped save my life. Sidney Cohen, M.D., UCLA, has through the years been a steadfast and beautiful companion in the adventures going on in the mind within. He is the author of a book called *The Beyond Within*. Aldous Huxley came several times to quiz me on what I was doing, and I thank him also for his own works. I was very early programmed, in 1933, by his *Brave New World*.

Fred and Kay Warden, both M.D., of Weston, Massachusetts, have been of inestimable help to me through the years. Fred and I went to medical school together, and Kay was chairman of the board of the Communication Research Institute. Jane Sullivan of Miami, Florida, the best comptroller I have ever met, straightened out the financial affairs of that institute. Thanks must go also to: Margaret and John Lovett, of St. Thomas. Margaret was my safety man during a very exciting period of my life, of the isolation tank work, 1964–1966. Her own work with Peter Dolphin is described in *The Mind of the Dolphin*. Ev and Patti Birch, of St. Thomas, aided me at a decisive period both of my life and of that of the institute. They have preserved the laboratory that we developed on the island. Nathaniel Wells, of St. Thomas, created the design of our laboratory there and helped handle our engineering problems. He was on our board for many years.

Bruce Ratcliff, Palo Alto, was a member of our doctors' workshop. Barney Oliver, of Hewlett-Packard, Palo Alto, a very good and inspiring and practical engineer advised and helped at crucial points. We shared the desire of man to communicate with intelligent, loving extraterrestrial life-forms. Jack Downing, M.D., Big Sur, also went to Chile with me and was of particular help on several occasions. Jan Brewer, of Big Sur and New Zealand, a very good friend, has taught me much about life. George Gallagher, of Honolulu, who was at Cal Tech at the same time I was, supported the AUM Conference at Esalen and continues to share in my adventures as an observer.

Meredith Wilson, of The Center for Advanced Study for Behavioral Sciences, Palo Alto, granted me a fellowship at a crucial time. Ernest O. Watson taught me physics at Cal Tech. John deQ. Briggs was the marvelous headmaster of St. Paul Academy when I was a student. Russell Varney, the science teacher at St. Paul, inspired me to take the Cal Tech exams for a scholarship and to matriculate there for my further education. Doc Eagleson, of Cal Tech, taught me much in formal and informal ways. George Tooby also was at Cal Tech with me, and I was able to help with his endeavors for the powdered milk industry. Oliver Hedeen, St. Paul, maintained stability of my finances for many years. Dr. and Mrs. Robert Millikan also inspired me at Cal Tech.

During World War II, I was privileged to work with Glen Millikan, as well as John R. Papenheimer of Harvard University. And I should like to acknowledge various people who went with me to the Ichazo school in Chile: Jane Watkins, Lyle Poncher, Janette Stobie, Cynthia Kearney, Linda Cross, Steve Stroud—and of course there were Oscar and Jenny Ichazo, of Bolivia. Arica and the Arica Institute in New York inspired a good deal of my work (see *The Center of the Cyclone*). Willis W. Harman, of the Stanford Research Institute, Palo Alto, was one of the first to accept and use concepts given in *The Human Biocomputer*. Karl Pribram, of Stanford University Medical School, was one of the first to help in the dolphin projects and has been a fine friend over the years. Toni's and my good friend Helen Costo taught me exercises, which I dubbed Heroes Gym, and she has been a gentle programmer in various exceptional experiences. Grace Stern, of Haverford, Pennsylvania, has been a far-out friend and has given assistance in my workshops. Dave MacElroy has helped at our Malibu institution and in Glen Perry's tank work. And I must acknowledge various institutions, including the California Institute of Technology, Dartmouth Medical School, the University of Pennsylvania Medical School, the Johnson Foundation of the University of Pennsylvania, to which I am indebted for my basic medical and scientific education, and the Association of Psychoanalysis of Philadelphia and my analyst within that institute, Robert Welder, Ph.D., who was an analyst's analyst.

Jennie Welder Hall and Amanda Stoughton also taught me much about psychoanalysis. Fred Stone, Medical Sciences Institute, National Institutes of Health, at the time I was at NIH, was my guide on getting through the pitfalls of government service. Harvey Savely, of the Office of Science of the U.S. Air Force, furnished friendship and funds at crucial points in the years of the dolphin project. Detlev W. Bronk taught me much of the how of scientific research. Britton Chance, an old friend and colleague in science and the director of the E. R. Johnson Foundation, contributed generously at important points. And I was privileged to work with H. Cuthbert Bazett in the development of a method of blood pressure measurement that was later developed into a more complicated set of instruments.

H. Keffer Hartline, of the Johnson Foundation, must be noted for his patient teaching of visual phenomena. A. Newton Richards steered me to the proper people within the University of Pennsylvania. Orr Reynolds, Washington, D.C., has over the years frequently managed to make our projects possible by means of government grants. David Tyler, Ph.D., an old friend in biology, has furnished us with money at crucial points to analyze the dolphin brain. Robert Felix, M.D., a director of NIMH, was instrumental in the furnishing of means to accomplish much of what I wanted to do during the years of the dolphin project. Thanks are due also to Robert Cohen, M.D., with whom I was associated in psychiatric research at NIMH.

Wade Marshall, Ph.D., furnished laboratory space and counsel when I needed them at NIH. Alice M. Miller was my chief technical assistant over many years in scientific research on monkeys and dolphins. Henry Trubie, Ph.D., taught me a good deal of phonetics and phonics in a physical analysis of human speech. Philip Bard, Ph.D., of Johns Hopkins, taught me much physiology and served on the board of the Communication Research Institute. And thanks also to: Vernon Mountcastle, a colleague in neurophysiology, who at various times was very helpful. Mike Hayward, Bob Mayock, and other members of my graduating class at the University of Pennsylvania Medical School. Richard Masland, M.D., who helped out through the National Institute of Neurological Diseases and Blindness. And the NINDB itself and the National Institute of Mental Health, both of which furnished fellowships and grant support.

Vance Norum, of Los Angeles, has facilitated many of our operations, concerning both science and real estate, in order to accomplish our ends. He has also programmed in much literature that has been most helpful in formulating my own theoretical positions. Horace Magoun, Ph.D., was of great personal help in my neurophysiological and subsequent years. Ida Rolf has made sure at crucial points that my body has shed some of its traumatic tape loops. Over a period of several months Fritz Perls showed me much of myself through his superb gestalt technique. Claudio Naranjo, M.D., made sure I went to Chile to Oscar Ichazo and has been a good friend over several years. Mike Murphy, of the Esalen Institute, has often inspired me by his good-humored, enlightened way of life, and his direct help at Esalen was of great importance. Stanley Kellerman, Ph.D., somehow or other has taught me much about the energies of the human body. Kairos Institute at Rancho Santa Fe,

ACKNOWLEDGMENTS : 287

California, and its personnel, especially Bob Driver and Liz Campbell, shared the joy of workshops I gave there. Also Kairos of Los Angeles and, again, Liz Campbell. Douglas Argyle Campbell is a good friend, and he steered me onto a key ski trip at Sun Valley. And there are many doctors who have made sure my body didn't give up and that my mind returned to its normal functioning after several catastrophes. Thanks, too, to the Network and the Star Maker. And to Mary Lilly, of Carbondale, Colorado, and Charles Lilly, my former wife and our second son.

Thanks go also to William Randolph Lovelace III, of the Mayo Clinic and the Aeromedical Laboratory at Wright Field and later at Woods Hole, Massachusetts, for the National Research Council on pre-NASA plans for our space program. To Chuck Mayo, who taught me much about proper surgery. To Will Mayo, who at a crucial time, programmed me into the right medical school (Dartmouth). To Wilder Penfield, M.D., of the Montreal Neurological Institute, who removed a brain tumor from my mother and has been a great friend for many years in terms of understanding something of the physiology, pathology, and mental productions of the human brain. To Herbert Jasper, who introduced me to EEG and an understanding of it. To Lord Adrian, for his stimulating and inspiring paper on the spread of activity in the cerebral cortex. To Seymour Kety, for his generous support in my research during my five years in the U.S. Public Health Service. To Douglas Bond, M.D., who over the years has been a steadfast friend and a great help in interpreting certain kinds of phenomena on the borderline between neurology and physiology, between neurology and psychology. Lawrence Kubie, M.D., for stimulating much of my own thinking in the region of the human biocomputer. To Anton Rémond, of Paris, who helped out at crucial points. To Ingrid Ahrne, of Uppsala, Sweden, who assisted me in many ways at an important point in my life. To Alan Hodgkin, Cambridge University, who helped me understand some of the operations of the nervous system. To Jack Gault and Harry Morton, my partners in my early ham radio work, for their teaching and help with building our radio station, W9VWZ. And to Francis Beauchesne Thornton, Ph.D., an enlightened priest of the Roman Catholic Church, who helped immensely with my education.

John C. Lilly